D1162560

THE WRITING CENTER
New Directions

SOURCE BOOKS ON EDUCATION
(VOL. 27)

GARLAND REFERENCE LIBRARY
OF SOCIAL SCIENCE
(VOL. 678)

SOURCE BOOKS ON EDUCATION

THE WRITING CENTER
New Directions

edited by
Ray Wallace
Jeanne Simpson

GARLAND PUBLISHING, INC. • NEW YORK & LONDON
1991

Library of Congress Cataloging-in-Publication Data

The writing center : new directions / edited by Ray Wallace, Jeanne
Simpson.
    p. cm. — (Garland reference library of the social science ; vol.
678. Source books on education ; vol. 27)
  Includes bibliographical references.
  ISBN 0–8240–7056–9 (alk. paper)
  1. English language—Rhetoric—Study and teaching. 2. Writing
centers. I. Wallace, Ray. II. Simpson, Jeanne H. III. Series: Garland
reference library of social science ; vol. 678. IV. Source books on
education ; vol. 27.
PE1404.W69445   1991
808'.042'07—dc20   90–48219
                                                   CIP

Printed on acid-free, 250-year-life paper
Manufactured in the United States of America

DEDICATION

This collection of essays is dedicated to all the Writing Center staffs across the United States who struggle every day to have their achievements acknowledged, their expertise rewarded, and their Centers adequately funded.

CONTENTS

PREFACE

This book uniquely addresses the needs of writing centers which have matured past the initial problems of establishment. Since the National Council of Teachers of English endorsed a resolution calling for the establishment of writing centers in all colleges and universities, nearly 90% of the institutions of higher education in the United States have developed writing centers or learning centers where writing is taught.

Clearly the writing center idea is well established in American education, and the methods and principles for developing them are well documented in writing center literature. Key earlier works by Steward and Croft (*The Writing Laboratory: Organization, Management, and Methods*, Scott, Foresman, 1982), Harris (*Tutoring Writing: A Sourcebook for Writing Labs*, Scott, Foresman, 1982), Olson (*Writing Centers: Theory and Administration*, NCTE, 1984), and Clark (*Writing In the Center: Teaching In a Writing Center*, Kendall/Hunt, 1985) describe how to start writing centers and gather support for them.

However, because the writing center movement is now nearly 30 years old, the number of well established writing centers is substantial. The increasing demand for writing center experience and the growth of graduate programs in which writing centers play a significant role creates the need for more sophisticated writing centers.With this demand has come the need for wider definition of the roles that these centers can have and should develop. These twenty-three nationally known writing center leaders/researchers offer this definition of the larger, cross-curricular, role of centers.

Hence, *The Writing Center: New Directions*, presents a much-needed investigation into how writing centers identify new roles, new constituencies, and new methodologies across our college and university curricula. The contributors, all leading writing center researchers and/or directors, describe center-based programs and methodologies successful in reaching new groups of students or programs successful in more effectively tutoring those students who have always come to the writing center.

Each essay describes how a college or university writing center has attracted a previously unreached student-group on campus or has modified its approach to tutoring a traditional student-group. Each essay focuses on how this group was served, what special writing skills were tutored, what administrative, linguistic, and rhetorical problems were dealt with, and how the center and the institution have benefited from the center's expansion into this area. This book offers fresh insight and concrete examples into the expanding role of writing centers in improving writing across the curriculum.

ACKNOWLEDGMENTS

There are many people we need to thank for helping us to develop this book. Chief among these is, of course, Gary Kuris, Vice-President of Garland Publishing Inc. who first believed in the project, and Dr. Phyllis Korper who helped us develop the manuscript. In addition, we need to thank all of the contributors for meeting our deadlines, for producing essays of such high quality, and for helping us deliver a book which offers so much hope for the future of our field.

We also need to thank Dr. Kerri Morris Barton, of The University of Tennessee, for her valuable design advice and help in preparing the final camera-ready copy.

We would like to thank our respective spouses and close family members for putting up with our long hours spent producing this work.

Introduction to the Collection

Ray Wallace
University of Tennessee

Jeanne Simpson
Eastern Illinois University

The challenges faced by institutions of higher education for the rest of the century also will be faced by writing centers. These challenges include dramatic shifts in the populations to be served, changes in the missions of colleges and universities and the resulting alterations in curricula, revisions of our ideas about how knowledge is made, used, and transmitted, and revisions of our methods for assessing our work. In the meantime, we will all continue to compete for funding under increasing pressures.

As these larger changes occur, there are parallel changes in the way writing is taught. While writing centers began as a response to the new writing pedagogy, the speed and size of the changes are so large that any writing center faces the possibility of obsolescence. However, the danger of being obsolete at the same time presents an opportunity for change, growth, and gaining strength. As they enter a "second generation," writing centers must plan and adjust to meet these challenges so that they can continue their tradition of serving students and other members of the academic community. The purpose of this book is to offer specific suggestions and ideas for how centers may achieve that goal.

The essays that follow address issues under various rubrics, including political issues involving funding and recognition for writing centers, pedagogical issues involving theory and methods for writing center instruction, administrative issues involving the planning and organization of writing centers, and assessment issues involving the study of how well writing centers do their jobs. Fundamental to all the essays is the principle that writing centers are dynamic, not static, that change and adjustment to new problems come with the territory.

Because writing centers inevitably face change, these essays offer writing center personnel opportunity to plan and develop responses to change. Anyone with experience in college or university governance knows the principle that the plan that is already prepared is usually the one that gets adopted. This collection provides ideas about what changes are likely to occur, how other institutions have faced them, where more information may be found, and what problems might be anticipated so that well-informed, timely planning can occur.

Donald E. Bushman begins this collection with an piece titled "Past Accomplishments and Current Trends in Writing Center Research: A Bibliographic Essay." Bushman's essay examines the major writing center research of the past two decades, with an eye toward both the accomplishments of past researchers and the trends developing that will help define the expanding role of the writing center of the future. Bushman claims that the advent of social constructionist thought in the teaching of writing has resulted in an explosion in the number of writing across the curriculum programs, peer tutoring programs, and writing-emphasis course offerings in all disciplines. This theoretical wave has also contributed to the increased importance being attached to writing centers on campus, transforming the writing center from the English department fix-it station to the center of learning for the entire academic population.

Bushman looks at writing centers and research associated with writing centers from three perspectives. First, an examination of past writing center research over the last two decades is necessary to discover in what ways we have defined ourselves. Second, from these definitions, it is then necessary to understand the major trends writing centers are driven by. Finally, the essay focuses on predicting the role of the writing center of the future, based on the current state of research and application in the field.

Bradley T. Hughes in his essay "Writing Center Outreach: Sharing Knowledge and Influencing Attitudes About Writing" notes that for too long, too many writing centers have been insular in their thinking and in their teaching, focusing their attention exclusively on their own programs and their own staff. Granted, such an approach made sense when writing centers began, but by continuing to do so, Hughes claims they are missing opportunities to share their knowledge about writing with faculty and students outside the confines of the writing center and to learn more about writing done across the curriculum. Hughes notes that one excellent way for writing centers to share their expertise, to influence and improve the dialogue about writing on their campuses, and to strengthen their own programs, is to develop an effective outreach program which, at faculty request, takes writing center instructors into classrooms across campus to teach brief units on writing.

Each year staff from the Writing Center at the University of Wisconsin at Madison make presentations to and lead discussions about writing with over a thousand students in classes across campus, ranging from History to Sociology to Nursing to Psychology. Through this experience, these writing center personnel have developed a successful model for soliciting outreach requests and for planning and delivering instruction, a model based on collaboration and shared responsibility with faculty. Such presentations serve many purposes and benefit everyone involved.

This essay argues for the importance of such outreach, discusses theoretical and practical principles on which it should be based, and illustrates these points with examples from Hughes' experience with faculty and courses in various disciplines.

Jim Addison and Henry L. Wilson in "From Writing Lab To Writing Center: Reinventing, Advancing, And Expanding" discuss the theoretical and practical considerations involved in reinventing, advancing, and expanding the writing center. The central issue is the process through which a writing center can broaden its mission and extend its reach to all segments of the academic community after it has evolved from its initial remedial nature. With the move from the remedial "lab" status, and all the negative baggage this label carries, comes the need to redefine mission, focus, and procedures of the writing center. This redefinition must include evaluations of location, administrative control, funding, staffing, and the need for future cross-curricular programs.

The authors focus on the writing center at Western Carolina University. They discuss how this writing center has evolved; the essay presents an important description of the metamorphosis from the remedial "band-aid" stage to a more fully developed stage in which the center serves the needs of the entire academic community.

Katherine H. Adams in "Satellite Writing Centers: A Successful Model for Writing Across the Curriculum" offers an interesting discussion of the role of writing center(s) in a writing across the curriculum project. At Loyola University in New Orleans, a liberal arts college with an undergraduate population of 3500, Writing Across the Curriculum operates a centrally located writing center where students from each discipline can come for tutoring. Trained undergraduates tutor 100 students each day, with another 100 coming to the center daily to use and train on word processors. This center also operates a writing fellows program, with tutors assigned to classes across the curriculum.

Besides this main center, Loyola also has satellite centers for specific disciplines. Loyola also operates a tutoring and computer facility designed for students in basic and advanced writing courses within the English department; this area has a small teaching room for advanced writing workshops. In the communications building, a computer-equipped classroom with graphics and desktop publishing software is available. Classes meet there in the morning; the room is used for tutoring in the afternoons and evenings. In the law school a Legal Writing Workshop is staffed by third-year law students. Adams claims this this tutoring center has been especially important for minority retention.

Loyola is now planning a graphics/writing center in the art department, a business writing center for the business school, and a writing center for students in the new extension program at City Hall. All of these sites involve cooperation between WAC and teachers in other disciplines for grant applications, lab administration, and tutor-training. They involve faculty development since the center must be formed to support the teachers' assignments and grading: they necessitate ongoing discussion of audience/purpose/speaker as well as the styles and forms of specific discourse communities. This essay discusses the goals of these satellite centers, their administration, their effect on faculty and students, and their positive relationship to the main writing center from which they have evolved.

Ray Wallace's essay "Sharing the Benefits and the Expense of Expansion: Developing a Cross-Curricular Cash Flow for A Cross-Curricular Writing Center" reports that the days of the writing center being regarded as simply a linguistic "band-aid" station have come and gone for most of us. In fact, many writing centers have deliberately dropped the "lab" nomenclature and replaced this remedial/quick service image with terms such as "Center", "Place" or "Resource." Wallace comments that just as the field of teaching writing has matured rapidly over the last twenty years, so has the way we think of our writing centers.

While our primary clients still seem to be those students enrolled in freshman and other English writing courses, writing centers all over the country are now being asked to help even more diverse groups. With the writing across the curriculum movement in full swing, writing intensive courses being developed every semester, and the ever-increasing awareness among faculty that writing can be an effective way of teaching many subjects, writing centers are becoming very popular, very quickly. Another fact is also apparent. The English department at most institutions of higher education cannot be considered a limitless source of money from which to fund the tutors needed in these various additional programs across the curriculum. Since most writing centers are funded by English departments and our primary clients are those enrolled in English, it only makes common fiscal sense to find other parties to pay for other programs.

Wallace's essay discusses three writing center-based programs at the University of Tennessee at Knoxville which are funded independently of the English department budget. The programs, the Educational Advancement Program, the College of Law, and the Athletics Program, all pay for writing center tutors and operating time from their own budgets. This essay looks at how these three programs are handled in the writing center, the advantages (and some disadvantages) to this funding method, and, finally, the author offers advice to other writing center directors on how to implement this type of additional funding in their writing centers.

Jeanne Simpson, in "The Role of Writing Centers in Student Retention Programs", challenges traditional views of the structures in which writing centers develop. She argues that the view of writing centers as dependent upon English departments is incomplete and ignores the institution-wide effects of writing center work. Simpson comments that the key to larger support within an institution is for a writing center director to understand the concept of retention. Retention of students is a major issue for all college and universities.

Successful retention happens primarily in the first few weeks a student spends on a campus. This fact holds for traditional eighteen-year old freshmen, transfer students, and nontraditional students. The goal of helping students to write better and the goal of meeting their needs within six weeks of their arrival on campus are not easily combined. There is, however, a need that occurs before the need for writing assistance: students need to connect with an institution in a positive way before they can become successful learners. The writing center offers a significant opportunity to achieve this vital connection.

Simpson notes that writing centers can improve retention by addressing these issues in tutor training, particularly how little new students often know about the conventions of college life. Record keeping systems also need attention so that they may be accurate and useful but not unpleasant bureaucratic hassles. Simpson claims writing centers probably can address these issues better than almost any other agency within an institution because tutorials are private and ungraded. Finally, she notes that writing center directors need to learn more about how retention affects governance on their campuses and use this information to further the interests of their centers. Understanding how retention affects the behavior of councils, committees, and other governing bodies is an important step in developing effective strategies for expanded funding and support.

William C. Wolff's essay "Writing Services: A New Role for the Writing Center and Faculty" notes that when staffing permits, directors of university writing centers should serve constituents other than undergraduates. Faculty and staff often appreciate colloquia and workshops that are not threatening, where each writer's work is reviewed with tactful suggestions. Wolff's article focuses on an advanced level of this type of collaborative learning; the writing workshop at Appalachian State University for faculty and staff was found to be highly valuable and effective. After an initial workshop with faculty from across the curriculum sharing a general peer commenting instrument, faculty were asked to develop a discipline-specific instrument for their own majors' use. This essay discusses the writing center's role in helping to develop this second instrument. Wolff offers valuable advice on how to reach faculty through this method and how faculty, in turn, can reach out to other faculty, students, and staff after some initial contact with a caring writing center.

Sallyanne H. Fitzgerald, Peggy Mulvihill, and Ruth Dobson in their essay "Meeting the Needs of Graduate Students: Writing Support Groups in the Center" examine the value of workshopping in the writing center. Specifically, collaborative writing as it is manifested in peer writing workshops provides the theoretical basis upon which the University of Missouri-St. Louis Writing Lab has developed graduate writing support groups. These three authors explain that graduate students are contacted and asked to submit times they are available to participate in such groups. Groups meet with a faculty facilitator. Initially, the faculty facilitator models peer workshopping; gradually, students assume more responsibility for workshopping each other's papers. Groups are limited to four or five graduate students, but occasionally the faculty facilitators merge small groups for a larger group meeting. Sometimes, the facilitator may meet with the individuals for additional tutorial assistance while the focus of the program remains the small peer workshopping groups.

Furthermore, this essay claims that the most recent graduate support groups are meeting the needs of international students for whom there are no other University English as a Second Language (ESL) services. Thus, in the case of ESL graduate students, the benefits relate not only to collaborative writing but also to second language facility. This essay also includes observations of workshopping sessions, advice about setting up graduate groups, a sample questionnaire to attract graduate students to the writing center, and personal accounts from facilitators.

Richard Leahy's essay, "A Lot of Pleasure, a Bit of Agony: Producing a Newsletter for the Faculty," explains that the Writing Center at Boise State University publishes a monthly writing across the curriculum newsletter that exerts considerable influence on campus. The newsletter, called *Word Works,* has just completed its third year and the thirty-second issue. In that time it has proven that reaching the faculty is a way to attract students to the writing center. This essay explains in detail how the newsletter is written and produced, with very limited resources, and shows that writing centers can follow Leahy's lead.

Word Works succeeds partly because it is not strictly a newsletter; it is, in a sense, a textbook in serial installments, teaching the basics about writing processes and writing-for-learning. It presents practical tips for using writing in the classroom, including such topics as designing assignments and responding to student writing. Some issues are also devoted to the more theoretical concerns about learning through writing. Some are aimed at teachers' own writing because Leahy believes faculty must understand their own writing processes in order to use writing well with their students.

The essay also reports on a readership survey designed to find out who reads the newsletter, what articles have had the greatest influence on writing in BSU classrooms, and what specific changes in teaching the newsletter has inspired. This essay concludes with a section discussing how Leahy expects the newsletter to evolve as BSU's Writing Center becomes involved in a proposed writing across the curriculum program.

Jay Jacoby and Stan Patten in "Changing the Ways We Teach: The Role of the Writing Center in Professional Development; Or, The Virtue of Selfishness" explain that from its inception, the Writing Resources Center at the University of North Carolina at Charlotte has viewed professional development as one of its central missions. Despite the rapid growth of client services and populations, professional development is still a cornerstone of the center. Jacoby and Patten note that at UNCC all tutors (undergraduate, graduate, and faculty) are trained and treated as peer professionals with the dual responsibilities of working as peers of clients and working and being treated as professionals.

This essay focuses on how the professional development of various tutor groups changes the ways in which writing is taught in the classroom. Specifically, three groups of tutors are discussed: faculty who teach composition, graduate assistants who move from tutoring to teaching in the second year of their assistantships, and finally students who are preparing for teaching careers in the public schools.

These authors note that tutors seldom begin work in the center with any background in tutoring. Thus, the center, through a required credit-bearing practicum and on-going support services, trains all tutors, paying particular attention to methods of intervening in the writing processes of others, to the dynamics (psychological, pedagogical, and political) of one-on-one tutoring, to the interactive dimensions of teaching writing, and to the implications of transferring tutorial pedagogy to the classroom environment. Central to this professional development is the belief that tutorial practice transfers more readily to the classroom than teaching practice does to the tutorial situation.

Robert Child's essay "Tutor-Teachers: An Examination of How Writing Center and Classroom Environments Inform Each Other" discusses an important issue in the teaching/tutoring of writing. Child looks at how tutoring styles and training can steer the actual teaching of writing in the classroom environment. In addition, Child looks at how classroom-based teaching styles and outcomes can be modified by tutor-training sessions in the writing center. Child discusses the findings and observations of both tutors and teachers at Purdue University, and he looks at how teachers and tutors can benefit from a thorough understanding of how to develop effective questioning strategies, to apply modeling theories, to develop objective agendas, to test, and to demonstrate authority in the writing process.

Maurice Scharton and Janice Neuleib in "The Gift of Insight: Personality Type, Tutoring, and Learning" note that personality type theory proposes that humans are divided into learning, decision-making, and coping preferences that produce distinct behavior patterns that can make or break personal and learning relationships. Properly understood, type theory can be a powerful tool for improving social, professional, and academic contacts of every kind. This theory has begun to contribute a powerful new method for improving tutoring in writing and learning centers.Tutors learn early to understand themselves as distinct individuals with characteristics that differentiate them from other tutors and from those they tutor. They also learn that they share characteristics with others in identifiable patterns which can in turn inform decisions about how and what to tutor and in what order. Both authors claim that an understanding of type theory can enable a tutor to analyze error more effectively and to plan an effective tutoring sequence for each student tutored.

Scharton and Neuleib explain that center administrators have found type knowledge invaluable in coping with the complex problems of staff training, supervision, and renewal. Books like *Please Understand Me* (Bates and Keirsey, Prometheus Nemesis Books, 1978) and articles like "On Gaining Insight into Ourselves as Writers and as Tutors" (Maid, Crisp, and Norton, *Writing Lab Newsletter* 13 June 1989, 1-5) aptly describe how knowledge of personality preference can resolve differences, organize teams, and enhance learning environments. Type theory finds wide acceptance in business, social organizations, the government, but has only recently been introduced to educational institutions. However, recently reading and writing centers have begun to lend direction to the use of personality type, but much more remains to be done.

This essay briefly reviews personality theory, and describes the ways in which this theory can change the administration of and tutoring in a writing center. The chapter includes practical workshop methods for introducing and applying type theory as well as advice on sources for workshop training of administrators.

Irene Lurkis Clarke in "The Writing Center and the Research Paper: Computers and Collaboration" notes that the Freshman Writing Program at the University of Southern California has developed a new computer project to assist students in writing research papers. Located in a Macintosh lab which is a component of the Writing Center, the new computer project enables Writing Center tutors and students to approach the research paper as a process of research-oriented activities. These activities include: analyzing key terms in a topic, understanding necessary background material, accessing information alphabetically, hierarchically, and associatively, reading critically, note taking, summarizing, paraphrasing, organizing large chunks of material, comparing, contrasting, analyzing and synthesizing. Working through several of these activities with Writing Center tutors also helps students to familiarize themselves with their topics, so that they can then formulate an informed position and effectively incorporate outside sources.

The new project, called "Project Jefferson," consists of a topic specific on-line information retrieval system, which enables students to access key terms, background information, and secondary sources for their assignments. The computer allows students to establish links between chunks of information, thus simulating the associate cross-referencing characteristic of the research process. It also enables students to write responses to pre-writing questions associated with their assignment, take notes, outline, and word process their papers. Ultimately, it will provide students with access to on-line data bases available in the university library. Writing Center tutors are thus able to help students utilize sources in their papers in their composition classes and ultimately to use the full range of library resources.

This new model has become the prototype for a new undergraduate teaching library soon to be built at USC and has thus become an important link between the Writing Center and other components of the university. The new library will incorporate a similar approach to conducting research; like "Project Jefferson," it will integrate into one workstation environment the many resources and tools that the student needs to do research, as well as provide a graduated introduction to these things. This essay presents the theoretical rationale and practical applications of this new Writing Center project and discusses some of the activities tutors and students work through on the computer.

Nadene A. Keene in "Portfolio Evaluation: Implications for Writing Centers" explains that at Indiana University's eight campuses in 1988 a system of portfolio evaluation was proposed for individual classes, in multiple sections of a course, in the major, as part of the capstone experience, or as a method of evaluating the writing competency of potential graduates. The proposed system not only applies to writing or English courses, however; portfolios were to be used across the disciplines. To date various portfolio pilot studies have occurred on several campuses.

Keene notes that Indiana University-Kokomo employs portfolio evaluation in two ways. First, portfolio evaluation was used in multiple sections of one course, English W132, a research oriented course required of all arts and sciences majors which emphasizes writing across the disciplines, i.e., in the arts, in the social sciences, and in the natural sciences. Subsequently, portfolio evaluation became an option in the first semester writing course required of all IU-K students, W131. Continued and increased use of portfolio evaluation will doubtless affect the Writing Center.

Keene warns that first writing center clients will need an increased awareness of multiple readers/audiences, some of whom may be from differing disciplines. Both clients and tutors will need a knowledge of various disciplines' conventions, forms, and jargon. Additionally, tutors will help students identify acceptable criteria for a variety of items, document and non-document, in the portfolio. Because most portfolios contain selected materials, tutors must be able to help clients with critical thinking skills in a variety of disciplines. In short, Keene notes that the addition of portfolio evaluation to college campuses means additional talents and responsibilities required of Writing Center tutors and administrators. But, Keene claims that for the Writing Center such additional responsibilities will also provide additional opportunities.

Donald Samson's essay, "Tutoring Technical Students in the Writing Center," explains that as more students majoring in the sciences, computer science, engineering, etc., make use of writing centers, and as peer tutoring is used more frequently in centers, student tutors majoring in English, journalism, and other fields in the humanities find themselves helping upperclass as well as freshman and sophomore technical students learn how to present information better in their writing. Samson notes that peer tutoring of "technical" students by "communications" students can involve work with writing assignments for technical courses in addition to assignments for composition or humanities courses. Training tutors to work with technical material presents different challenges for a Writing Center director and staff. Peer tutoring of technical students is more effective than peer editing, which traditionally profits technical student clients more than communication student tutors. Tutors can be trained fairly easily to use strengths in communication to help technical students, but traditionally tutors have received little in return besides teaching experience. However, the Writing Center director can devise writing center assignments that profit both groups. Samson claims that having the tutors help the technical students with writing about science or technology enables technical students to develop their ability to communicate technical information and enables communication students to learn principles of science or technology from their peers. Success with these assignments requires that the Writing Center director define both groups of students, what the different tutors are to do and how to do it, and that he or she develop effective writing assignments. This essay examines how tutors and clients can be prepared for this collaborative peer tutoring that helps writing center tutors as well as technical student clients with valuable experience and skills.

Karyn Hollis in "More Science in the Writing Center: Training Tutors to Lead Group Tutorials on Biology Lab Reports" reports that although she has found that faculty in the Sciences are eager to use the writing center to improve their students' writing skills, writing center staff often have a hard time finding ways to help these students. Typically, the prose of science students is filled with intimidating terminology and processes with which tutors are very unfamiliar. Hollis explains that when faced with a paper from Biology 101 on Mendelian genetics and the *Drosophila melanogaster*, tutors are inclined to throw up their pens in despair, even though they notice familiar problems of organization or diction in the student writing. This essay describes the success achieved with these students, including how the tutors prepare for specific peer editing sessions, conduct the sessions themselves, and solve the problems typically encountered. Hollis claims that students, faculty, and tutors have expressed satisfaction with this peer-group methodology which is firmly grounded in composition and writing center theory. She further notes that this peer group technique has also been easily adaptable to other departments and programs across campus.

Curtis E. Ricker's essay "Creating a Writing Center to Assist Developmental Studies Students Across the Curriculum" notes that writing centers have traditionally been a component of English departments -- staffed, housed, and administered by those departments for the primary purpose of providing tutorial assistance to students with their writing problems. Such an objective, though certainly noteworthy, often narrows the type of assistance provided. In order to broaden the areas of help available to students, Ricker notes that Georgia Southern has supplemented its English Department's Writing Center by creating a Learning Resources Center that crosses the curriculum in the services it provides. Located in the college library, it contains the Academic Computing Center and the Tutorial Center. Heavily used by students from all subject areas, the Academic Computer Center is equipped with IBM and Apple and/or Macintosh computers in a networked environment. Many of these stations are linked to the mainframe computers of the University System Computing Network, providing access to Plato, the Cyber, and much computer-assisted instruction. Computer software is also available in multiple subject areas, and student assistants are available to help users.

Ricker explains that the Tutorial Center division of the Learning Resources Center offers an alternative to the customary Writing Center approach. Available to any student on campus, the Tutorial Center assists those experiencing difficulty with academic assignments or wishing to improve their academic skills. The peer tutors in the Tutorial Center are supervised by faculty from the Department of Developmental Studies in the areas of English, mathematics, reading, and study skills. One-on-one tutorials are supplemented by computer-assisted instruction, audio and videocassettes, and selected texts. In addition, faculty from other academic departments regularly present workshops that relate to specific instructional areas.

Ricker notes that the benefits of such a system are obvious. Besides the customary referrals to the Writing Center for those students doing poorly in writing, any instructor can refer students to the Tutorial Center for help in any subject matter -- including writing -- and since colleagues regularly present workshops, most instructors across the campus are aware of the assistance available. In addition, since the Learning Resources Center is one stop on the mandatory orientation tour, almost all students can locate that one area on campus where they can go to get, or be referred to, help in any subject. And, Ricker finally notes, because the Tutorial Center has such close ties to the Department of Developmental Studies, those "at-risk" students who are initially placed in developmental studies courses become acquainted with the assistance available from the Center during that crucial transition period of their freshman year.

Christina Murphy, in the final essay of the collection, "Writing Centers in Context: Responding to Current Educational Theories," comments that the emergence of writing centers as an important aspect of supplemental instruction has been one of the most significant developments to influence literacy education in America over the past twenty-five years. Like all changes in instructional practice, this emergence has taken place within a conflux of contending socio-political forces and amidst contending theories of the purpose of higher education; yet few theorists have examined writing centers from the perspective of the conflicting ideologies that vie to shape their structural and philosophical identities.

Drawing upon the distinctions developed by Stanley Aronowitz and Henry Giroux in *Education Under Siege*, this essay discusses the conservative, liberal and radical theories of education's role within society and applies these concepts to writing center theory and practice. Specifically, this essay develops three premises: (1) that each of these philosophies makes legitimate claims on what the character and identity of a writing center should be within education; (2) that the conflict amongst these views derives from the humanistic versus the technopragmatic concepts of education and from the ways educational systems reflect social and political realities; and (3) that the responses writing centers make to these conflicting ideologies will determine whether writing centers will serve instructional aims of self efficacy and self-enrichment or administrative aims of the quantitative assessment of identifiable literacy skills.

The history of writing center books and other publications has been marked by a spirit of helpfulness. The tradition of strong networking and generous exchange of information and ideas has helped make this book possible. We hope that readers will continue that tradition by using and refining what is presented here and by distributing what they learn among the writing center community in more articles, papers, workshops, books, consultations, letters, and simple conversations. Our discovery of so much expertise that we could draw on suggests that there is plenty more out there.

Past Accomplishments and Current Trends in Writing Center Research: A Bibliographic Essay

Donald E. Bushman
University of Tennessee

At the 1990 Conference on College Composition and Communication in Chicago, a roundtable discussion entitled "The Writing Center as Research Center: Issues and Directions" focused on the place of writing centers and the current state and writing center-related research in the academic community. Among the particular issues addressed were the following:

*Session chair Harvey Kail discussed how writing center professionals feel the need to be "at home" in the university setting and how the unique service writing centers offer needs to be more fully recognized not only by our peers but by ourselves.

*Lil Brannon suggested that writing center professionals do their identities a disservice by insisting upon research which focuses upon distant, theoretical concerns ("Research with a capital R"). In the tutoring which is a part of the writing center's everyday operation, she said, we find fertile ground for the sorts of ethnographic research and contextual knowledge which ought instead be our concern. Tutoring itself ought to be justification enough for a writing center's existence considering the research possibilities it provides.

*Lisa Ede called for more center-based research grounded in social-constructionist theory, saying that we must continue to stress the benefits of the social context of writing in the center in order to overcome the traditional paranoia over the center's collaborative nature. This, she said, is the first step in overcoming the writing center's "marginalization" within English Departments.

*John Trimbur talked, as well, about overcoming the outsider status of writing centers, suggesting that writing center researchers need to make the first move: Trimbur suggested that center-based research ought to be sent to a variety of composition journals and that our making use of the term "writing center" in an essay's title may, unfortunately, needlessly limit that essay's appeal to our peers.

One of the participants of the roundtable commented that, compared to writing center-related sessions at past CCCC meetings, 1990's was notable for the large room in which it was scheduled and the great number of people--many not directly affiliated with writing centers--in attendance for a Saturday morning. None of the roundtable participants

27

had, in fact, prepared enough handouts to supply everyone in attendance, suggesting that the growing interest in writing center research caught even the most active researchers themselves off guard.

The problem of the writing center's "marginalization" and our attempts to bring writing center research to the fore of composition studies was an issue raised by each of the roundtable participants. Recent research in the major professional journals suggests that writing centers are, indeed, becoming less marginal, that the gap is being bridged between the writing center's theoretical and pedagogical concerns and those of the composition classroom. One-to-one tutoring, the basis of writing center pedagogy, is being used more often and with greater effectiveness by classroom teachers from across the curriculum as a way of promoting learning through writing in a collaborative context. This essay is devoted to reviewing past work on writing center-related issues, such as the theoretical basis of the writing center, the role of the peer tutor, and the current state of writing center research.

The Writing Center in the Academic Community

One of the most frequently-cited essays in the history of writing center-related issues is Stephen North's "The Idea of a Writing Center." North's essay is one of the most concise statements of the theory which underlies writing center operation: "in a writing center the object is to make sure that writers, and not necessarily their texts, are what get changed by instruction" (438). He states further:

> Whereas in the "old" center instruction tends to take place
> after or apart from writing, and tends to focus on the correction
> of textual problems, in the "new" center the teaching takes
> place as much as possible during writing, during the activity
> being learned, and tends to focus on the activity itself. (439)

In his essay, North mentions briefly a *College English* article dating to 1950, Robert H. Moore's "The Writing Clinic and the Writing Laboratory." Therein, Moore creates a distinction between a writing "clinic"--what most researchers now refer to as a "center," a place of student-centered, individualized writing instruction--and a writing "laboratory"--a classroom-type atmosphere with mandatory attendance and where grammar drill and practice are the main tools of instruction. Moore's "laboratories" are remedial in the most pejorative sense. He states:

The writing clinic works with the individual student. The writing laboratory on the other hand, is far more likely to work with the individual as a member of a group with varying problems. It is more economical than the clinic, in that one instructor in a given hour can work with ten or twenty students where the clinician can scarcely work with more than four at most. Further, the laboratory can more successfully be used as the sole remedial agency, if the institution is willing to provide only one. (391)

Moore's essay raises many of the same concerns--funding, staffing, administering--that are at issue with writing center professionals today. What ought no longer to be an issue, though, according to North-- thirty-five years after Moore's essay--is the theoretical basis of writing centers: "Our job is to produce better writers, not better writing" (438). However, North notes sadly that

[t]he grammar and drill center, the fix-it shop, the first-aid station--these are neither the vestiges of some paradigm nor pedagogical aberrations that have been overlooked in the confusion of the "revolution" in the teaching of writing, but that will soon enough be set on the right, or done away with. They are, instead, the vital and authentic reflection of a way of writing and the teaching of writing that is alive and well in English departments everywhere. (437)

Similarly, in 1985, then-NWCA vice-president Jeanne Simpson, in "What Lies Ahead for Writing Centers: Position Statement on Professional Concerns," notes that she still finds "many writing center people who see no problem with giving a writing center a strictly remedial focus. This, to me," she says, "is anathema" (35). Overall, though, Simpson is more optimistic than North, stating that "writing centers have arrived"; however, she says, even though "the academic world now accepts writing centers," we would be foolish to become complacent about our roles in the university community. "The changes in writing centers--in what they mean and how they have been used, funded, and administered over the last decade--should tell us that fluidity is a fact we must accept. Writing centers will unquestionably continue to change" (35). Simpson urges writing center directors to listen to each other and to ask questions of each other, to consider who we are and where we are headed as professionals. Our continuing to be accepted in the university community, Simpson stresses, depends ultimately on how we view ourselves and how we portray ourselves to administrators, those to whom we must finally answer; we must think big: "the more professional we are, the more we can ask for; the more we ask for, the more likely it is that we will be recognized as professionals" (36).

Although Simpson's NWCA "Position Statement" provides "guidelines for developing job descriptions for writing center directorships and for evaluating the credentials for these positions" (37), a survey of freshman English directors, conducted by Gary Olson and Evelyn Ashton-Jones and published in 1988, shows that the role of writing center director is still "ill-defined," existing somewhere between "teacher, scholar, and administrator" (19-20). Undoubtedly, this lack of definition in writing center directors' roles does nothing to decrease the marginal status of centers as a whole, but the problem of defining our professional status is, ultimately, ours to correct. Since our departments and employing institutions have not heeded such professionally-endorsed position statements as Simpson's, the solution to the writing center professional's ill-defined role lies in our continuing to conduct and publish the sort of research urged by the CCCC roundtable participants. Defining the role and the importance of tutors in the writing center--how they should be trained and how they collaborate with students to produce better writing is primary to the role of the center in the academic community.

The Peer Tutor in the Writing Center

The publication in recent years of such books as Carol Feiser Laque and Phyllis A. Sherwood's *A Laboratory Approach to Writing*, Emily Meyer and Louise Z. Smith's *The Practical Tutor*, and Muriel Harris's *Teaching One-to-One*, ought to tell us that tutor training has become serious business. Textbooks such as Donald Murray's *A Writer Teaches Writing* and Charles Dawe and Edward A. Dornan's *One to One: Resources for Conference-Centered Writing*, too, show that the need exists for texts that translate the peer tutorial method to the classroom.

The concept of the "peer tutor," however, has been hotly contested in the last ten years. The peer tutor is a necessary part of many writing centers, especially those in secondary schools and smaller colleges without graduate programs. But even many of the well-established

writing centers at large state universities--those schools whose centers
see 40-50 students daily--must make use of undergraduate tutors from
across the curriculum. Often at issue, however, is whether these tutors
can truly be considered the "peers" of those they assist in the center and,
if so, how tutors can work most effectively.

The place and the value of peer tutoring, how to train tutors, and
tutoring's relationship to collaborative learning has been widely
discussed in writing center research in the last decade. In his "Peer
Tutoring and the 'Conversation of Mankind,'" Kenneth Bruffee suggests
that the value of peer tutoring is found in its ability to change the
social context in which people learn by replacing the traditional,
hierarchical model in academics (that of a teacher lecturing to a student)
with a model based on cooperation and collaboration. Bruffee argues
(via literary theorist Michael Oakeshott) that what we refer to as
"reflective thought" is both "organically and formally" related to human
conversation. "Reflective thinking is something we learn to do, and we
learn to do it from and with other people. We learn to think reflectively
as a result of learning to talk" (6). It follows, Bruffee insists, that "[i]f
thought is internalized conversation, then writing is internalized
conversation re-externalized .... By writing, we re-immerse conversation
into its social medium" (7). Hence, in the conversational nature of peer
tutoring is the root of better thinking and better writing.

Bruffee also cites Thomas Kuhn as one who argues that knowledge
is a social artifact created by a community of like-minded peers. In the
peer tutoring situation, then, knowledge is created through the
collaborative efforts of the tutee, who provides "knowledge of the
subject to be written about and knowledge of the assignment," and the
tutor, who provides "knowledge of the conventions of discourse and
knowledge of standard written English" (Bruffee 10). By providing a
community of "status equals" in which to create knowledge, Bruffee
says, peer tutoring helps both tutor and tutee learn the "skill and
partnership" that characterize the communities in which writing is done
outside of school, "in business, government, and the professions" (8).

The problem with the notion of "peer tutoring," though, according
to John Trimbur (in his "Peer Tutoring: A Contradiction in Terms?") is
the "cognitive dissonance" it creates within the tutor, who is at once a
peer, but who is also a tutor invested with "a certain institutional
authority" (22-23). Undergraduate students who are employed as peer
tutors by writing center directors are, generally speaking, "highly
skilled academic achievers" and "independent learners," Trimbur rightly

notes. "Rewarded by the traditional structure of teaching and learning," he says, "tutors have often internalized its values and standards and, in many respects, remain dependent upon its authority." Such tutors, then, feel a loyalty both to their fellow undergraduates and to the "academic system that has rewarded them" (23).

To deal with this dissonance, Trimbur proposes a "developmental sequence" of tutor training

> which would begin with a Bruffeesque approach to peer tutors as collaborative learners. [T]his stage is most significant because it demands that students unlearn some of the values and behaviors-- the competitive individualism of traditional academics--that have already rewarded them and shaped their identities as students. (26)

It is vital, Trimbur concludes, that we do not turn tutors into authority figures, that, ultimately, it is the "peer" half of their identities which must be fostered. We must teach tutors to "unlearn" the traditional, hierarchical academic model in order "to resocialize tutors as collaborative learners within student culture" (27). In "The Politics of Peer Tutoring," Trimbur and Harvey Kail propose a similar tutoring strategy, but in this essay they ground their justification in the sociological and cultural theories of Richard Sennett. Through the collaborative context of peer tutoring, Kail and Trimbur state, students are lead through a "crisis of authority" which demystifies the notion of the teacher as an omnipotent authority figure. "What students gain is the ability to reinterpret . . . power by defining the authority of knowledge as a relationship among people--not a hierarchical structure of generation and transmission" (12).

While Muriel Harris agrees that the peer tutoring environment provides a rich learning context for students, she notes (in "Peer Tutoring: How Tutors Learn"), as well, that tutoring "create[s] a uniquely beneficial learning environment for those selected to be tutors" (28). These student workers gain knowledge of grammar, theories of learning, problem solving strategies, and audience awareness. Most importantly, though, tutoring helps to develop tutors' cognitive abilities, which translates into improved revising skills. They develop the ability "to read a paper and . . . to compare what they see in it with what the writer had intended to write" (32). Lil Brannon and C. H. Knoblauch, too, suggest that the best tutoring derives from a "philosophical awareness . . . of how people learn and how learning can be encouraged" (46).

In *Lives on the Boundary*, Mike Rose suggests another sort of awareness tutors must have, aside from how to help a writer make effective choices for revision. The language we use when dealing with writers, Rose suggests, has much to do with how they view their status in the academic community:

> We still talk of writers as suffering from specifiable, locatable defects, deficits, and handicaps that can be localized, circumscribed, and remedied. Such talk carries with it the etymological wisps and traces of disease and serves to exclude from the academic community those so labeled (210).

Although Muriel Harris suggested a few years ago that, "despite the anti-doctor attitudes, a medical image of what we do is not as repugnant as it might sound at first" ("Theory and Reality" 5), she stated during a writing center-related session at the 1990 CCCC in Chicago that we must be sure to avoid "the grammar of isolation and defeat" when commenting--orally or in writing--on a student essay, stressing instead that writing is a skill that matures and is in no way an outward manifestation of one's self-worth.

The Writing Center Researcher

Discovering how learning is enhanced through the collaborative efforts of tutors and tutees is the primary objective of writing center research. If writing really is the social activity that current theorists insist it is, then the writing center, Lisa Ede says (in "Writing as a Social Process: A Theoretical Foundation for Writing Centers?"), ought to be the best place to uncover some of the specific details of this social interaction. Ede wants to explode the:

> general perception that writing centers are "extras," helpful additions to composition or writing across the curriculum programs that fall into the nice-to-have-if-you-can-get-it-but-not-essential category . . . [and] place writing centers at the heart, rather than the periphery of current theory in composition studies. (4-6)

In order to give credence to the idea that writing is best viewed as a collaborative activity, Ede explores the notion of "authorship" as it has developed historically. She notes that it was not until the Romantic era that there existed a "fully conceived argument for the primacy of the individual imagination," from which developed our modern notion of authorship as ownership or "intellectual property rights" (8). It was, Ede notes, the "impact of Cartesianism, which established epistemology as the central branch of philosophy" and the typical Romantic "image of the solitary writer working silently in a garret" that informed those who came to believe "that the individual thinking and writing in isolation is the source of all truth worth knowing" (8-9). It is an unfortunate fact that the people who are most skeptical of the collaborative atmosphere of writing centers are very often our English department colleagues whose "immersion" in the "solitary writer" theory prevent them from fully accepting the writing center's mission (9).

Ede suggests that writing center professionals can best legitimize their research by immersing it in the theories of the various fields from which the social-constructionist model grew--"philosophy, education, sociology, anthropology, psychology, and literary criticism" (10). Ede urges that we contribute to and test the current theoretical wave by capitalizing on the social atmosphere in which we work to do "case studies" and "detailed ethnographic analyses" of the collaboration we see every day in the writing center (11).

The same sentiment is expressed by Kail and Kay Allen ("Conducting Research in the Writing Lab") and by North in his "Designing a Case Study Method for Tutorials: A Prelude to Research," wherein he justifies case study or ethnographic methods of research in the writing center as the most beneficial because of their close relationships to the daily, pragmatic nature of tutoring. Despite the fact that the information gathered in such research may not be altogether significant outside of the immediate context of the tutorial environment--that one is confronted with the "difficulty of transporting 'knowledge' across methodological borders"--North suggests that, as writing center professionals, the tutorial-social environment ought to be our primary concern: "We need to remember who we are and where we set out from . . . " (96-97). The best method for writing center research ought to mirror the daily activity of tutoring.

In "Writing Center Research: Testing Our Assumptions," North provides two sample research projects suitable to the writing center environment. The first project involves videotaping a series of tutorials by a number of "good" and an equal number of "not-so-good" tutors (these judgments would be made by their directors and fellow tutors). The experimenter and tutor would then view the tape and go through a "stimulated recall session," which would be taped, transcribed, and analyzed to determine if any significant differences exist in the way "good" and "not-so-good" tutors operate (30-31).

There is also a need, North adds, to study the effect of tutoring on the many "drop-in" students who enter our doors. To see whether a single tutorial has any effect on such a writer, North suggests a study which analyzes pre- and post-tutorial protocols of students working on a specific writing task (he suggests, for example, law school applicants working on entrance exams) and compares these protocols (the experimental group) with the single protocols of the untutored (control) group (32). While this model for research could be attempted at any central or decentralized writing center, North's first research sample has implications for both the tutorial models Kail and Trimbur outline, voluntarily-attended writing centers and curriculum-based tutoring programs.

Research possibilities such as those suggested above are critical to the further growth--both theoretically/pedagogically and physically/economically--of writing centers. Such research serves not only to justify a center's existence to administrators, but it also shows the rest of the university community that writing center professionals have the ability to do honest-to-goodness research and that such research is aimed--like that of the classroom teacher--at improving student writing. Brannon and Knoblauch say it best: "[F]ar from performing an adjunct or support service, [writing center tutors] do essentially the same work as their classroom counterparts--and do it under conditions that can be particularly beneficial to writers" (44-45).

Ede cites Marilyn M. Cooper's essay "The Ecology of Writing" as representing a model of the tutorial-type instruction that is branching beyond the writing center and into the classroom. Cooper's essay is one of the best statements on the social-constructionist model of writing, one which suggests the limited scope of the cognitive process theory and its "solitary author" (365). The "ecological model of writing," Cooper says, is based upon the idea "that writing is an activity through which a person is continually engaged with a variety of socially constituted systems" (367). These systems--for no two are the same--are "inherently dynamic" and "concrete," she says. They are tailored to the needs of a particular writing task, and they are such that they "can be investigated, described, altered; they are not postulated mental entities, not generalizations" (368-69).

These "ecological systems" are, in a sense, the foundation of the writing center environment. The individualized, student-centered approach we take is similarly dynamic: we rarely travel the same instructional path with any two students. Thus, writing center tutors must take a similarly "ecological" approach, taking into account each student's relationship to his or her respective "environment." Tutors do not follow a given model with any two students because no two students can claim exactly the same environment; students enter the center at various stages in the writing process with different assignments, different levels of competency, and different fears or concerns about writing. Thus, Cooper says, "The systems are not given; not limitations on writers; instead they are made and remade by writers in the act of writing" (368). This very idea is at the heart of North's philosophy on the writing center's reason for being: "The only composing process that matters in a writing center," North insists, "is 'a' composing process, and it 'belongs' to, is acted out by, only one given writer" ("Idea" 439).

As Cooper's essay suggests, writing center/tutorial research and research on writing in both the classroom and the workplace are, in many ways, on a parallel course. Case studies and ethnographic research are becoming widely accepted as the most beneficial methods of studying the collaborative nature of the process of writing. And as the many scholars here cited insist, writing center professionals must, in order to bring writing centers to the foreground of composition research, take advantage of the opportunities for such research in the center. As writing center administrators and tutors, our struggle for acceptance in the academic world--our attempt to overcome our marginal status--has been made worlds easier by the current acceptance of the social-constructionist model of writing, for we are a part of the making of knowledge every time we engage in one-to-one instruction with a student. It is up to us to capitalize on our favorable positions and to make the writing center the center of writing research and instruction on campus.

Works Cited

Brannon, Lil, and C. H. Knoblauch. "A Philosophical Perspective on Writing Centers and the Teaching of Writing." In Olson, 36-47.

Bruffee, Kenneth A. "Peer Tutoring and the 'Conversation of Mankind.'" In Olson, 3-15.

Cooper, Marilyn M. "The Ecology of Writing." *College English* 48 (April 1986): 364-75.

Dawe, Charles W., and Edward A. Dornan. *One to One: Resources for Conference-Centered Writing.* Boston: Little, Brown, 1981.

Ede, Lisa. "Writing as a Social Process: A Theoretical Foundation for Writing Centers?" *Writing Center Journal* 9.2 (Spring/Summer 1989): 3-13.

Harris, Muriel. "Peer Tutoring: How Tutors Learn." *Teaching English in the Two-Year College* 15.1 (Feb. 1988): 28-33.

--------. *Teaching One-to-One: The Writing Conference.* Urbana: NCTE, 1986.

--------. "Theory and Reality: The Ideal Writing Center(s)." *Writing Center Journal* 5.2/6.1 (1985): 4-9.

-------. *Tutoring Writing: A Sourcebook for Writing Labs.* Glenview, IL: Scott, Foresman, 1982.

Kail, Harvey, and Kay Allen. "Conducting Research in the Writing Lab." *Tutoring Writing: A Sourcebook for Writing Labs.* Ed. Muriel Harris. Glenview, IL: Scott, Foresman, 1982. 233-45.

Kail, Harvey, and John Trimbur. "The Politics of Peer Tutoring." *WPA: Writing Program Administration* 11.1-2 (Fall 1987): 5-12.

Laque, Carol Feiser, and Phyllis A. Sherwood. *A Laboratory Approach to Writing.* Urbana: NCTE, 1977.

Meyer, Emily, and Louise Z. Smith. *The Practical Tutor.* New York: Oxford UP, 1987.

Moore, Robert H. "The Writing Clinic and the Writing Laboratory." *College English* 7 (1950): 388-93.

Murray, Donald. *A Writer Teaches Writing.* 2nd ed. Boston: Houghton, 1985.

North, Stephen M. "Designing a Case Study Method for Tutorials: A Prelude to Research." *Rhetoric Review* 4 (Sept. 1985): 88-99.

-----. "The Idea of a Writing Center." *College English* 46 (Sept. 1984): 433-46.

-----. "Writing Center Research: Testing our Assumptions." In Olson, 24-35.

Olson, Gary, ed. *Writing Centers: Theory and Administration.* Urbana: NCTE, 1984.

Olson, Gary, and Evelyn Ashton-Jones. "Writing Center Directors: The Search for Professional Status." *WPA: Writing Program Administration* 12.1-2 (Fall/Winter 1988): 19-28.

Rose, Mike. *Lives on the Boundary: A Moving Account of the Struggles and Achievements of America's Educational Underclass.* New York: Penguin, 1989.

Simpson, Jeanne H. "What Lies Ahead for Writing Centers: Position Statement on Professional Concerns." *Writing Center Journal* 5.2/6.1 (1985): 35-39.

Trimbur, John. "Peer Tutoring: A Contradiction in Terms?" *Writing Center Journal* 7.2 (Spring/Summer 1987): 21-28.

Writing Center Outreach: Sharing Knowledge and Influencing Attitudes About Writing

Bradley T. Hughes
University of Wisconsin-Madison

The history of writing centers is largely one of expansion. As this current volume attests, writing centers are constantly inventing new forms of instruction and reaching new audiences. To the individualized instruction that defines them, writing centers (my own among them) have added such activities as instruction in word processing, classes on writing essay exams and book reviews, and peer review workshops for graduate students. More and more writing centers have also begun teaching, at faculty request, brief units on writing within selected courses across campus. This last type of writing center instruction, which is the subject of this essay, is most commonly known as outreach. More than just a sign of writing centers' creativity and vitality and more than just the attempts of writing center directors "to stake out as large a claim as they can in more visible or acceptable territory" (North 446), though it is both of these, outreach can be seen as a natural and logical extension of writing center talk. Outreach gives writing center instructors opportunities to share experience and knowledge with faculty as well as students; and as writing centers mature, this knowledge grows ever more valuable within the university.[1]

---

[1]Throughout this essay I use the more common term "writing centers" to refer to both writing centers and writing labs. I use the term "instructor" to refer to the professional staff in writing centers. In most programs, it is likely that the professional staff will do the bulk of outreach work, though certainly student tutors can play an important role in outreach. Kim Moreland's article about an outreach program at Brown University illustrates the important role student tutors can play. Certain kinds of outreach--especially the instruction I describe in this essay that requires consultation with faculty and that builds from year to year--do, however, require the involvement of a professional staff, as Hayhoe discusses (252). In a recent article, Karen Rodis makes a case for the value of professional staff in a writing center (55-56). To her arguments that professional staff enhance the reputation of a writing center and help establish respect among English Department faculty, I would add that they provide the knowledge

Generally, outreach can be divided into two categories based on its purpose. Designed to inform and recruit students, the most common kind of outreach consists of brief visits to classes by writing center instructors who introduce the writing center and explain how students can best use it as they work on course papers. Sometimes these presentations take the form of demonstration tutorials of the sort described by Stephen North (441). The other form of outreach is more instructional in its aim and requires a much more substantial commitment from both course professors and writing center staff. This type of outreach takes writing center instructors into classes to teach brief units on writing designed to help prepare students to write particular course papers. As Rebecca Howard explains, this instruction can be "a valuable tool for teaching composition strategies to students and composition philosophy to their professors" (39).

There is a small but useful literature about outreach. Numerous possibilities for outreach have been suggested by, among others, George Hayhoe (247-248), Joyce Steward and Mary Croft (55-56), Kim Moreland, Bradley Hughes (28), Joyce Smoot, David Klooster (2-3), and Barbara Brooks (137-138). Two more substantial articles about outreach explore the connections between writing-across-the-curriculum and writing center instruction in regular courses. In an important article, Carol Peterson Haviland describes several examples of writing center outreach at Montana State University, where outreach is part of the university's writing-across-the-curriculum program. Howard's essay "*In-Situ* Workshops and the Peer Relationships of Composition Faculty" considers both the theoretical and practical dimensions of composition instructors teaching within classes in other departments. Building on this literature, we need to continue to define what writing center outreach is, to explain its benefits, to establish its relationship with writing-across-the-curriculum, and to articulate a set of principles for guiding it.

Over the past five years, outreach has become an important part of our writing center at the University of Wisconsin at Madison, a part that strengthens in valuable ways the rest of what we do. During the fall semester of 1989, for example, we made presentations about the writing center (the first type of outreach I have identified) to over 1600 students in some 25 courses, and we taught units on writing (the second

---

and continuity necessary to develop and sustain a substantial outreach program.

and more important type of outreach) to over 700 students in 15 different courses. The courses in which we made presentations and offered instruction ranged across the disciplines, from a graduate course in library science to a graduate business course on operations management; from a senior thesis class in landscape architecture to a course in experimental psychology; from an introductory course on English and American literature to a women's studies course on race and ethnicity. Through this experience, we have developed a successful model for soliciting outreach requests and for planning and delivering instruction.

An Argument for Outreach

There are, of course, certain prerequisites for developing an outreach program, the most important of which is adequate staffing. As Hayhoe points out, "a lab that expands its services in the directions I have indicated [directions which include outreach] must have a director who is free in terms of both available time and institutional policy to explore these possibilities" (252). There must be support, Hayhoe continues, from a university's administration (252). And if there is a writing-across-the-curriculum program, a writing center must have its support and cooperation. If these conditions exist, there are, I think, compelling arguments for writing centers to invest energy in developing a carefully conceived outreach program. As other advocates of writing center outreach have argued (Haviland 30, e.g.), outreach benefits everyone involved: students receiving the instruction, faculty who have requested and participated in it, and center staff who design and deliver it. Those benefits can be seen from these different perspectives.

1. Through outreach, students and faculty learn directly about the writing center, and more students come for tutorial instruction. Student and faculty attitudes about writing centers are perennial concerns in our field. As Stephen North explains, we are widely misunderstood; and despite North's excellent article, which I now share with new teaching assistants in my department, the situation has not changed.

Some professors do a good job of explaining the writing center to their students and encouraging them to take advantage of center instruction; in fact, faculty endorsements can be highly persuasive to students. But I wince when I hear about how some other faculty describe the writing center to their classes (albeit with good intentions) or when I read some of the descriptions of the writing center that appear on paper assignments ("If you are having trouble writing in English, go to the writing center"). During class presentations, we work to confront directly some of the misconceptions about the writing center, and the handouts we distribute do the same. We stress that there is nothing inherently remedial about writing tutorials; that no one learns all there is to learn about writing once and for all; that writers go on to write in new fields, at new levels, and in new genres; and at those times they can benefit from additional instruction. And we explain that good writers, their professors included, share their work in progress with trusted colleagues for a critical response while a paper is still changeable. Students in the class sometimes volunteer testimonials about their previous experiences at the writing center, endorsements that are far more convincing than anything our staff could say. Of course, our audience for this presentation includes the course professor as much as the students, for we are hoping to change the way faculty understand and talk about writing center instruction in the future. There is no doubt that, when they are well done, these presentations work; students come for tutorials as a direct result of the presentations made in their classes.

2. **Through outreach, all the students in a class receive practical and timely advice about writing course papers.** As we know, students often struggle with assignments--unsure of what is expected of them and of how to start and thus they are prone to procrastination, and reluctant or unable to articulate precise questions to elicit clarification and advice. Among the experienced professional staff of a writing center, those who have worked with students on writing assignments from a variety of disciplines, there is a wealth of knowledge waiting to be tapped for outreach instruction, knowledge from which students can profit. This knowledge ought to be shared beyond the confines of writing center tutorials, and it deserves to be valued publicly, where teaching is centered on our campuses--in the classroom. Well-designed outreach instruction that engages a writing center instructor, the course instructor, and the students in a conversation about the paper assignment can do much to clarify expectations and to help students get started on a writing project. And outreach instruction reaches all the students in a course, something writing center tutorials, unless they are a required part of a course, never do.

3. Through outreach, writing center staff learn more about writing in different disciplines. Outreach necessitates learning--about the kinds of writing done in different disciplines, about the teaching methods and philosophies of different instructors, about the needs of different students at different levels of study. Most writing center directors would acknowledge that they and their staff need to learn more about writing outside their own fields, but it is easy never to find time for this kind of learning and instead to postpone it because of more pressing needs; outreach presentations, with their built-in deadlines, provide the incentive to follow-through with these good intentions. And the benefits rebound, as samples gathered for outreach become materials for staff training; as outreach handouts are used in other writing center teaching; as faculty met through outreach participate in future staff meetings to talk about writing in their field; and as these faculty participate in writing-across-the-curriculum seminars and become informed supporters of the writing center.

4. Through the dialogue essential to outreach, valuable connections are established between the writing center and faculty in different departments. To develop an effective outreach program, writing center staff and course instructors must collaborate. As part of our planning for outreach, we commiserate about problems and jointly seek solutions; we discuss goals for writing assignments and methods for teaching writing; and we offer suggestions about ways to help students succeed with writing assignments. During classes, we serve as catalysts to get faculty talking productively with students about writing. In fact, this consultation, tailored individually for instructors, parallels and exemplifies what we do in writing center tutorials for students.

Although she is describing the work of writing-across-the-curriculum composition instructors at Colgate University rather than that of writing center instructors, what Rebecca Howard says about the benefits of collaboration about writing across the curriculum applies equally well to outreach done by writing centers:

> Greater numbers of faculty in the other disciplines are coming to see writing faculty not as technicians from the Academic Fixit Shop but as full participants in (and sometimes enablers of) the liberal arts traditions. They are increasingly willing to set aside counterproductive visions of writing instruction as inherently

normative or remedial. They are realizing that writing faculty have a content for their instruction--that we are working from a disciplinary base, the discipline of composition, which itself facilitates learning in the other disciplines of the university. (45)

In fact, I would argue, as Howard does, that by offering tangible assistance to faculty through outreach, we do much to encourage cooperation between faculty in other disciplines and writing faculty, cooperation that is essential to the success of writing-across-the-curriculum.

Principles and Methods for Outreach

To be successful and satisfied with the outreach they do, writing centers need to have a clearly defined philosophy and set of principles for their outreach programs. Otherwise, it is easy to get trapped in unproductive and awkward teaching situations--to be asked, for example, to do the impossible, to perform a miracle in 15 minutes of class time; to develop a class presentation without information the professor should provide about the writing assignment and the needs of the class; to act as a substitute teacher while the instructor is attending a conference; or to deliver instruction that we know is not appropriate for students, instruction that is too brief or too general, and as a consequence to regret at leisure what we agreed to do in haste. In our case, such principles have evolved from experience more than they were established in advance; indeed, our mistakes and failures have taught us much about how to approach outreach. The principles I outline here should be seen as guidelines, not rules, for outreach. Effective cooperation with faculty requires that we balance these principles with flexibility and that, as Howard recommends, we effect change diplomatically (45). For outreach to be successful we need to:

1. **Make it easy for faculty to request outreach presentations and instruction.** For years, in a memo sent to all faculty and instructional staff on my campus, I offered to make presentations in classes. The response was, however, underwhelming: the same two or three instructors, ones with whom the writing center had been collaborating for years, requested presentations, but the group was growing no larger. Then we featured outreach more prominently in the memo, listed some courses in which we have done outreach in the past, and added a tear-off form for faculty to request presentations. Under

the heading "Lab Staff Are Available to Visit Your Classes," the memo reads,

> *We have found that students are more likely to visit the Writing Lab after they have met one of our staff members. We would be happy to send one of our instructors to your classes to make a short presentation about Writing Lab services, or we would be pleased to consult with you about the writing component of your courses. If you would like such a visit, please complete and return the form below.*

The form requests basic but essential information about the course; the number, types of, and due dates for writing assignments; the number and level of students enrolled; the time and location of class meetings; and times we should try to call the professor. Simple as it sounds, this one change has led to a dramatic increase in requests for outreach presentations and instruction and has provided us with information, in a convenient form, necessary to begin planning the presentation.

2. **Communicate and establish expectations in advance.** We have found that it is easy to miscommunicate about outreach, especially for faculty to have unrealistic expectations for what we can accomplish in a brief period of time. As a consequence, we now painstakingly gather information before a session and establish clear expectations. In an initial phone conversation, I explain that I would be happy to make a brief (ten minute) presentation about writing center instruction or that I would be willing to plan together a more substantial presentation or workshop designed to help students write a particular course paper. And I always mention that the center has done such instruction with many faculty in different departments; in other words, I do not want faculty to think that they have to be pioneers. Even for a brief class presentation, I ask questions about the assignment, about the students, and about the professor's response to students' writing in the past; I ask to have copies of the course syllabus, of the writing assignments, and of sample papers if possible. In other words, I want to have as much information as possible so that I can tailor my presentation to the class and so that I can offer suggestions to help instructors with the writing assignments they make. (The paper assignments from outreach courses are then placed in a notebook in the writing center so our instructors can read them over and be more prepared to work with students from

those courses.) My questions also alert faculty that the writing center is serious about its instruction. Almost always I try to time outreach presentations to coincide with the period when students will actually be writing a paper for the course. To do so often contradicts the timing that faculty propose. They often ask center staff to speak in their classes early in the semester even when no paper may be due for months; by that time students have long forgotten what they heard about the writing center and about writing their paper. As Wendy Bishop points out based on her recent study of recruiting students for the writing center, students need to be reminded of the benefits of writing center instruction "several times during the semester" (39).

3. **Collaborate with the course instructor--in advance and during the class, and try to make students active participants in the outreach session.** For more substantial outreach instruction, I meet with the faculty member to negotiate what we will do during the class session. Course instructors should help decide what to cover in the class and they should, to some degree, participate in the teaching. Faculty need to analyze what they want students to do with their writing assignments and to decide what they value in papers; planning an outreach session requires this kind of analysis. With very few exceptions, I refuse to make an outreach presentation without the professor present. I have, before I knew better, allowed myself to be put in the position of a substitute teacher who was completely ignored by the class, and on other occasions my presentation has been the only thing standing between students and the end of the class hour--both impossible situations. Faculty signal to students the importance they attach to a subject by the degree to which they involve themselves in teaching it. Besides, students often--indeed they should--have questions about writing a particular assignment and about writing in a particular field that only the course instructor can answer.

During outreach presentations, course professors and writing center instructors can collaborate in different ways. Some professors will never feel comfortable leading a discussion about writing (though I try to emphasize to them how much they know about writing in their field, intuitively if not explicitly), while others want the variety an outside instructor brings to a course. That is fine, but in such cases I make sure during the class to direct questions about the assignment to the professor and I encourage students to do the same.

In some cases, our outreach has been so successful that we have made ourselves obsolete by transferring responsibility for the writing instruction completely to the course professor. Far from being a problem, this seems ideal. Our recent outreach work in a history course on American education, religion, and the media illustrates how this can happen. In our meeting in advance of the class I could tell that the instructor had clear ideas about what he wanted students to do in their course papers and that he was willing contribute significantly to the session. At my urging and mostly on his own initiative, he decided to lead the class himself (something he had not originally intended to do); he wrote up a full-page handout explaining his assignment in more detail and offering advice about approaching it; he created brief sample papers in response to the assignment for the class to discuss, papers that illustrated the difference between analysis (what he wanted in this particular paper) and summary (what he wanted them to avoid). During the class itself he talked with his students about the process of writing in general and shared some of his own approaches to writing, and he led a discussion of the samples (no small feat in a lecture of 100 students). All that was left for me to do during the class, besides describing writing center instruction, was to ask the instructor questions designed to clarify points he was making and to offer a few additional pieces of advice. We have had a similar success with outreach in a bacteriology class. We originally developed materials to help students write lab reports in that class; now the course instructor, with our enthusiastic support, teaches the unit on writing herself using our materials.

4. **Develop effective materials, tailored to the class, and offer specific advice, tied to samples.** Writing center instructors should never go to a class without handouts. While some general writing center handouts may be applicable, ones customized for the particular class are preferable. It may be time consuming, but it is worth the effort to write up some brief points of advice to help students with their paper assignments. The best materials for discussion during an outreach session are sample papers written by students in the same class in previous semesters (saved by the instructor for such a purpose and used with the authors' permission). I would recommend discussing at least two papers so that students see that there is no single right way to approach an assignment. With these samples, the course instructor can set a high standard, and reading and discussing them gets students actively involved in the class and thinking critically about writing,

rather than passively receiving information. The samples help students understand what the assignment entails and prepare them to begin writing. In addition, they provide a means to ground the discussion of writing in specifics.

5. **Remember the limitations of outreach.** Just as no lecture or presentation about writing can address all the different needs students have, neither can an outreach session. After all, it is brief and, no matter how customized for a particular class, is still to some degree general and abstract. And, as we know, students learn about writing by writing, not by listening to a presentation. For these reasons, writing center staff should, as part of outreach, encourage students to come for tutorials as they work on their course papers. And staff should encourage faculty to build into their writing assignments opportunities for students to receive responses to their writing--from peers and the professor--while it is in progress.

6. **Know the limits of the writing center staff.** As with other forms of writing center instruction, it is easy to become a victim of success in an outreach program. In other words, writing center directors need to guard against allowing outreach to overwhelm the resources of their staff or to reduce time available for tutoring. If students who are encouraged to come to the writing center discover that there are no tutorials available, they will only be frustrated and discouraged, and so too will the center staff. The goal should be steady, manageable growth; this kind of growth in outreach can in turn bolster arguments for increased staffing.

Writing center directors also must be careful not to force staff into outreach teaching if they are not interested or qualified. Outreach teaching can be difficult because there is something ad hoc and unpredictable about it; some staff enjoy the give-and-take with faculty and students in a classroom and thrive teaching under such conditions, while others are uncomfortable. There is more to this issue of staffing outreach than might first appear, since in most outreach the personal connection that is established between the course professor and the writing center instructor is crucial to success. Sallyanne Fitzgerald explains that a successful outreach instructor is good at creating "personal contacts" and has a "willingness to respond" to faculty in other departments and readily makes an "effort to investigate the skills required by disciplines other than English" (13). To the course professor, one particular member of the writing center staff comes to represent the writing center, and the professor generally wants to have this same person back to speak in future classes and often refers students directly to him or her. While this personal bond represents a strength in outreach it also reveals a certain frailty. If there are not instructors who possess these traits and who have adequate time for work with faculty in other departments or if key people leave the writing center staff, an outreach program can decline rapidly. Fitzgerald recommends that

> giving lecture demonstrations [the kind of outreach instruction I have been discussing] should be someone's fulltime commitment, not an occasional, voluntary service. We need to hire a faculty member to publicize the lecture demonstrations, to make the personal contacts with faculty, and to do the presentations in consultation with the faculty and other writing staff. Such a person could make this service the success it once was. (13)

7. **Keep careful records.** Writing centers should carefully track the development of their outreach programs so that they can share information with deans and department chairs about this contribution the center is making to writing instruction on campus. Beyond this, records can help centers learn from experience--to see which instructors request repeat presentations and instruction; to follow-up with those instructors who do not in order to find ways to improve; to measure and report back to course instructors how many students, after an outreach presentation in a course, have subsequently come to the writing center for tutorials. We have found it helpful to have center instructors complete a brief report after making an outreach presentation; this report includes not only facts about the session (date, course, professor, etc.) but also advice for other staff who might do outreach in the same course in the future.

8. **Take a long-term perspective on outreach.** It takes time to build a reputation for a good outreach program. It takes time for faculty to think in what are perhaps new ways for them about assignments, or about responding to student writing, or to talk in new ways about writing with their classes. Requests for brief presentations in one semester can grow into more substantial collaboration in the future. If we are strongly committed to using outreach to advance one of the

central goals of writing-across-the-curriculum--that is, changing approaches to teaching--we should not expect immediate reciprocity. We should be willing to make the first move, to give something of value to faculty and their students, something worth giving up class time for.

Some Examples of Outreach Instruction

I would like to conclude by describing in some detail three very different outreach programs our writing center has developed in the past few years. These examples illustrate, perhaps better than abstract principles or prescriptions do, an approach to outreach and the possibilities inherent in it. Because these are essentially success stories, let me add that by no means has all of our outreach been ideal. The most common problem we encounter is the case of faculty who request outreach but will not provide sample papers or even help us plan a session or respond to what we have done. In these cases, we take a patient, tactful approach, but eventually if there is no improvement, we let the outreach lapse.

What characterizes the three successful outreach programs I will describe is the change we have seen take place in the professors we have worked with and in the activities that take place in the classes we visit. These faculty members have become increasingly willing to participate actively in planning sessions and to change the way in which they incorporate writing into their courses. The first example involves a senior level sociology course on applied research methods. For the past four years, the professor of this course and I have collaborated on developing and teaching a two-hour unit on writing. At first, the outreach consisted largely of presentation--I presented principles I thought would be helpful to students as they wrote papers for this class (reports on their research) and as they prepared for the writing they would do after graduation. But over the years, partly as a result of the collaboration established through this outreach, the professor has changed the writing assignments she makes, and the outreach itself has changed to suit them. Students now write a brief paper (a critical analysis of a reading) before the outreach class; during the week after the writing center instruction, students read and comment on their peers' work and revise their papers (a pattern that is repeated throughout the semester). The outreach class is designed to prepare students to act as a critical reader and to revise their own work. During the class, we discuss a handout I bring on guidelines for peer review and we practice responding to papers by discussing samples written for the same assignment in previous years. Through this discussion, we attempt to identify characteristics of successful papers of this type, and thereby establish criteria students can use to guide their review of their peers' work and their revisions of their own. During the outreach session, this professor prefers to have me lead the discussion, but she plays an important role: she frequently offers examples drawn from her discipline to illustrate general points I am making, she responds to students' questions, and she shares with students advice based on her own experience as a scholarly writer. In order to give students more guidance about writing, the professor has also begun requiring students to read Lee Cuba's *A Short Guide to Writing about Social Science*, which the class discusses periodically throughout the semester.

In our work with a large (150-student) survey course on health care systems, we have witnessed a similar change. For several years, we offered, in the discussion sections of this course, brief introductions to writing research papers designed to help students write the one long paper due at the end of this course. Despite this instruction (and certainly not to our surprise), the faculty in this course continued to be unhappy with the papers they received. The faculty eventually chose to switch to a series of short papers designed to foster critical thinking about the issues taught in the course. Students now write a half-page summary of a class lecture or article; a summary of two readings that take opposing views on a controversial health issue such as drug and alcohol abuse; three brief descriptions of social or domestic abuse, each aimed at a different audience--readers of a local newspaper, second grade students, and a congressional representative; an annotated bibliography that includes differing perspectives on a topic; and a concluding paper in which students explore how their thinking on a health issue has changed during the semester.

To help prepare students to write these papers, the writing center created an hour-long outreach program. We developed handouts, which we discussed during the session, which include sample summaries of sources and annotated bibliographies; the examples come from papers the professor provided from previous semesters. We also introduce students to the basics of the APA documentation system, which they are required to use in their papers.

Our work with an intermediate level course on the geography of Africa illustrates once again that the impact of writing center outreach goes far beyond the instruction we provide in a class period. Actually the history of it seems to lend itself to narrative. At the end of the fall semester two years ago, an assistant professor in the geography department called to arrange an appointment. The tone of her voice warned me that something was wrong. When we met she explained that she was very disappointed with the research papers she had just graded, and, in effect, she wanted to know why I was not doing my job. After explaining that I try not to accept responsibility for the way the 43,000 students on my campus write, I asked her to tell me about the assignment and to describe the problems in the papers. I then offered to develop an outreach presentation with her for the next semester, but she declared adamantly that she would not sacrifice a minute of class time for work on writing. Students should, in her opinion, already know how to write by the time they go to college. Choosing not to press her on this, I suggested ways we might get students from her class in the next semester to come to the writing center for individual instruction and for classes we offer on writing research papers. I also mentioned that many faculty find they are happier with the results when they require students to submit a draft of a longer paper for peer review or faculty criticism a month or so before the final due date and then have students revise based on the responses. She told me that she would think over my ideas and get back to me.

The next semester this professor asked me to consult with her about the assignment before she gave it to her class (she had included several intermediate due dates for parts of the paper). She also asked me to teach a special evening section of the writing center's class on research papers, and I agreed. Not a week passed before she called me and asked if I would do the presentation during the regular class hour, and I readily agreed; her students had rebelled at the idea of attending an extra evening session. For the class I assembled a packet of information about writing research papers (including handouts on posing good questions for research, on patterns for organizing a research paper, on evaluating sources, and on paraphrasing and documenting sources) and samples that we discussed during the outreach session. In advance of the class, the professor solicited questions from the students for me to discuss, and these questions provided an effective means to open up a discussion of research papers; during the class, the professor participated actively, modifying or clarifying points I have made, responding to questions from me and from the students. A number of students from this class came to the writing center for tutorials both before and after they submitted their first drafts; and the professor was happier with the papers she received, though by no means was a miracle worked. Most important to me is that writing center outreach helped serve as a catalyst for this instructor, as well as many others like her, to find new ways to talk with her students about their writing and to help them succeed with writing assignments.

Works Cited

Bishop, Wendy. "Bringing Writers to the Center: Some Survey Results, Surmises, and Suggestions." *The Writing Center Journal* 10.2 (1990): 31-41.

Brooks, Barbara. "Writing Across the Curriculum." *The High School Writing Center: Establishing and Maintaining One.* Ed. Pamela B. Farrell, Urbana: NCTE, 1989. 137-141.

Cuba, Lee J. *A Short Guide to Writing about Social Science.* Glenview, IL: Scott, Foresman, 1988.

Fitzgerald, Sallyanne H. "Successes and Failures: Facilitating Cooperation Across the Curriculum." *Writing Lab Newsletter* 13.1 (1988): 13-15.

Haviland, Carol Peterson. "Writing Centers and Writing Across-the-Curriculum: An Important Connection." *The Writing Center Journal* 5.2 (1985): 25-30.

Hayhoe, George. "Beyond the Basics: Expanded Uses of Writing Labs." *Tutoring Writing: A Sourcebook for Writing Labs.* Ed. Muriel Harris. Glenview, IL: Scott, Foresman, 1982. 246-253.

Howard, Rebecca M. *"In-Situ* Workshops and the Peer Relationships of Composition Faculty." *WPA: Writing Program Administration* 12 (1988): 39-46.

Hughes, Bradley. "Reaching Across the Curriculum with a Writing Center." *Illinois English Bulletin* 74.1 (1986): 24-31.

Klooster, David J. "Tutee Training, Or It Takes Two to Collaborate." *Writing Lab Newsletter* 13.4 (1988): 1-4.

Moreland, Kim. "The Writing Center: A Center for Writing-Across-the-Curriculum Activities." *Writing Lab Newsletter* 10.3 (1985): 1-4.

North, Stephen. "The Idea of a Writing Center." *College English* 46 (1984): 433-446.

Rodis, Karen, "Mending the Damaged Path: How to Avoid Conflict of Expectations When Setting up a Writing Center." *The Writing Center Journal* 10.2 (1990): 45-57.

Smoot, Joyce. "Public Relations and the Writing Center Director: Making the Center Visible On and Off Campus." *Writing Lab Newsletter* 11.1 (1986): 6-8.

Steward, Joyce S., and Mary K. Croft. "Presentations to Classes."
*The Writing Laboratory: Organization, Management,
Methods.* Glenview, IL: Scott, Foresman, 1982. 55-56.

From Writing Lab To Writing Center: Reinventing, Advancing, And Expanding

Jim Addison
Western Carolina University

Henry L. Wilson
University of Tennessee

The transition from writing "lab" to writing "center" implies more than a change in nomenclature. This simple surface shift in terminology represents dramatic alterations in the underlying philosophy, role, and functions of a writing center in the academic community. In fact, the implications of the change from lab to center represent in capsule form the entire metaphorical and ideological metamorphosis that the idea of a writing center has undergone over the last twenty years.

As long as the writing "lab" remained a mere lab, the metaphorical baggage associated with more familiar labs served as an obstruction to the full development of the potential power and effectiveness of the writing center. After all, a "lab" is most commonly associated with images of dry, objective "research," rather than with the promotion and development of living, growing organisms such as developing essays, term papers, and other publications. While it is true that "lab work" can to an extent connote a sort of hands-on, trying out experience (Harris, 6), the overall flavor of the concept of "lab" does not lend itself well to the process view of writing: a lab is often more backward-looking rather than forward-looking, in that the initial focus of a tutoring session is on the "sick" writing project brought into the lab for diagnosis and analysis. Thus, a student taking a paper to a "lab" is likely to assume that his writing efforts must somehow be sick or in need of the sort of treatment dispensed along medical lines--in this case, quick band-aid remedies like proofreading and the inevitable red-pen dissections of the dead, finished product.

In the writing "center," on the other hand, the idea of a centralized location from which writing emanates directly into the academic community takes hold. In addition, the strong nucleus of a writing center serves as a focus or lightning rod into which the various scattered writing tasks and activities from all across campus can radiate inward. And, as Stephen North has pointed out, the idea of a true writing center expresses itself at the local level in a focus on improving the writing skills of the individual writer, rather than on merely making changes within a text; thus, tutoring efforts can in effect transcend the limits imposed by a single text, and thereby be projected into longer range

goals (438). Taken as a whole, the concept of a writing "center"
conveys a more vibrant, comprehensive, and forward-looking point of
view than the tired, fossilized concept of writing "lab."

The specific experiences of the writing lab/writing center at
Western Carolina University serve as an instructive mirror to the
metamorphosis reflected by these change in nomenclature. Located in
the small mountain community of Cullowhee, North Carolina, WCU
was the site of an interesting, rather lab-like experiment in itself for the
development of a now-thriving writing center serving the needs of the
entire academic community. Like many early attempts at founding a
centralized location for the individualized teaching of writing, the "lab"
at WCU was initially not the outgrowth of any centralized plan or
"mission"; instead, the lab was simply thrown together by a new
department head who recognized the need for some form of more
individualized writing instruction for developmental or remedial
students. More specifically, when Dr. Marilyn Jody assumed the post of
department head in the late 1970's, she authorized the use of a regular
instructional classroom for the exclusive use of students enrolled in
"Remedial" English 100. Only a very limited supply of tutoring
materials, workbooks, etc. were available for the students remanded to
the writing lab. Typical of these early stages of the evolution of the
writing center, the tutoring and instructional activities which actually
gave the lab a reason for existing had to mold themselves--sometimes
very awkwardly--to the limitations and constraints imposed by the
environment in which the tutoring occurred. As William O.
Shakespeare has pointed out:

> Because writing centers are a relatively new academic
> institution, many of our facilities are less than adequate.
> There is neither adequate space, configuration of space,
> nor placement of the facility for students' convenience. (11)

Only later in the process of writing center evolution does the much
more sensible step of molding the surroundings to the specialized
instructional demands of individualized tutoring take hold.

Aside from the simple physical constraints offered by impromptu,
jerry-built facilities, the initial tendency to use the writing lab only as a
sort of band-aid station for those afflicted with chronic writing ills
creates impediments to growth. Students "remanded" to the center often
resent such treatment; aside from not being entirely clear about the

meaning of the word "remanded," students at WCU were not very pleased with the extra scheduling burdens and demands placed on them by their "banishment" to the Writing Lab. As any practicing tutor can attest, a surly, resentful student who would rather be elsewhere makes a difficult tutee.

Yet another problem attendant to the early "lab" stage of writing center evolution is the problem of faculty attitudes toward the lab. According to Ben Ward, who assumed control of the WCU writing lab in 1981, the initial problem faced by writing center directors at this juncture is not so much changing the image of individualized writing instruction among the faculty as it is to create some sort of image to begin to work from. When Ben arrived in Cullowhee, awareness of the writing lab among the faculty and staff at the University was practically non-existent. The general attitude seemed to be that the writing shortcomings of the academically underprepared were indeed best kept restricted to the safe, antiseptic confines of the lab.

Perceiving the importance of broad-based faculty support to the healthy early growth and development of the writing Lab, Ben set out at once to raise the level of awareness of the Lab among the faculty all across the WCU campus. He began to attend religiously all departmental meetings so that he could thereby spread the good word about his now-growing writing lab. He also availed himself of the opportunities offered by the presence of a captive, and at least potentially sympathetic, audience at these meetings to distribute assorted handouts, data sheets, and flyers now being produced in his aptly named center for writing.

In the fall of 1982, The Writing Lab moved to a more centralized location in the WCU library. At this point, Ben Ward furthered his efforts to raise the profile of individualized writing instruction at the university. With the clerical support of a half-time secretary, Ben sent notices to faculty all across campus notifying them of the existence of the Writing Lab/Center, and outlining some of its major services and functions. In addition, the center began to send more in-depth and detailed weekly reports to faculty members whose students had received tutoring during the past week. From the beginning, these reports were highly detailed and specific about the writing problems faced by the tutees and the areas in which they had received help. In this way, faculty members began to get a much clearer notion of the value and importance of having a thriving, well-supported writing center on campus.

Anyone charged with the development and expansion of a writing center is faced early-on with the challenge of finding adequate funding for the project. The situation faced by Ben Ward was no different. Initial funding for the early "lab" stage had been more or less appropriated from the incidental overflow of a federal grant (Advanced Institutional Development Grant), which had been assigned to WCU for more general expansion and development of academic opportunity programs--such as career counseling. Subsequently, the writing center at WCU had to get by on a hodgepodge of monies from a variety of sources. Aside from the English Department's support--which largely took the form of funding the stipends of the graduate students tutoring in the center--the writing center at WCU during these years also received funding from the Instructional Services Office and the Department of Academic Affairs, which paid the wages of the undergraduate tutors employed in the center.

As the level of awareness of the Writing Lab/Center continued to rise on campus, so did the degree of respect and attention granted to the center. In 1982, the English Department created the Writing Center Advisory Board, a committee entrusted with guiding and promoting the Center's now campus-wide activities. Thus, the faculty department with the most at stake in the prosperity and growth of writing across campus had taken a significant step toward granting legitimacy to individualized writing instruction. A step toward gaining even wider acceptance occurred at this time with the establishment of the North Carolina Writing Project. Funded by the Governor's office, this project provided considerable financial and moral support to writing centers all across the state, including the now steadily-growing center at WCU.

During the mid 1980's the Writing Center at Western Carolina University continued to expand its role and mission. Now under the direction of James R. Nicholl, the English Department began additional outreach and community involvement programs, including a Summer Writing Project for the training of writing teachers at the community college level. In so doing, members of the English Department interested in the promotion of writing at WCU continued in their efforts to build a solid PR foundation for the future growth and prosperity of the writing center. One sure-fire way to ensure the long term growth of a financially demanding educational endeavor is to create a strong need for and level of awareness of the project among the surrounding non-academic community. Financial resources from within the academic community are often unpredictable and erratic--especially for relatively

new projects such as writing centers--and these funds tend to dry up at
the worst possible moment. If allies of the writing center can find ways
to extend the reach of the center beyond the narrow confines of the
academic community, the center stands a better chance of withstanding
these inevitable droughts and moratoriums in funding.

Such far-sighted planning began to pay off in the late 1980's. In
1987, the WCU writing center hired a full-time secretary to handle the
voluminous paperwork now being generated through the scheduling of
appointments, the compiling of reports to faculty, and the keeping of
accurate records of writing center tutoring sessions. The director of the
writing center was thus freed to spend more time on promotion,
publicity, planning, and tutor training. Upgrading this last element was
a crucial factor in the progress of the writing center at WCU. Before
Ben Ward assumed control of the center, no real tutor-training program
existed; graduate students were simply assigned to the center as part of
their required duties, and undergraduate peer tutors were selected solely
on the basis of a one-time, first impressions interview. Indeed, the
predominant attitude toward staffing the center during this era seemed to
be that anyone with a modicum of verbal skills could help diagnose and
treat the grammatical ills of developmental students. Ben changed all
this. He initiated mandatory weekly staff training sessions for all tutors
working in the center, as well as scheduling guest speakers at intervals
to further his tutors' awareness of trends and developments in the
teaching of writing. Ben also made it a point to distribute assorted
handouts, flyers, and leaflets from other centers across the country to
promote a sense of community and shared endeavor among his writing
center staff. Additionally, Ben dramatically expanded the Writing
Center's holdings in process-centered textbooks, and created a mandatory
reading list focusing on these texts for his tutoring staff. Thus, his
tutors were well on the way to becoming practicing professionals rather
than merely well-meaning, but largely untrained, amateurs.

With the rapid growth of the writing center and its overall shift in
emphasis came a significant shift in its clientele. From the initial
restricted stage of serving the needs only of those students officially
designated "remedial," the center expanded its role to serving the writing
needs of students enrolled in the full spectrum of English department
classes. But expansion did not stop there. By the fall of 1986, more
than 50% of the students who sought help at the Writing Center at
WCU were referred from classes outside the English department. Efforts

to expand the role and mission of the Writing Center at Western Carolina were clearly beginning to pay off.

The final major obstacle blocking the development of the Writing Center's full potential was cleared in the fall of 1988 with the appointment of a writing specialist as the full-time director of the Writing Center. Prior to this period, writing center directors had carried out their administrative duties in conjunction with a variety of other responsibilities; these directors often bore such titles as "learning skills coordinator" rather than simply "Writing Center Director." The result of such a fuzzy, unfocused allocation of responsibilities was often unfortunate for the best long-term interests of the writing center; directors whose job security rests solely on the growth and prosperity of the center are more likely to succeed at their tasks than directors who are juggling several potentially conflicting programs and duties. Additionally, if the writing center director's primary area of training is specifically in writing--rather than more broadly in English or Education--he or she is more likely to be at the forefront of research into the complexities of the composing process, and thus better able to infuse the center's tutoring core with the proper instructional fire and orientation.

The major philosophical shift that occurred in the Writing Center produced significant consequences. When the new director took over the operation of the center, he officially changed the name of the entity to the University Writing Center and then codified and made widely available through publication a clear statement of its mission. Before this date, the lab or center still remained little more than a quick-fix or "band-aid" to stem the blood flow of various remedial ills. Mission was vague or ill-defined, the lab's identity was confused and ambiguous, and the prospects for the entity remained in a holding pattern, as if the lab were waiting, somehow, for a divinely inspired take-off. Up to this point in its evolution, the writing lab was still seen as a place of remediation, a refuge of last resort for the terminal, the desperate. Business was slack by present standards. Lab personnel worked with 330 students the previous semester, providing help with word and sentence-level problems. Typical of the problems addressed by the full-time, non-faculty administrative assistant and the quarter-time, non-teaching administrator were low-level grammatical and usage issues, word-choice decisions, and misspellings. Few, if any, of the seven or eight undergraduate writing tutors who staffed the lab worked with text-level concerns. Few, if any, had even rudimentary training in anything more than error detection. So, the lab, as it approached the fall of 1988, was proceeding, haltingly, with its mission still ill-defined, its status remedial, and its administrators and tutors more and more disenchanted with the prospects. Anyone eavesdropping or who stopped to chat with a tutor after a session could clearly feel the wind picking up. After years of lying becalmed, the lab was to feel the winds of change.

Initially, the Director, a Ph.D. in English, with an M.A. in Composition and Rhetoric, was appointed half-time. His first act was to hire, early in September 1988, a full-time Assistant Director. She had an M.A. in English and had substituted, quite ably, for the previous Administrative Assistant on an earlier occasion. She had also taught in both the Department of English and in the School of Business. And she knew both how to teach effectively and how to work with people. She was also outgoing, and that, the Director knew, would be a real advantage in what he saw as one of her primary duties--outreach and public relations. Hitherto, the lab had remained fairly isolated, partly because neither of the people in charge had faculty status. Although they attempted to connect through the sending of regular reports to faculty about how their students were doing in tutoring, the results were typically disappointing. The problem, it seems, was that the faculty-- particularly the faculty in English, the largest such unit on campus--did not trust or respect the lab. There was the sense that somehow unqualified people were using somehow suspect means to tutor students, who themselves were under suspicion. Of what--no one was quite sure.

So, into this breach stepped the new staff. Yet, it was a staff with several built-in advantages over its predecessors. First, their credentials were less likely to be challenged or dismissed. After all, the new Director was a tenured Associate Professor of English, and this in itself communicated something about the value that both the School of Arts and Sciences and the University itself attached to the Center. Second, their networked connections in both the Department of English and the School of Business helped with initial Center contacts. Third, because of the nature of the appointments, the status of the Center was seen by the general faculty as enhanced. Faculty--even in English--were now more willing to send their students, to require their coming, to emphasize the importance of writers working with other writers in a one-on-one format. So, immediately, there stretched before the new Center almost infinite possibilities.

Even before he appointed the new Assistant Director, the newly appointed Center Director had been at work. His first priority was to hire a staff of tutors who would be capable and who could earn the respect of the faculty whose students came to work on their writing. Whereas before the fall of 1988 students hired as tutors had not been systematically screened, now a selection mechanism was put in place. In addition, the new Director began to actively recruit excellent undergraduate students, particularly those in the now-burgeoning Honors Program. For each student applicant--even those he knew to be strong--he required a writing sample based on a previous Advanced Placement Exam topic, a fifteen-minute interview, and engagement in a series of role-playing activities which simulated likely writing center situations. Only after each applicant had gone through this entire process, and only after he was certain that the would-be tutor could himself write well and interact with writers well, did the Director hire him. And in this way the staffing proceeded along logical, consistent lines. By the time the Assistant Director came aboard in mid-September, the Center was staffed with quality undergraduates, as well as graduate students who had taken a methods course in the teaching of composition. And there was reason for cautious optimism that things were at last beginning to turn around. The wind was blowing from a new direction.

Using the time line that follows, it is easy to trace the evolving nature of the University Writing Center, from its incipience as a Center (in the fall of 1988) to its state today (late spring 1990). Under each date, specific changes in Center operations, as well as specific additions and deletions, are listed. These, when read sequentially, provide a systematic overview of how what had been a lab evolved into a Center, and how that Center continues to evolve, to adapt to the changing needs of the whole academic community.

FALL 1988
1. New Center Director and Assistant Director assume their responsibilities.
2. Secretarial support continues to be half-time, shared with an adjacent unit.
3. Writing Center tutors are no longer "chosen primarily on the basis of a personal interview, appearance, and personality" (Ren Decatur, "Brief Comparison Study," WCU May 3,1988, 4).

4. Role and Mission are clearly defined. The Role and Mission Statement reads as follows:

> *In order of priority, the Center's first operating principle, beyond establishing and maintaining rapport with WCU students, is to get students to take and maintain a positive attitude toward their writing. A second principle is that the writer does his or her own writing. Tutors will not write papers; they will, using common tutoring procedures, guide the student writer through the drafting process, which eventually leads to the finished text. A third principle is that in one-to-one tutoring, higher-order concerns (like invention, thesis generation, structuring, and developing with specific examples) take precedence over lower-order ones (like syntax, micro-structures, usage, punctuation, grammar, spelling, and dialect). Finally, the mission of the University Writing Center tutors is fulfilled when they have guided a student writer through the composing process so that the piece of writing is significantly improved (not perfected). The student must retain ownership of and investment in the piece of writing; otherwise, the Center and its tutors are doing a disservice to the student, the student's instructor, and the learning process.*
>
> (modeled on Tom McLennan's statement at UNC--Wilmington)

5. Outreach begins as Director and Assistant Director conduct mailing to the entire faculty, asking for the opportunity to come and speak about what the Center does and can do for both students and faculty.
6. Initial mini-courses (intensive workshops on specific topics or problem-areas, such as "How to Document a Scientific Paper," "How to Summarize a Journal Article in the Social Sciences," etc.) are authored by the Assistant Director.
7. Systematic staff training begins. Both staff and tutors attend weekly staff meetings where interactive involvement in both higher-order and lower-order writing concerns is the norm. Workshop sessions typically address such problems as (a) getting students to write clear thesis statements, (b) getting students to brainstorm, and (c) getting students to provide specific, concrete details to support their assertions. Such regular tutorial meetings are in contrast to pre-fall 1988 staff meetings which "focused on menial tasks aimed at problem-solving in remedial areas" (Ren Decatur, "Brief Comparison Study," WCU, May 3, 1988, 5).

8. Center budget increases, on the recommendations of the Chair of the English Department and the Dean of the School of Arts and Sciences, by 50% over pre-fall 1988 figures.

9. Director gives two presentations at national conferences. The first--one based on collaborative research between himself and a graduate student writing tutor--is given at the Penn State Conference on Rhetoric and Composition, and the second--one based on Center research into student composing methods--is given at the Miami Sentence-Combining Conference.

SPRING 1989

1. A former graduate assistant assigned to the Writing Center as a tutor completes research for and finishes the first M.A. thesis done on writing at Western Carolina University. The student's topic, for which data were gathered at weekly tutorial meetings, involved discovering if and how case studies or scenarios about typical writing tutorial situations could help in the training of writing tutors. The researcher leads tutors through four role-playing exercises designed to provoke a discussion of the strategic knowledge involved in the tutoring process.

2. Assistant Director works in earnest to develop a whole array of University Writing Center Mini-Courses. She sends out a memo requesting that faculty from all disciplines request those Mini-Courses that specifically apply to their field and their teaching needs. A list of Mini-Courses offered in Spring 1989 reads as follows:

Note Taking as a Writing and Study Skill
How to Organize an Essay Question Response
How to Summarize a Journal Article
How to Write a Critique
Resume Preparation
Job Search Letters
How to Write a Research Paper
Paraphrasing and Research Documentation
Punctuation, Especially the Comma
Editing to Eliminate Fragments, Run-ons, and Comma Splices

For the Spring Semester there were four mini-courses presented to 160 students in the Writing Center itself and nine mini-courses given to 385 students in classes in a variety of disciplines.

3. Director and Assistant Director provide Writing Center Information Sessions to 419 students and 22 faculty.

4. Director and Assistant Director offer students, for the first time, two new mini-courses on "Tips for Taking Various Types of Tests" and "Strategies for Doing Well on Essay Examinations." These are presented as preparation for the two English Department common examinations--at both midterm and final. One hundred-fifty-two students attend these pragmatic, highly interactive sessions.

5. Director revitalizes the University Writing Center Advisory Board, adding members and changing its charge such that interdisciplinary input is received regarding Center operations. In regular meetings, Advisory Board members suggest future directions for the Center and ways of handling difficult logistical and political problems. Besides obvious Board members--the Chair of the English Department and the Director of Freshman English--outside members in Reading and Instructional Services provide diverse and especially helpful perspectives on Center strengths and weaknesses.

6. Systematic resource acquisition begins in earnest. Center purchases forty-two important books on tutoring, conferencing, collaborative learning, and composition and rhetoric. In addition, fifteen copies of *Training Tutors for Writing Conferences*, by Reigstad and McAndrew, are purchased and loaned out to tutors for as long as they work at the Center. Later in the semester two videotape programs are purchased--one of "Donald Murray in Action" and the other "The Writing Workshop: A World of Difference" by Lucy McCormick Calkins. All of these resources are regularly used for both day-to-day tutoring in the Center, for outreach workshops and classroom sessions, and for staff training.

7. Regular and systematic Writing Center evaluation begins. A questionnaire soliciting information on how effectively the Center is meeting the needs of both students and faculty is designed and distributed. Response is significant, and several areas for change are identified through this process. Future plans are to work with a psychometrist to design a more scientific questionnaire and to develop a longitudinal study, which traces the effects that attending the Writing Center has on student grades and attitudes.

8. Publicity is increased--WWCU, the local campus radio station, carries spots; *The Western Carolinian*, the student newspaper, runs advertisements; *The Sylva-Herald*, the weekly county-wide newspaper, provides copy of special Center events and activities. In addition, *The Reporter*, the faculty and staff newsletter published by the WCU Office

of Public Information, carries a page-one story on The University Writing Center, its new mission and its growth.

9. Regular, computer-generated, individual tutoring reports are sent out weekly to faculty whose students work on their writing with tutors. These reports, although versions were sent out before Spring 1989, now begin to contain detailed, specific information on what was worked on in the tutorial, who tutored, and for how long.

10. Director accompanies six Writing Center tutors to the Southeast Writing Center Association Annual Meeting in Knoxville, TN. Plans are made to visit other writing centers throughout the Southeast and to regularly, as travel funds allow, attend other writing center conferences. Tentative plans are made to propose a session for the next National Writing Centers Association meeting or for the regional affiliate.

11. Limited word-processing capability arrives at the Center. Students can now compose electronically and receive help with on-screen revision. Because of limitations of Center space, however, further expansion of word-processing in conjunction with one-to-one tutoring is put on temporary hold.

12. Tutor training begins to include videotapes of the tutoring process and interactive involvement of the tutors in problem-solving of crises which they identify.

FALL 1989

1. Center purchases eighteen additional writing texts, concentrating on those that emphasize the tutorial process. For example, multiple copies of *The Practical Tutor*, by Meyer and Smith, are purchased and made available to tutors.

2. Center purchases *The Tutor's Guide* videotape series (developed at UCLA), and begins using it in role-playing situations as a part of staff training.

3. Center purchases software programs to support word-processing-- Microsoft Word, Microsoft Write (an inexpensive student-writer version of Word), and other similar programs--and puts them on Macintosh hard drives for students to access.

4. Center subscribes to *The Writing Center Journal* (NWCA/NCTE) and *The Writing Lab Newsletter* (Purdue), and encourages tutors to write articles for both based on their own tutoring experience.

5. University outreach by the Center grows dramatically as 170 faculty (out of 300 total) are contacted and worked with, either through mini-

courses or through informational sessions about what the University Writing Center does and can do for both faculty and students.

6. Center expands its services to graduate students and faculty, working with 108 graduate students and five faculty in one-to-one tutorials.

7. Center expands its services to include more and more work with ESL students, particularly Oriental graduate students accepted into the Master's program in Industrial Technology. Relatedly, Center purchases a number of ESL and TESOL publications and teaching aids.

8. For the first time, Center succeeds in tutoring students from every Department and every School of the University (37 departments and 6 schools).

9. Center obtains additional equipment monies to fund new tables and chairs for tutoring, new word-processing stations, and new conference seating for staff tutorials.

10. Center decides to expand its hours of operation, adding Sunday 3-9 pm to the daily schedule, which runs 9-9 M-Th, 9-3 F.

SPRING 1990

1. University Writing Center holds "Open House" in its newly refurbished Hunter Library location. University Chancellor, several Vice-Chancellors, and Academic Deans meet with Center personnel and discover the kinds of work that have been going on there. In preparation for the "Open House," Center tutors prepare a poster session illustrating Center accomplishments over the past year (Spring 1989-Spring 1990). Striking statistics from the posters include these:

> 92 mini-courses presented in the past year
> 76 different professors worked with through outreach efforts
> 36 general information sessions presented
> 5277 student contacts through outreach efforts (WCU's enrollment is 6000 students)
> 2936 individual students tutored in the Center in the past year
> 8213 total student contacts within the past year

2. Center solicits design of University Writing Center logo. Two student designs are accepted--one to be used on bookmarks to be given out in information packets at freshman orientation, and one to be used on screen-printed t-shirts to be given to tutors at the "Open House."

3. University Writing Center stationery, personalized Writing Center pencils, and informational bookmarks are contracted. Pencils and bookmarks are to serve as reminders; both contain Center phone number and hours of operation.

4. Assistant Director and graduate tutors develop a videotape on how the Writing Center serves WCU students and faculty. The videotape, made in cooperation with the Media Center, contains edited interviews with six students and nineteen faculty. In each segment, which is accompanied by music and graphics, faculty who regularly assign students to the Center and students who regularly attend talk about their experiences with tutoring.

5. Center Director solicits contributions to the Kim L. Brown Award for Excellence in Tutoring Fund. The fund, now totalling over $1000.00, is named for one of the Center's best and brightest tutors, whose tragic death touched everyone on the staff. Now, at each year's Honors and Awards Night (April 23, 1990, this year), one of the University Writing Center's tutors is recognized and rewarded for excellence in the art and science of tutoring writing. A perpetual plaque, prominently displayed in the Center, keeps outstanding achievement prominent in the minds of both the tutors and those who come to be tutored.

6. Center is selected as one of six key units on campus to be visited by the University of North Carolina Board of Governors. Director, Assistant Director, and tutors prepare a presentation and a packet for each visitor. Each packet contains the Center's Role and Mission Statement, Strategic Plan for 1990-92, a sample Mini-Course, a chart showing levels of activity in the Center since the Hunter Library fire of 2/25/89, and University Writing Center personalized pencils and bookmarks.

7. One of the Center's writing tutors is awarded a Fulbright Scholarship for study in Germany.

8. Center staff meet with administrators to request additional space and secretarial support for the Writing Center. Business, having increased by over 200% in the past two years, has outgrown the allotted library space. There is a promise to make additional space the highest priority for next year's budget. After years of being at the bottom of the heap, the Center has bright prospects for future growth. The winds are changing again, and the unaccustomed breeze feels fresh and good.

These, then, have been some of the changes in the University Writing Center over the years. Budget, staff, facilities, outreach, advertising, numbers of faculty and students served, and recognition both within the academic community and outside in the UNC system have grown. Perhaps one indelible way to trace the evolving nature of the Center is to look back at how the Writing Center, as entity, has been described in *Western Carolina University General Catalog* copy over the period:

1982-83 and before: No mention of a writing center, lab, or facility of any kind

1983-84 and 1985-86: Listed under Instructional Services Center heading as follows: *"For students, the center is the source of assistance in basic skills development, primarily through a writing lab. A staff of faculty, graduate assistants, and peer tutors is available to help with all sorts of writing tasks related to their courses of study and with general skills development."* (*General Catalog* 11).

1987-88: Listed under Instructional Services Center heading as follows: *For students, the center is the source of assistance in basic skills development, primarily through a writing laboratory* (*General Catalog* 9). Note that the only change is "lab" has now become "laboratory."

1989-90 and 1990-91: Listed under University Writing Center heading as follows: *A staff of faculty, graduate assistants, and peer tutors is available to assist students in developing skills for preparing term papers, creative writing projects, articles for publication, and other purposes. Faculty members are encouraged to refer students to the center for general development of writing skills.* (*General Catalog* 10).

From nothing to "lab" to "laboratory" to University Writing Center in seven years; it's been a whirlwind of change. In a way, the profound nature of the changes and their frequency have represented something of a paradigmatic shift, a means of speeding up the typically slow evolutionary process--of watching the slow reptilian "remedial" crawl forth from the ooze to claim his birthright, his rightful, central place within the community of the species. "Life is flux, and flux is life," according to Lucretius. Those at the Center can identify with that.

WORKS CITED

Harris, Muriel. "Theory and Reality: The Ideal Writing Center (s)." *The Writing Center Journal.* 6.1, 4-9.

Jody, Marilyn. Personal Interview. March 13, 1990.

North, Stephen. "The Idea of a Writing Center." *College English* 46.5 (September 1984).

Shakespeare, William O. "Achieving the Ideal Writing Center by Establishing the Role of the Writing Center within the College or University." *ERIC.* ED 261 403.

Ward, Ben. Personal Interview. March 13, 1990.

Satellite Writing Centers: A Successful Model for Writing Across the Curriculum

Katherine H. Adams
Loyola University/New Orleans

In 1987, when I arrived at Loyola University in New Orleans as director of writing across the curriculum, I found what may be a typical approach to writing at small liberal arts colleges. In a curriculum that is heavily weighted toward general studies requirements and with a faculty/student ratio that allows for fairly small sections, students already did a great deal of writing in their classes, usually essay exams and short papers. A few teachers in upper-division classes also made assignments reflecting the discourse of their communities: research projects in biology, product campaigns in advertising, site visit reports in nursing. Our faculty were generally convinced of the importance of writing in college classes as preparation for all careers.

In their assignments and classroom style, teachers followed a traditional approach to writing instruction. Especially in arts and sciences courses, they assigned similar projects. Students generally narrowed a large topic assigned from the class material, marshalled their own opinions and/or those gained from research and their texts, and wrote personal reflection, summary and argumentative papers usually longer, but not much longer, than the 500-750 words of freshman composition essays. In many classes, assignments were given in class and never mentioned again until the papers were due; little attention was paid to process or audience. Most teachers had not considered informal writing as a tool for ongoing critical thinking.

Although the faculty cared about teaching writing, they were not necessarily eager to alter their current methods. Since, as at many schools trying to preserve their tradition as liberal arts colleges and also become research institutions, faculty taught three or four courses per term, did an amazing amount of committee work, and were expected to publish, they were certainly aware of their already overburdened days; they were reluctant to add more work to their schedules; and they reacted negatively when asked to participate in any mandate to change instruction if it came from a seemingly less busy administration or new "directors" functioning as part of it. In Toby Fulwiler's terms from a recent talk on barriers to writing across the curriculum, they were also plagued, as are we all, with academic inertia, with a reluctance to change what they had done before.

Since our faculty was already assigning writing and working hard at teaching, I wanted writing across the curriculum to seem like a service to them, something to help good and overburdened teachers, lessening their work load, extending their successes, standing by them in the effort, practically and realistically. I put change in their methods as a secondary, down-the-road, indirect goal, as part of a support system created through satellite writing centers.

Our First Writing Center and Writing Fellows Program

Writing Across the Curriculum began with a main writing center in a central location which provides 25 Macintosh computers for writing, word processing software like MacWrite and Microsoft Works, and reference books on writing. Three or four undergraduate peer tutors, who take a training course during their first term in the center, are always on duty to provide help with the computers and writing instruction. We do not require appointments. Students often come to the center on their first visits to use the computers; then they ask for computer assistance; and then they speak with a tutor concerning their writing, perhaps first just about punctuation or grammar, but maybe the next time about prewriting or a rough draft. The computers draw in students who would not go to see writing tutors in another location. Over 200 students, from our enrollment of 5000, come in each day to use our word processing equipment and computer instruction; at least 70 also work with writing tutors each day. Our users represent each class year fairly equally, from 17% freshmen to 29% seniors, with 9% from our graduate programs. Users generally come in once or twice a week, and they see tutors to discuss their writing during one out of four visits, or perhaps once every two weeks, with more visits before paper deadlines and exams. In our second year, 95% of student respondents rated the computer instruction as excellent or good, 88% found the writing instruction excellent or good, and 11% rated it as average. When asked about the results of their spring tutoring, after two months of school, 66% indicated that the sessions had already improved their writing skills.

As faculty become familiar with our services, and especially when they understand that tutors will ask the right questions but that the student will still be doing her own writing, they feel well served by the writing center. They can refer individual students for extra help, recommend tutoring to their entire classes, and also receive word processed papers. They can bring by their assignment sheets and make sure that we will provide appropriate help when their students come in. Teachers feel that the offer of help reinforces their own standards: that they can make more difficult and more frequent assignments, demand a better quality product, and give lower grades for poor papers. A survey conducted during our third year indicated that 80% of faculty respondents were telling their classes about the center; 71% were recommending its services to individual users; and 60% had altered their assignments and grading because of the center's services.

Besides our drop-in center, I also instituted a writing fellows program for tutoring entire classes, modeled after Tori Haring-Smith's program at Brown University, but now adapted to our campus. In this program, I talk to the teacher about her assignments before the term begins and assign tutors to her class, usually one tutor for each four students. During the term, each student meets with a tutor to discuss drafts of major class assignments. We have also created many variations to this model: for a music history class, our tutors and the instructor mark the drafts of two major papers, and then conferences are voluntary; for a religious studies class, we have half-day sessions when students can drop in to discuss their essays with tutors scheduled especially for them; in a political science class, tutors spend a class hour discussing general problems in the drafts and then individual students can meet with them later.

This writing fellows program is an important extension of our drop-in center because it leads students to our services who would not come in voluntarily. Students with the worst problems may not come to a center because they are embarrassed to show their writing. Also, we rarely see as drop-ins the better students who may feel too confident to think they need tutoring, but who can become better writers by getting beyond the generalized thinking and pedantic style that Maxine Hairston describes as typical of advanced students. Students of both types will return after an initial required visit if they find help appropriate to their skill and confidence levels.

The discussions with teachers which this program entails also have an important effect. As a teacher explains an assignment to us and answers our questions, she sometimes rethinks it and recognizes confusions, and may then do a better job of crafting her writing prompts and explaining them to her classes. Our Institute for Ministry's extension program, for example, regularly assigns a "reflection paper" for which they want students to combine material from personal experience, readings, and class discussion to define ministry or another key concept. Many students become very upset about this major project, and some have left the program because of it. Their anxiety and confusion have in part stemmed from uncertainties felt by the workshop leaders and paper evaluators. My conferences with the director led to a style manual with sample structures and to in-service meetings for evaluators that have clarified and improved the assignment, helping both staff and students.

Informal sessions with teachers can also lead to discussion of new types of assignments and class structures, perhaps involving writing to learn, different audiences for writing, critique groups, and discipline-specific writing. From such discussions have come learning journals in math classes, practice notebooks in voice classes, rhetorical situations in art history assignments, and critique groups in British history classes.

The College's Discourse Communities: Opening Satellite Centers

Our initial center has served students and faculty across the arts and sciences and in our music school quite well. It works for this group, we think, because at Loyola these students form a type of discourse community. To serve members of other communities, which experience is teaching us to recognize, we have opened satellite centers, not just new versions of our first center, but different facilities for serving different populations.

Kenneth Bruffee has talked about a community in which peer tutoring can flourish as "a group of people who accept, and whose work is guided by, the same paradigms and the same code of values and assumptions" ("Peer Tutoring" 8). He cites Rorty, Geertz, and Perry as he asserts that college work should stimulate the student's growth toward membership--and communication abilities--in a field of study ("Social Construction"). As Geertz asserts in *Local Knowledge*, one's discipline provides "a cultural frame that defines a great part of one's life"(155) ..."a world we inhabit" (160): as Bruffee echoes, "who, what, and where we believe we are" ("Social Construction" 788). Growth toward membership in an academic community does occur in college, and more so in graduate school, but the community of a particular major is not the strongest one at our school, or probably at many, especially for arts and sciences majors. Loyola students take an average of 36 hours of an 128 hour degree in their major field. They commonly change majors once or twice, often finally deciding during the junior year. Most arts and science majors will not work within history, political science, or whatever their major field when they graduate. When they are taking five courses per term, perhaps two are in their major; writing is also required in the other courses.

Many undergraduate students who may be beginning to enter the discourse communities of their professions are before that semi-comfortable members of a larger undergraduate community: they work around similar deadlines, they compare notes on the professors' requirements and grading; they discuss their performance on tests and papers. This community exists in the cafeteria and dorm, in the hallways and classrooms. Students are already accustomed, also, to recognizing the superior skills of certain members of that community and thus turning to them for academic help, because they are "good in English" or they have already taken the class. They also encounter dormitory assistants who offer advice and help them with problems.

The undergraduate writing center can provide a space where that community relationship, which is stronger for upperclassmen, those who live on campus, and more out-going students, can be extended to all types of students and can facilitate learning. A writing center can look like a community place, if, as in our center, it is housed in a large open room in a central location where students can sit near each other reading, writing, using computers, and meeting with tutors. My tutors try to reinforce the notion of community by making everyone feel welcome, sharing their own problems, joking and prodding others as they might in a dorm environment. The student can feel like learner and teacher, like a peer, since here two expert circles overlap, with the student having more knowledge of the subject matter and particular course and the tutor having more knowledge of writing. Such a center works well because it draws on the strengths of a positive community, one that many students already exist within, and one that can make word processing and writing less threatening and more successful.

These arts and sciences students do not only form a discourse community because of their daily contact and their work on the same assignments; they also have similar writing experiences and skills. Loyola students are commonly not developmental; a smaller part of our business concerns work with grammar and punctuation than might be true at other schools. Our students' freshman experience centers on 750-word rhetorical analyses of a writer's appeals, claims, and fallacies. They have little fluency with other forms of summary and argumentative writing. My experience at the University of Tennessee

was similar. There students entered college with the five-paragraph
theme down pat and then had two more semesters of it. They knew how
to write a funnel introduction, a tripartite thesis, clear topic sentences, a
classification or comparison pattern, and a summary-plus conclusion.
But what neither group has been taught, and perhaps are not ready to be
taught in freshman composition, is how to forge an organization to suit
their content, audience, and purpose and how to write an essay of more
than three or four pages. Even in sophomore literature courses, their
own composition teachers complain that the students seem unable to
structure an essay, but there they are not handed a form. Besides lacking
experience with creating new essay types, they also seem vaguely
displeased with their past instruction, and low on confidence.

Although the assignments might be a comparison of Descartes and
Hobbes in a philosophy class, a score analysis in music, or a lab report
in biology, these students need help with understanding the assignment,
doing primary and secondary research, forging a thesis, planning an
effective structure, revising for unity and clarity, and proofreading. The
same questions--simple ones like "what was the assignment?," "where
is your thesis?," "why did you put your points in this order?," "do you
have enough evidence/facts/examples here to make a complete
paragraph?," "do you need to state your opinion more clearly?"--can
help them, in all these situations, with creating their own thesis and
essay structure. Tutorial sessions can also provide the "you can do it"
message which these students need.

On our campus, the arts and sciences disciplines, then, have formed
a natural community--one marked by student collegiality, common
tasks to perform, common strengths and weaknesses as writers, and a
common place of work. These four factors can create the successful
boundaries of a writing center at any school. They are not necessarily
boundaries that just contain undergraduates; our religious studies
graduate students fit within this group. They don't necessarily follow
college lines since students from our music school function well within
this group and those in our journalism department do not. When
students go beyond these boundaries--into physically separate locations
and groups, into different assignment types, and into different skills and
needs--a campus may choose to open other writing centers to serve
these students, as we have at Loyola.

One such "satellite" was already functioning well at my campus, as
at many others, and can be a model for expansion. Most schools already
have writing labs that serve freshmen in their basic composition classes

who may have severe grammar problems, little knowledge of essay structure, and poor reading skills. English departments choose (and specifically train in the writing required in the freshman sequence) tutors, many of whom are English majors, who succeeded in those courses. These English majors are representatives of their community, in the same way that my liberal arts majors represent the larger arts and sciences population. These tutors correspond with the teachers and the director of composition, creating the important triangle of tutor/teacher/student which the writing fellows program provides at the main center. The director of composition chooses, trains, and monitors these tutors in consultation with the writing across the curriculum office. This lab is equipped with IBM computers, Textra software for easy word processing, and reference books concerning grammar, spelling, and essay form.

Another group of students best served apart from the arts and sciences community are those in our journalism program. This is the largest of our majors--at 600 students--with courses taught in a building separate from our arts and sciences complex. These students write news articles, feature stories, press releases, and other forms of journalism and public relations writing in a shorter paragraph and brisker style than required for most class essays. They often have better writing skills than other undergraduates, or, if they don't, they are still different because they think they do or should. On our campus, they also form a different social and activity group, tied to our campus newspaper. For this group, we have established a separate writing center modeled on the others: with a location in their building, with tutors from that major who are given training concerning journalistic types of research and writing and the appropriate tutorial questions for those genres, with reference and style books pertaining to that field and with appropriate software, such as Pagemaker for desktop publishing. These tutors are trained by a journalism professor who helps with monitoring the center.

We have also established a separate writing center in our law school, located down the street from our main campus: again to help students with the research, audiences, and forms appropriate to that discipline, primarily the law exam, brief, memo, and letter, and to provide software, like Cite Write, that can enable these students to write as professionals. Here the tutors are third-year law students, members of the peer community. Part of their training is given by a professor of legal writing who also helps with monitoring them.

As we have witnessed the success of these separate centers and found through experience the boundaries of our communities, we have begun planning for two more separate facilities: a writing center for our business and computer science students and a graphics/writing facility for our art, graphics, and advertising programs. We also want to initiate writing fellows programs from each center so that faculty will be working with tutors specially trained to deal with writing in their disciplines. We also plan to open a speech center where tutors can help students with their speaking skills.

These facilities are all run by writing across the curriculum, which consists of an administrative assistant and me. Our law facility can run without daily maintenance; these law students, after training sessions, open and close, tutor each afternoon, and keep daily records without much supervision. But satellite centers with more extended hours and undergraduate workers require on-site supervision. We have found several alternatives to provide that supervision. In the basic skills center, the director of composition provides monitoring, from an office located outside of it. The communications center has a faculty advisor; we are also hiring a graduate student in communications to provide on-site supervision. This combination of graduate assistants, faculty advisors, an administrative assistant, and a writing-across-the-curriculum director is some days stressful, but it is working well on our campus. Further growth may necessitate another full-time faculty or staff position.

Our satellite centers currently provide a great deal of lab assistance at a fairly low cost. We have gotten grant donations from a local educational foundation to buy our computers, printers, and software. In the main, communications, and basic skills centers, the tutors are work-study students and so their pay has not presented any extra budgeting. Faculty advisors are "paid" with release time from their teaching loads. Law school tutors receive some pay and course credit.

These centers have brought writing into a central role on our campus, provided support to students and faculty, reinforced good teaching, and helped teachers to understand various approaches to writing. Their presence on our campus has been important for admissions and student retention. Adequate support can help teachers and students raise their expectations--so that students can be given challenging writing prompts and can work within a supportive writing community to respond to those prompts at the best possible level, thus preparing to write as professionals.

Works Cited

Bruffee, Kenneth. "Peer Tutoring and the 'Conversation of Mankind.'" *Writing Centers: Theory and Administration.* Ed. Gary A. Olson. Urbana, IL: NCTE, 1984. 3-15.

---------. "Social Construction, Language, and the Authority of Knowledge: A Biographical Essay." *College English* 48 (1986): 773-89.

Fulwiler, Toby. "Friends and Enemies of Writing Across the Curriculum." *Conference on College Composition and Communication.* Chicago, March 1990.

Geertz, Clifford. *Local Knowledge: Further Essays in Interpretive Anthropology.* New York: Basic, 1983.

Hairston, Maxine. "Working with Advanced Writers." *College Composition and Communication* 35 (1984): 196-204.

Sharing the Benefits and the Expense of Expansion: Developing a Cross-Curricular Cash Flow for a Cross-Curricular Writing Center

Ray Wallace
University of Tennessee

Introduction

For several years we, in this relatively new branch of the writing field, have been wrestling with various metaphors to describe what exactly it is we do in the rooms provided for us to tutor in. Indeed, perhaps it is this very newness that compels us to argue about what we are doing, to define our boundaries, and to describe our goals. We still seem to be mapping procedural cornerstones by which to build a writing center philosophy to guide further movement. However, such heated discussion has had at least one important result -- we are beginning to see our usefulness to other departments and services across campus and, as such, we are beginning to realize our own worth as academic colleagues, peers, and professionals. It is with, and through, the emergence of this recognition that the writing center must develop and grow. To this end, first we must dislodge the negative image of the lab, an image we have foisted, or allowed to be foisted, on ourselves for quite some time.

From Lab to Center

In North's (1984) early work (or relatively early work given our newness), the image of the band aid station was used to describe the type of facility we were. North was correct to present such an image because this is how our rooms had been seen, and, in some cases, continue to be seen. However, we cannot be blamed for this evolution due to two very important factors. First, this was the type of facility we had the philosophical tools to build. Second, this was the only type of service we could build given the resources available to us.

We developed writing labs -- another metaphor for places of experimentation and less-than-perfect handling of problems -- to help our students improve as writers at a time when the emphasis on the writing process had not yet reached our shores. We also developed labs because even we thought of writing as a task primarily residing in English departments -- writing across the curriculum movements are of course very new innovations on our campuses. We were provincial in our view of how writers wrote and we were provincial in our view of where writers wrote.

We also developed labs because we were not given (nor did we think to ask for) enough money or space to build anything other than this. Thus, it became a self-fulfilling prophesy that labs would spring up because labs were all that were planned. Since we had reinforced the idea that the most important writing went on in English departments, it made perfect sense to develop a facility to look after the writers in these departments; those enrolled in freshman composition courses were targeted as the clients we needed to reach.

The Idea of The Writing Lab

Before this discussion goes much further, however, it should be remembered that writing labs are still here with us, and indeed, they still are providing a valuable service in the departments in which they were developed. One of the most obvious writing labs which come to mind is at a very large and influential school; Muriel Harris directs the Writing Lab at Purdue University. This facility and several others around the country do incredibly complex and varied work across their campuses (see also Freisinger and Burkland, 1982). However, I would argue that these facilities are misnamed, and this misnomer is the result of overlooking or de-emphasizing the very varied services which differentiate labs from centers.

Nevertheless, there are many correctly-named labs operating on campuses across the country and many of us direct or tutor in these facilities. Given the many discussions of our facilities over past years we can generalize that a lab is usually a place:

* funded by a single department, English in most cases
* where freshmen come to get help
* where the focus is on error
* which is badly staffed
* which is not held in very high esteem in the academy
* where "bad" people are sent (even remanded)

Usually, these labs are set up and funded by a single department, most often English. As such then the primary purpose of such a facility must be as a service to the department which initiated it. In addition, usually the first- and second-year students are the ones who attend the lab, and these are the same students enrolled in the introductory writing courses.

Try as hard as we can, yet the tutorial focus in many of these labs is on error. This occurs either because the faculty will only send students with graded papers to be "gone over with a tutor"; a double problem of misunderstanding the composing process and the place and role of tutoring in this process. The other reason the focus on errors is prevalent in tutoring labs is due to lack of staff or guidance. Many labs (not all) are ineffectively staffed or directed, given the lack of tutors, either peer or not, and the fact that many lab directors are not given enough release time to oversee their tutors and to provide the effective tutor-training sessions they need. Both this lack of tutors and the lack of a lab director to constantly oversee and train only leads to ineffective tutoring, especially tutoring based on a response to the errors the student has already produced. While a student's writing errors are an important aspect of many tutoring sessions, there are other much more important areas in the composing process that need to be stressed before the tutor discusses surface, or product, problems. Thus, when a writing lab tutoring session focuses only on, for example, the fragments and comma splices a freshman writer produces, the tutor often fails to discuss, explain, and clarify ideas of invention, rhetorical choices, stylistics, and the benefit revision holds for this writer.

Yet another problem the lab may suffer from is one of image (Olson, 1984). The problem of image is two-fold, one at the departmental level, and second at the college/university-wide level. If the lab is set up to deal with freshman writing problems, then only the composition staff will see its importance (if even they see this). Given the relative lack of prestige most writing personnel hold within their own literature-based programs, combined with a general lack of enthusiasm for freshman composition in general, and one begins to see the lab as yet another remedial crutch for those "who do not belong in school to begin with." Secondly, if the department faculty feel this way about the lab, the overall faculty from across the discipline may soon catch this disease. If the most influential people in the English department (not usually writing personnel) view the lab as remedial, then this view will spread quickly at meetings and get-togethers where faculty members from across the curriculum meet.

On a more positive note, writing labs across the country do still serve a useful purpose in many academic institutions. We see they are useful because so many English departments publicize them as offering a valuable service to the levels (in reality, one level) of students they serve, and we in the writing field should never forget that before we can move beyond the departmental level to develop wonderfully inventive writing across the curriculum projects and upper-division writing emphasis courses, freshman writing skills (both process and product) must be improved.

But note the dilemma of the two-edged sword here and what this says about the importance of writing in many of our institutions. True, it says that writing is important at the early levels, but, it also says that one-to-one writing help is not as important later on. The very department which supports us feels that we are there to service the recalcitrant masses, to bring them up to a level where others can then work with them. There is little need for the writing lab after the freshman/sophomore years because we have tutored those astoundingly rampant errors out of our students and they will be "fit" to move on to more important matters.

One of the most obvious ways in which this stigma is shown is in the amount of money (or percentage of budget) which is given over to outreach programs to other departments, publicity brochures for around the campus, and forays into other student groups we could possibly serve. In the writing lab world precious little money can be spared to seek out clients from other parts of the campus. Our primary goal is to meet the needs of our own charges, and our budgetary overseers feel less kind to requests for other services than they do for increased tutorial services for more freshmen writers.

The Idea of The Writing Center

While we have been quick to understand the limitations of the writing lab as we have defined it, much is happening across campus which would seem to suggest that a lab is not the ideal facility to improve writing that it once was. Indeed, with the advent of the writing across the curriculum approaches to cross-campus writing effectiveness and the idea that writing belongs in all departments has come an obvious and loud call for improved facilities, for what I see as a move from the writing lab to the writing center (see also Baltrinic, 1988 and Smith, 1986).

Writing centers are concerned with more varied types of writing than labs are. The writing center then is usually a place which:

* serves the needs of a much wider cross section of the academy

* works with writers at all levels
* focuses on process and product
* encourages both developing and advanced writers to attend
* promises well-trained and abundant staff
* is well-funded -- usually by more than one department

By definition, the writing center should be a center for writing for an entire academic institution. This means that freshman composition students should be welcomed into a writing center, but they should be aware, as should their instructors, that they will be tutored along side other writers from other departments, both undergraduate and graduate (and even faculty and staff), who may have very different writing dilemmas and needs. Given these different levels of writers from disciplines across the curriculum entering our facilities, several changes need to be made in image and substance.

While the lab was often a place to send students <u>after</u> the fact (after the paper had been written, read, and graded), the center must be a place to send writers <u>during</u> the writing process. Therefore, the center must be sold as a place to get help on composing issues rather than editing issues (although this must not be disregarded). The way to stress this is of course to publicize: to call faculty and staff, to write to students, faculty , and staff, and to generally promote the writing center at venues where students, faculty, and staff will be present.

As such then it is vitally important to change the type of clients who will use the center. We must work hard to erase the image of the drill lab from the center. We need to get upper division writers coming into the center to work on their higher order writing skills, and we need to make certain the powers that be (whether these be deans, professors, instructors, or secretaries) know that these types of writers are coming to use our facilities.

Another difference in the writing center is the need for more staff. A tutoring staff that worked in a writing lab will in all likelihood be too small and too narrowly focussed on English composition errors to help solve many cross-curricular composing/writing problems. Therefore, as writing center directors it is up to us all to develop a larger and more-widely trained tutorial staff. This can be done with help from other departments or from our own department (Scanlon, 1986 and Wallace, 1988).

Finally, it is important to realize that a writing center that claims to serve the needs of many writers from many different disciplines will be an expensive operation to run. Most English departments will not be able to shoulder all of this increased financial burden, and so the other aspect which differentiates the center from the lab is that there is (or should be) outside funding entering the writing center to help pay for this new outreach across the curriculum. It is this point that perhaps is the most tentative in the move from lab to center, and it is the area that those who are contemplating the move from lab to center must be most aware of.

The Present Situation

While it is certainly true that the lab/center nomenclature debate continues (that our newsletter uses "Lab" in its title and our major journal uses "Center" in its title should be indication enough), one fact is clear. We are moving away from the idea of the lab and towards the idea of the center.

It is apparent from this volume and from others in the field, the various conferences we attend throughout the nation and beyond, and our three widely read and cited publications, that the idea of writing centers (from this point on defined as broad-based centers of writing for all levels of writers across our campuses) is now well-established in the writing field; we have shown our importance to the writing across the curriculum movement, as well as education in general.

There are not many colleges and universities (not to mention the ever-increasing numbers of high schools) in this country which do not have some type of writing tutorial facility -- a writing center, a writing lab, or a writing lab acting as a writing center. Indeed, many graduate programs in rhetoric and composition advertise their ability to give graduate students valuable writing center/tutorial experience in their respective writing centers.

The idea of a writing center has arrived. We have arrived! We have our own regional conferences, we have our own organization, we have three quality publications --*The Writing Center Journal, Focuses*, and *The Writing Lab Newsletter*. We have contributed a number of quality books and collections of essays written about writing centers, we have had several writing center researchers publish articles in the leading writing journals in the field, we have had presentations on tutoring at both national and international conferences.

The future also looks bright. We see graduate students wanting writing center experience before they graduate; yes, actually wanting to work in the center, no longer having to be coerced into it with promises of fewer papers to grade or the chance to look good on a resume. We have seen both empirical and theoretical dissertations on writing centers in which researchers have moved beyond how to set up a new writing center to what we can accomplish across the curriculum through the well-established center. We know we have arrived when we see writing centers being set up, modified, and advanced in high schools (Farrell, 1989).

Writing centers, after they have been modified from their original lab status, are still very important places in English departments since they become advertisements for what it is we do best -- teach writing -- and, once this modification is complete, the center becomes equally important across campuses. While we still help many freshman composition students (since this population never goes away) understand how to fix fragments and comma splices and how to organize introductory academic prose, we now do much more than this in the center. Now we are involved in writing across the curriculum programs, in the training of faculty and graduate students in more effective writing emphases to their various courses, to the production of outreach workshops across the campus, to how to document effectively in the hard sciences, to how to write for publication in the social sciences. We are now seen on campus -- we are not stuck in some little corner of the Humanities building --we are linked to computer labs and mainframes. When the academic term starts, campus offices want to know our hours. We are interviewed by the campus newspaper, fraternities and sororities want us to hold workshops for them, educators from across the campus call to ask can we help with their majors' writing improvement, other educators call to use our resources in developing syllabi to include writing as a mode of learning. We have grammar hotlines which reach out across the campus and into the community. We train the writing instructors of to-morrow. These people often enter our centers as teachers of writing based in classrooms and we show them what it means to be teachers and tutors of writers both in the classroom setting and in the conference setting. We hold training sessions, we invite speakers and researchers to speak every semester to our tutors about how they teach writing (Brown, 1990), and we instill both theory and practical rationale into our charges. We develop a community of writers, with a community center for their use.

The Problem With Funding

It is obvious that writing centers are more effective in reaching and helping various writing groups on campus than are the relatively less well-organized labs around the country (Harris' lab at Purdue University notwithstanding).

However, institutions of higher education in this country are facing quite serious financial problems because of decreasing student enrollment in both the universities themselves, and, more importantly, the liberal arts divisions. With demographic data showing students choosing to enter the business and hard sciences arenas more frequently than the humanities, the funding problems for writing centers (based in the Humanities) is beginning to become a problem.

The writing center at the University of Tennessee, Knoxville has faced many of these funding problems, and we have developed some solutions that have helped lessen the financial burden of the English department to fund our center solely. The university has seen its enrollment drop from a high of a little over 30,000 students at the height of the baby boom ten years ago to a current enrollment of just under 25,000 to-day. In a state which lacks any state income tax structure, the university achieves its funding budgets based on a formula directly linked to student enrollment. Even as the largest state-supported school in the state, we have still felt the purse strings tighten as enrollments decline. In fact, this essay is being written at a time when the university is going through what the administrators euphemistically call "impoundment." Departments have had to return previously budgeted money back to the administration, who in turn return it to the state because even fewer students enrolled this academic year than we thought would.

All writing center directors know that when the administration starts looking for areas to cut back funding on that their writing center is often near the top of the list. One of our constant struggles in this field is to get those people in power to understand that we are providing an important service to many students and faculty outside a traditional classroom setting (some administrators think that writing centers are credit-bearing classes); they seem to understand and commend us when the finances are stable, but when they are not, then we had better look for money from other quarters. This is the case at Tennessee.

Defining Funding For The Writing Center

My philosophy of writing centers is that if disciplines from across the curriculum use our services then they should help pay for them. Applying this philosophical definition can help the director look at other avenues of funding to alleviate the financial difficulties inherent when writing centers expand and universities contract. While the English department at the University of Tennessee still pays the lion's share of center's operating budget, we have been very fortunate to have been able to supplement this budget with self-sufficient cross-curricular programs. I offer these programs as examples of what other writing center directors can do to supplement their operating costs.

The end of year report is perhaps the most important document in the writing center's library. Here the director can, if records have been kept in sufficient detail, tell at a glance the number of clients who have been served, how often they have come to the center, and, most importantly, their majors. From this information, the writing center director can decide which departments to ask for financial help for the next academic year.

Of course, it is not as simple as just calling a department head on the phone and saying: "did you know we had one hundred and fifty of your majors visit us last semester in the writing center? Would you like to pay for a tutor?" However, it is the writing center director's task to show this department head why he/she should help pay for the operation of the writing center. To do this most effectively, the writing center director must:

* gather statistics on group of majors attending the center
* outline these majors' most common writing problems
* develop links with the faculty who send many students
* design a writing-center program specifically for each major
* submit this proposal to the department head.

Since you should already have had quite a lot of communication (through the usual tutoring reports, phone calls, query memos about assignments, and even perhaps in-class presentations about what the writing center can do for these students) with individual discipline-specific faculty, the proposal for a more structured writing emphasis program should probably be shown to these people first. Then as a group you can work on streamlining the proposal before it reaches the department head (although, in reality, the department head will soon

hear you are planning this proposal from his/her faculty members).
Once you have outlined the goals for a formal writing-center based
component to this major you can discuss the financial aspect of the
program with the head of the department.

One goal has to be remembered when you talk to the administrative
head of any program or major -- you want this person to pay for the
service you are willing to provide; you do not want to add another
program to your already over-worked writing center and pay for it out of
your own meager budget. The goal is to improve writing across the
curriculum, but, bluntly stated, it is also to make sure this
improvement is not solely coming out of your pocket!

The most commonly paid for budget items in these specially
designed programs are graduate assistantships to hire additional tutors.
Many departments are quite happy to do this if these personnel are
trained to meet their students' specific needs. Other departments are also
willing to pay for books, supplies, and computer equipment.

The Supplemental Writing Center Programs At UTK

The writing center at the University of Tennessee is not unlike
other centers at schools of its size. Each semester we have between 14-
20 tutors (all English majors working on their M.A. or Ph.D degrees)
in the central program. We are open around forty hours a week
(including two evenings), we have four computers in the center and two
networked computer labs (Mac and IBM) within a thirty second walk,
for a total of forty-five computers for our clients to use. We have a
grammar hotline, we offer outreach sessions in other departments, and
we have a solid tutor-training program before anyone tutors. Starting
next academic year, all newly admitted M.A. students will have to
spend one year in the writing center before teaching their own
composition classes. This last academic year we saw approximately five
thousand students receive tutorial assistance.

While the central budget for the writing center is run as part of the
English department's overall budget, we have been fortunate to start
three supplemental programs which have helped pay for themselves and
even helped with the day to day cost of operating the central writing
center itself. The programs we have been able to develop have been
with the Law School Program, the Athletic Program, and the
Educational Advancement Program.

A. The Law School Program

The Law School Program is beginning its third year of operation and we have seen it evolve into something very special indeed. We have worked closely with both the Dean and the Associate Dean of the Law School to set up this program, and with modifications each year we are now quite happy with what the program is doing for both the Law School and the writing center.

Program Description

The first year Law students all must take a writing course in the Law School titled Legal Process I. In the past, the four professors who taught the four sections of this course had been displeased with the type of writing skills they had to work with in these classes. Many of the students were sent to the writing center to get help on various areas of their writing. However, the then director of the center initiated the first year of the program with the Law School to help meet these students' needs in a more formal setting.

The first year of the program was modeled on the Brown University tutorial model, and four instructors were hired as special writing center-based law tutors. The Law School paid for these tutors, and the tutoring took place in study areas near the writing center. A writing center tutor was assigned to a Legal Process I class and to the professor teaching this class in order to help improve the use of writing in the class and the students' writing skills.

In the past two years we have seen many modifications to this program. To begin, the Law professors, the Law students, and the writing center tutors found the Brown model to be unwieldy. The tutors were hired for ten hours a week but complained about having to tutor all forty students per class during this time. They were quickly overrun with students who did not know why they had to come to see the writing center tutor -- this was due to a lack of communication between deans, professors, tutors, and director.

However, now we have been able to streamline this program to make it more effective for all those concerned. The Law professors wanted the tutors to be physically closer to the students; the students had complained about having to leave the Law School to walk to the Humanities Building to be near the writing center. The deans of the Law School had two new rooms built in the Law School and we had our first satellite writing center (for further information on satellite writing centers see Adams essay in this volume).

The writing center staff working with this program, by now all graduate students working on Ph.D's in the English department, were able to take many of our writing center materials over to this satellite center. In addition, a diagnostic writing instrument was devised and given to all 160 students at the beginning of the Legal Process I term and only the most serious problem writers were asked to see the writing center tutors first.

One problem the writing center staff had had with the program previously was that they felt (as did the Law professors) that they were not associated with the class closely enough; it was as if only the worst writers were sent to see these people. The Law professors decided that the writing center tutors would be introduced at the beginning of the term and would be present when the diagnostic essay results were being discussed (since both tutor and professor commented on each paper).

As director, I had to remind the Law professors to keep stressing that the writing center tutors were there to help with any writing problem, and this reminder combined with the tutors' presentations in front of the whole class to discuss specifics about the writing process (invention, revision, stylistics, editing, etc.) helped the students to see the tutors as professionals.

Benefits to the Writing Center

The most important benefit to the writing center is that we hired four new tutors who were paid for by the Law School; the tutors are graduate students who can put this cross-curricular writing experience to good use when they go out on the job market. Also, since the Law School's academic calendar is shorter than the general university one, the writing center tutors involved in the law program finish their duties in early November each year, while their peers in the central writing center must continue to the middle of December. Since this program occurs in the fall semester of each academic year, I have four fully trained tutors to come into the writing center in the spring semester to replace graduating tutors or tutors who leave the center to assume other departmental research and teaching fellowships.

In terms of the financial arrangements, the writing center and the English department benefit quite well through the program. The graduate students are selected for the program, and teach one less course (one instead of two) for their assistantship. The Law School pays the department the salaries of four replacement instructors (considerably more than the graduate students' stipends) to teach the courses the graduate students are no longer teaching. Finally, the Law School also pays the writing center a percentage of the director's overall salary to train the tutors in the special skills legal writers must be aware of. This additional money has been used to buy both hardware and software for the central writing center (we rely heavily on Posey's 1989 article in helping us make computer decisions).

B. The Athletic Program

Another group of students we had seen entering the writing center in quite large numbers were the students involved in the men's athletic program (the University of Tennessee, Knoxville separates male and female athletic programs). It was fairly obvious why so many athletes would come to us. Being involved in a "big-time" NCAA athletic program such as football, basketball, track, tennis, or swimming takes a great deal of time out of a young person's already hectic academic schedule. A center which offers one-to-one tutorials not only offers academic help but a friendly personal service that many athletes need. We seldom found students who fit the image of the lazy scheming "jock" so many academics are quick to foist on athletes. These were, for the most part, earnest young people trying to balance two "careers" at once.

Program Description

The program with the athletic department has been in service now for two years, and, like the Law School program, it has gone through some modifications to help better meet the needs of both athletic department and writing center.

The athletic department funds one graduate assistantship from the English department for an entire year, pays all fees in addition to the usual tuition waiver, and even buys some of the tutor's books for his/her graduate courses. In return, the writing center tutor works for ten hours a week either in the central writing center or in the satellite athletic writing center which has just been developed.

The tutor, usually a Ph.D candidate, is in charge of working with all the athletes who come to the center while he/she is on duty. In the past, this tutor has been based in the central writing center and so when no athletes came in for tutoring appointments or none simply walked in, the central writing center was able to use this tutor as a general writing tutor.

The athletes who enter the writing center all are indicative of the clients we get in the center from the general population of students. Some are enrolled in freshman composition classes and need tutorial services related to the types of writing areas one runs across in such courses, but others are enrolled in upper division courses where they are asked to produce even more subject-specific writing. Therefore, this tutor must be trained in a number of different tutoring methods to meet these varied needs.

In addition, with the introduction of the new satellite writing center in the athletic complex, will come added responsibilities for this tutor (and added benefits). This facility has just added microcomputers to help these clients with word processing, and of course the tutor can take whatever materials are needed from the central writing center over to these rooms to help the students.

This program has been successful. Both the Athletic Department and the writing center has been pleased with the results. The graduation rate for athletes is now higher than that of the general student population here at UT, and the athletes seem to like working in both writing center facilities.

Benefits to the Writing Center

Again the major benefit to the writing center is that we get another tutor paid for by someone other than the English department. The tutor also benefits because the rate at which the athletic department pays the assistantship is actually a little higher than the rate the English department pays and so the tutor ends up getting more pay than his/her fellow English department graduate students, and has his/her books and fees paid also. In addition, this tutor is on assistantship for an entire year, but only tutors the usual two semester academic year.

The writing center also benefits when the athletes do not use the writing center in as many numbers as expected (this does not happen very often however). The writing center gets a free tutor to help work with the already over-crowded general writing center. Finally, even the English Department benefits because it has a free assistantship to offer one of its many fine applicants who just did not "make the cut" given the limited number of total assistantships it can pay for.

C. The Educational Advancement Program

Another supplemental writing center program that has worked very well for us has been the one we developed through the Educational

Advancement Program (EAP). This is a federally funded program aimed
at helping those students who are first members of their families to go
to university, those students indicated as having high potential but who
have come from less than perfect academic environments, and those
from ethnic populations which are considered minorities. The EAP
offers one-to-one tutorial services for its members in reading, writing,
and mathematics; the writing center is proud to operate the writing
tutorial services for this program.

Program Description

EAP pays for one graduate assistantship in the writing center each
academic year. This tutor (again, usually a Ph.D candidate) is in charge
of all the tutoring of EAP students (ten hours a week) and is also in
charge of all record keeping related to this program.

The EAP students are free to enter the writing center at any time
(as are any of the students from the other two programs mentioned in
this essay); however, we stress that they have had a tutor specifically
trained and paid to deal with them on a one-to-one basis. The tutor is
responsible for letting the EAP office know when he or she will be
tutoring and the EAP office then informs all its students of these hours.

We have tried as much as possible to tutor on a one-to-one basis
students in the writing center, but sometimes we have been asked to
work with small groups of students in documentation lessons for the
MLA and APA styles and other research-related topics. Most often these
requests have come from EAP, and we are very happy that those
students understand that we can help them improve all aspects of their
writing in all of their classes.

Incidentally, the EAP is a support organization developed to help
students succeed academically during their first two years of
undergraduate work at the university. However, we have many EAP
students who finish their first two years of university having made use
of our services for all two years who then keep returning throughout the
remainder of their academic careers. In fact, it is the EAP students who
hold the records for numbers of visits to the center in any semester.

As a federally-funded project, this supplemental program in the
writing center is the weakest in terms of possible renewal for much
longer. Federal grants do not last forever, but we are honored to have
been included in the grant. The EAP director is hoping that the
university will notice how well the students have done and continue the

program with "hard" money for then on. However, until the grant runs out, the writing center will be an integral part of this program.

Benefits to the Writing Center

Again, the fact that the writing center tutor is being paid for by someone other than the English department is a great benefit to both the center and the English department. In addition, the tutor is given valuable cross-curricular experience to add to his/her resume at the end of his/her academic career with us.

The Educational Advancement Program is very pleased with the tutoring that has taken place in the writing center. Many of the students who finish their first two years with us go on to talk to incoming students about the benefits of attending the writing center and this is obviously very important for future clients. In addition, other Education Advancement Programs from around the country have asked to visit the writing center at UT to see how we work with the program here.

This program also operates like the Athletic Program in that when no EAP students arrive in the center we are free to use the EAP tutor for general writing center tutoring.

Special Considerations

All three of these programs, the Law Program, the Athletic Program, and the Educational Advancement Program, involve some special considerations on the part of the writing center director. The students involved in these problems may at first seem very different from one another, but they are not. Tutoring these students may seem the same as tutoring general population students, but it is not. Finally, working with the finances of these programs may seem a very simple matter, but it is not.

All the students in these three programs are special. They are involved in a program set up to help then succeed academically. True, the law students may seem to be more grade conscious at first, but all these students have a very strong desire to prove to themselves and then to those around them that they are "successful." It takes a special kind of tutor to work with people who are either afraid of failing for the first time or for the twenty-first time. It is the writing center director's responsibility to choose carefully the tutors for each program.

In terms of tutor-training, the writing center director must simply count on extra time being spent developing subject-specific tutoring guidelines for these special tutors. While all these tutors attend our general Monday morning tutor-training session, they must also attend their own program's tutor-training session as well.

Finally, the financial arrangements for running these special programs take time to negotiate; writing center directors might like to think they have the barganing powers of a East/West Arms Reduction Negotiator, but after the first confrontation with an experienced and knowledgeable office administrator over a financial matter the director will soon lower his/her goals a little. Good paper-work is important.

Developing Other Supplemental Programs

At present these are the three supplemental programs we have developed and conducted under the auspices of our writing center at the University of Tennessee. However, we will be starting other programs in the forthcoming semesters, either fully or partially funded by an outside body rather than solely by the English department.

The College of Liberal Arts has instituted a Freshman Success Program for across the college and the writing center has been asked to handle two programs to help improve writing skills of these incoming students. The 103 and 104 Programs are supplementary programs to our freshman composition requirements. Each program will be developed out of the center and will be staffed by seven additional graduate tutors. The College of Liberal Arts will pay for these graduate students, and for additional computers for the writing center. Students selected for the 103 and 104 programs will receive extra tutoring in writing for at least two hours a week. The 103 program will focus on invention and revision skills, and the 104 program will focus on developing critical thinking and research-based skills.

In addition, the Governor's School for the Sciences is based here at the University of Tennessee, in Knoxville. This program selects the best science and mathematics students from around the state to take part in a four-week summer institute with some of the best professors from the university. Since these students will also have a technical writing component to their four-week institute they will be able to use the writing center facilities in the summer. Specifically, the students will be working on the VAX system to complete their writing assignments, and the Governor's School has bought the writing center a 2400 baud modem and an account on the university mainframe system to help develop an on-line grammar/writing hotline. After this program is completed in the summer, the writing center will get to keep the modem and account; we will be starting an on-line (Electronic-mail based) grammar/writer's hotline for the entire community.

Finally, while these two supplemental programs will soon be joining the other three already successful programs, we have other projects in the early developmental stage. We seem to be getting quite large numbers of students taking the Communications Exam (in fact one of our statistics shows that we have a 100% pass rate for those we work with to retake the exam after failing it once) in order to take upper division journalism and communications courses. They usually fail the grammar and writing sections. We will be suggesting a supplemental program with the School of Communications very soon. In addition, we have decided to also suggest a supplemental program with the Women's Athletic Program.

Conclusion

Moving from a writing lab to a writing center is necessary for more and more tutorial facilities in institutions of higher education around the country. Writing specialists have been effective in their jobs of informing teachers from across the curriculum of ways in which writing can be used as a mode of learning and how writing can improve a student's understanding of a specific discipline. One of the most important services we in the writing tutorial world can offer is professional, efficient support for these cross-disciplinary personnel; we do this best by developing writing centers which focus on discipline-specific writing in as many disciplines as we can.

Traditionally, the funding of narrowly defined labs has been left to a single department, usually the English department. However, if we are to provide expanded service beyond the needs of this one department, in other words really provide a full list of services and not just deal with the few students who happen to come into to see what a writing center is or who are sent by the few professors who understand what a center can do for them, then we had better decide quickly who will help pay for these expanded, professional, and efficient services.

As writing center directors we owe it to ourselves to search for outside funding for at least some of the day-to-day running of our centers. When we show that we can provide a quality service, a service streamlined to meet the writing needs of several different writing groups on campus, then we will gain even more clientele from across the campus.

Funding is going to be a very important issue in the advancement of writing centers over the next decades. We must develop additional sources of funding for our centers as more and more financial strain is placed on dwindling English departments facing low enrollments since more students are selecting majors in business and the hard sciences. If we in the writing center world want to be taken seriously in academics, to be seen as professional peers and not just a service branch of the English department, then we will have to start acting like professionals. Professionals, by their very definition, get paid for the services they offer.

Works Cited

Baltrinic, Barb. "Extending the Writing Center." *Writing Lab Newsletter* 31.1 (Sept., 1988): 7-8

Brown, Lady Falls. "Stable Concept/Unstable Reality: Recreating the Writing Center. " *Writing Lab Newsletter* 14.8 (April, 1990): 6-8

Farrell, Pamela B. (Ed.).*The High School Writing Center: Establishing and Maintaining One*. Urbana: NCTE, 1989.

Freisinger, Diana, and Jill Burkland. "Talking About Writing: The Role of the Writing Lab." *Language Connections: Writing And Reading Across the Curriculum*. Eds.Toby Fulwiler and Art Young. Urbana: NCTE, 1982:167-79 .

North, Stephen M. "The Idea of A Writing Center." *College English* 46 (1984): 433-36.

Olson, Gary. "The Problem of Attitudes in Writing Center Relationships." In *Writing Centers: Theory and Administration*. Ed. Gary A. Olson. Urbana, IL: NCTE, 1984. 3-15.

Posey, Evelyn "Purchasing Software for the Writing Center." *Writing Lab Newsletter* 13.9 (May 1989): 6-8.

Scanlon, Leone. "Recruiting and Training Tutors for Cross Disciplinary Writing Programs." *The Writing Center Journal* 6 2 (1986): 1-8.

Smith, Louise Z. "Independence and Collaboration: Why We Should Decentralize Writing Centers." *The Writing Center Journal* 7 (1986): 3-10.

Wallace, Ray. "The Writing Center's Role in the Writing Across the Curriculum Program: Theory and Practice." *The Writing Center Journal* 8.2 (Spring/Summer 1988): 43-48.

The Role of Writing Centers in Student Retention Programs

Jeanne Simpson
Eastern Illinois University

Retention is the magic word from the department level right on up to governing boards and legislatures. Funding, support, everything is based on how many students an institution gets, keeps, and graduates. Writing centers can play a significant role in retention efforts, but before they do, their directors need to understand what retention means and how centers affect it. After spending six years helping to develop a coordinated university retention program, I have learned some valuable lessons in this respect.

Retention is a concept that is often misunderstood. It does not mean hanging on to poorly prepared students beyond a reasonable point, though that is a common misinterpretation. Rather it means students' persistence in an institution. Sometimes it includes graduation; sometimes it means other goals, such as achieving transfer to another school. Retention means that students find a reasonable fit between their needs and the offerings of an institution. Retention is not simply a matter of keeping enrollments up, which can be done with an admissions revolving door. Retention means steady, significant, measurable progress.

A good retention rate suggests that a school is attracting and keeping students who are well matched to its style and mission. Such matches do happen serendipitously, but not often enough. Consistent retention success requires effort and planning, and one of the keys to this success is to begin as soon as students arrive on campus. Much of retention happens in a few key weeks, the first ones that a student spends on a campus; this pattern applies to traditional 18-year-old freshmen, transfer students, and non-traditional students, though it is especially important for the traditional freshman (Upcraft, 1984). As colleges compete for a dwindling pool of these students, more and more are developing retention programs aimed at the freshman year.

Writing centers need to identify the roles they can play in these retention efforts by examining the specific activities that are known to enhance student success. Among these are academic assistance, mentoring, and developing friendships and other peer relationships. Four segments of campus life seem to have the greatest effect on student success: residence halls, academic assistance programs, advisement, and orientation programs (Upcraft and Gardner, 1989). Any writing center can be involved, directly or indirectly, with all four.

Residence halls are the primary source of information about campus services for most freshmen. For this reason, writing center publicity and out-reach programs should certainly involve the residence halls on campuses where they exist. For example, the Residence Assistants in the halls are, in most instances, required to offer regular programs for the student they serve: mini-workshops offered out of writing centers can fill this need easily.

Obviously, the role of a writing center as an academic assistance program is the most germane to retention. There is more to it than simply offering tutorial help, however. There is a need that occurs before students need help with their writing: students need to connect with an institution in a positive way before they can become successful students. The writing center has a significant opportunity to achieve this connection.

Writing center directors need to address retention issues in tutor-training, particularly the issue of how little students often know about the conventions of college life. In a freshman orientation course, for example, I discovered that most of my 25 freshman students did not know what being on the dean's list meant; most believed it involved academic probation. They did not distinguish between *preregistration* and *prerequisites*. They were unaware of the university catalog's significance, considering it to be simply more slick recruitment material.

Tutors can be an important source of accurate information, provided they learn to listen to and observe their students carefully. Writing center personnel can find ways to supply information to students without embarrassing or frightening them, probably better than almost any other agency within an institution because tutorials are private and ungraded. "Learning assistance programs can identify and catch students not normally seen as attrition prospects" (Walter, Gomon, et al., 1989).

However, first tutors must themselves be trained so that they have accurate information about the school and its systems. While tutor training programs obviously should address issues of teaching writing first, they can appropriately include sessions on all academic assistance programs available on a campus, review of the general education requirements for degrees, and information about library services, for example.

Tutors may not need to know everything about a campus, but they do need to know whom to ask. The names, telephone numbers, and office locations of key personnel should be immediately accessible to tutors. A knowledgeable tutor can intervene early in the office-to-office runaround that students often complain about; getting a clear answer and straight directions to the right office has a significant role in retention as well as in encouraging repeat visits to a writing center.

Including this kind of material in tutor-training, especially for peer tutors, has the added advantage of strengthening the tutors' own academic survival skills. Just because such students are knowledgeable about writing does not necessarily mean that they are as well informed about other segments of campus life.

In tutor-training sessions which address academic survival, tutors need to understand that it is an issue of enormous importance. They can hardly overestimate the lack of information the average freshman student suffers from. Such students may not know that they can drop a difficult class or even that classes are not routinely held in residence halls, both instances of problems I have encountered. What may appear to be a writing problem may be much more. While tutors do not need to be able to solve all problems, they do need to be prepared to recognize multidimensional difficulties when they see them, and, above all, tutors need to be able to offer a helping hand. The discovery of a single instance of helpfulness can keep an otherwise discouraged student in school. Every year, hundreds of students simply leave school, packing their bags and going home without attention to any official withdrawal procedures. Writing center tutors should recognize that one part of their duties is to find ways to prevent such departures.

Freshmen suffer from lack of confidence as well as a lack of information. Attendance at a writing center, voluntarily or otherwise, can exacerbate low confidence, and writing center tutors must cope with this problem before any real tutoring can occur. The most effective approaches approximate the mentoring and friendship formation that are known to improve retention. Such simple things as smiling, learning people's names correctly, doing a little follow-up on how things are going, can make a significant difference for these students.

A second approach to the confidence issue is to look again at procedures within the writing center. Do the procedures of record-keeping and running tutorials intimidate? Often the goals of keeping track of who uses the center and of supplying that information to teachers and administrators obscure how those procedures affect students' attitudes toward writing center services. It is easy to become yet another uncaring bureaucracy if students have to navigate a system that makes access to tutoring a lot of bother.

At my university we discovered that a triple-carbon form intended to track high-risk students actually had the effect of running them off from all tutorial programs because it was so intimidating. We got better results when we ditched the form and used a more informal-looking (but equally official) slip sent through campus mail. The lesson we learned from this experience was to consult students as we redesigned our forms. They had plenty of good suggestions, and the act of consultation was itself an important ice-breaker.

The one advantage to the original form which we sought to keep was close contact with students' advisors. One copy was supposed to go to the advisor; the problem was that we had no way of identifying the advisor unless the student told us. Development of a central advisement program for all freshman students simplified the problem; now the writing center and the advisement center work closely to exchange information and track freshmen. Originally, our efforts focused on at-risk students, those with low ACT scores, for example. A close examination of the problem, however, revealed that the traditional definition of at-risk students was insufficient and that too many freshmen were getting into academic difficulties without knowing where and how to get help. We have developed brochures, handouts, and survival manuals to distribute to entering freshmen, and cooperation between advisement and the center is much closer. At schools where central advisement does not exist, this problem may be large; even so, for a writing center to have a list of all entering freshmen and their advisors would be a good start in developing effective means of early intervention.

An alternative to using a form to acquaint students with writing center services is involvement with orientation programs and courses. Many colleges offer student success courses designed to develop study skills, time-management skills, and knowledge of the academic and personal support programs available on a given campus. Students in such courses often earn points every time they use an assistance service. Their visits may be aimed at specific issue, but they also are frequently for the purpose of learning what a center does, where it is, who is there. The response can be very positive, in part because there is no risk, no embarrassing revelation of error.

It is simple for writing centers to become involved in such programs. They are excellent opportunities for distributing materials about writing center services. In many programs, guest speakers attend the classes to offer short workshops or question-answer sessions. Writing center directors and tutors easily fit into this format. Writing center directors are also obvious candidates to teach such courses and to participate in workshops to prepare teachers for student success courses because they already have the mentoring style which is a key to most orientation programs.

Writing centers, then, are not just about writing, they are about student success. If writing center directors adopt this larger view, it affects how they approach the politics of administering a center. While centers have usually been more than just departmental in their structures, regarding them as integral parts of retention efforts requires taking a full, institution-wide view of their services. Thinking about centers in this way should encourage a review of goals, purposes, methods, and policies to be sure none of these is too parochial.

The nature of the center's record-keeping may shift somewhat, as well. It is and has always been difficult to correlate writing center visits directly with success in writing courses; the same is true for their effect on retention because there are too many other variables to consider. Nevertheless, directors have to use numbers to justify funding and staffing. Connecting record-keeping with retention offers several ways to reach this goal. For example, tracking how many entering students use the center during their first six weeks on campus affords a means of assessing how well the center is distributing information to new students. Student persistence is easier to track than writing improvement; students who use writing center services can be sampled periodically to determine their cumulative grade point averages and accumulated hours, indicating reasonable progress. If most of the center's clients are at-risk students, this information is particularly important, though it is a useful measure of the effectiveness of any assistance program. It also has the virtue of being a measure easily understood by administrators and governing boards.

Understanding and using the concept of retention requires one more step. Retention is not a separate, free-standing goal for any institution. It is connected to the specific academic goals of the school. A small liberal arts college will have somewhat different retention goals and methods from those of a large university with graduate programs. Most of us have a general idea of the goals of our institutions, but may not be aware of the specific retention rate and how it compares with those of similar institutions. If a retention system is working well, the goal may be maintaining the status quo; if not, the goal may be achieving a specific percentage. Gathering this information and determining its effects on a writing center requires understanding the decision-making process of an institution. Where is assessment of retention done? How? By whom? Who sets retention goals? Who determines the means of achieving those goals?

Directing a writing center is such an absorbing job that it is easy to keep a local focus -- the writing center. Many decisions made in councils, committees, senates, and so on do not directly affect the center, so directors do not necessarily pay attention. We tend to be committed to teaching writing, not to institutional politics. But while the decisions themselves don't always affect the center, the decision process does. Writing center directors need to attend carefully to the process at their institutions. We should go to council and committee meetings as often as possible. Directors don't necessarily have to be on these councils and committees; in fact, simply observing them first will clarify which ones are most important and which, perhaps, a director might want to join. Attending these meetings will help directors in several ways: we will learn what positions our colleagues take on various issues, we will learn specifically how governance works on our campuses, and we will give our centers and our positions as directors greater visibility. We will also find how large a role the concept of retention actually plays in institutional politics and develop a clear idea of how to be involved with it.

In understanding these systems and the role of retention on a campus, writing center directors should avoid the mistake of equating the standard career path with power-holding, decision-making structures. Writing center directorships are usually low-level administration, frequently associated with English departments, and not always reflective of the center's campus-wide mission. For directors designated as faculty, the standard path through the professorial ranks, department chair, dean, provost or vice-president determines job retention, promotion and tenure. This path may not, however, be used for setting student retention goals and making budget decisions. Understanding how to protect one's employment status is not necessarily the same as understanding the whole institution's systems. Because retention echoes throughout any school, connecting a writing center's goals and systems to retention issues requires a thorough understanding of the whole picture.

All institutions have loops around their official power structures which lead to the real one; in most institutions, retention is one on-ramp to this loop. Writing centers and retention are a natural combination.

This natural, potent combination is a way for writing center directors to provide significant leadership to all of us whose concerns are addressed by the Wyoming Resolution and the National Writing Centers Association's Position Statement on Working Conditions for Writing Center Directors (1985), as well as helping students to stay in school. Writing center people have always known that writing is central to successful education; what we have needed is a means to convince others. If we face indifference, misunderstanding, wretched budgets, and unmotivated students, we need more than just to believe in what we do. We need to ask if we look at the centers where we work in a large enough context. Do we have a clear enough understanding of where and how the decisions are made which affect us? Have we developed means of evaluating our work which make sense in terms of larger, institutional contexts? Are we using the structures of our schools to the best advantage? Are our goals fully consonant with institutional goals?

Because we believe so strongly in what we do, because we have dedicated so much effort, time, energy, and brainpower to the task of developing and supervising writing centers and to the instruction that goes on inside of them, we sometimes suffer from forest-and-tree syndrome. We must remember that writing centers are like knowing how to write well: not the end itself, but the best means to other ends, including retention.

Works Cited

"Position Statement on Professional Concerns of Writing Center Directors." *Writing Center Journal*, Spring/Summer 1985, 36-39.

Upcraft, M. L. (ed.) *Orienting Students to College: New Directions for Student Services*, no. 25. San Francisco: Jossey-Bass, 1984.

------------, John Gardner, et al. *The Freshman Year Experience*. San Francisco: Jossey-Bass, 1989.

Walter, Timothy, Audrey Gomon, et al. "Academic Support Programs." *The Freshman Year Experience*, Ed. M. Lee Upcraft, John Gardner, et al. San Francisco: Jossey-Bass, 1989.

Writing Services: A New Role for the Writing Center and Faculty

William C. Wolff
Appalachian State University

I

Academic communities are challenging the coming of the twenty-first century with continued efforts to foster more widespread and sophisticated literacy. For this purpose, many institutions have identified and developed new services to organize and integrate writing skills among their various constituencies: students, faculty, staff, administration, and other interested groups. One important group of services where these needs can be met is the writing center.

Most publications relating to writing centers have been directed toward the tutoring of students because the traditional student has been the major focus of academic communities. Bene Scanlon Cox directs her attention and guidelines to students' "immediate needs" addressed by trained instructors (81). The students' needs may be met in a number of ways, three of which are: first, one-on-one tutoring sessions; second, collaborative learning; and third, peer tutoring (See Bruffee, "The Brooklyn Plan," "Staffing," and "Two Related Issues"; Harris, *Teaching One-to-One* and *Tutoring Writing*; Olson ed. *Writing Center*). But the development of writing among faculty, those who deal directly with student writing, will insure clear and detailed assignments from which students learn to write for specific audiences, for readers trained in different disciplines.

Susan H. McLeod of Washington State University and Laura Emery from San Diego State University have developed "a weekly writing workshop for faculty who want a supportive audience, friendly editorial help, and a definite deadline for the papers they write" (65). The workshop was based on various important theories of learning. Taking his cue from Michael Oakeshott (199), Kenneth Bruffee proposed that peer tutoring was partially justified by Burke's "Conversation of Mankind" ("Peer Tutoring" 3). He recognized Stanley Fish was right in proposing that all writers' thoughts and "mental operations. . . have their source in some or other interpretive community" (14). About the same time as Fish made his observation, Richard Rorty applied Thomas Kuhn's proposals about scientific communities and their thought to other communities where knowledge is produced, traditions

110

preserved, and where symbolic structures, mainly language, are applied and developed, in order to justify among knowledgeable peers some form of belief in each others' works (Rorty, *passim* ; See Bruffee, "Liberal," 8-20).

A more comprehensive community, academic establishment, uses forms of discourse in which writers within the various disciplines ask peer readers to accept their authority -- if not all of their premises. William Perry proposes that such writers refer to specialized data that are related to known contexts in ways that establish the writers as colleagues and peers (see Bruffee, *A Short Course* 221). But more often than not, these methods are applied only to the teaching of students. Because of this limited exposure, too often the writing center has been viewed as a place used only for aiding and helping to retain undergraduate or high school students in school. Unfortunately, literature is sparse about the Center providing an appropriate environment for writing among scholars teachers and graduate students.

This article focuses on a different level of collaborative learning: a writing workshop at Appalachian State University for faculty and staff which was found to be highly valuable and effective. The writing workshop is, in many ways, a model from which writing center directors could shape other such workshops at their own institutions. Appalachian's grouping began with the Director, the staff member who wrote an instrument on creative writing, and professors of psychology and language arts, later growing to include faculty from community leadership, management, and health care administration.

In a time in which academic institutions are talking about the importance of writing across the curriculum, the writing workshop for faculty and staff would bring together groups who all too often do not even converse much -- except about the time or the weather. The workshop can become a place of sharing knowledge and recognizing talents previously unknown. Too many faculty take shelter in their own disciplines by talking and writing only there and reading professionally only in their own specialties. Staff share their talents with other staff segregated, so to speak, from faculty. But this situation need not continue.

Community was developed in Appalachian's workshop because personal risk was minimized and trust developed in a milieu in which the members encouraged the building of writers as writers -- as well as the construction of their texts. The members seemed to intuit the need to give succor, to add support, even decorations, to personal and written constructions. They did not dismantle.

This obvious comfort with collaborative learning among a group trained to think and write alone inspired an outward direction for the members' new insights and energies. Why couldn't, the Director asked himself, those who collaborate in the Center workshop do the same with their colleagues, even with their students? Why couldn't they create writing workshops even in their classes, just as he did? And so the Director shared with them an instrument he developed for leading students in their revisions of papers written for courses in freshman English and Advanced Writing:

Workshopping Class

Exchange papers. Read the paper you get at least twice and then answer the following questions in writing. Your purpose is to make editorial suggestions that will help the writer revise in order to improve on an initial effort.

1. Is there a clear specific statement of purpose-- a thesis -- and does it appear in the beginning? In other words, do you know in the beginning what the paper is about?

2. Do you understand exactly what the writer is saying in every sentence, every paragraph? If not, which passages are unclear?

3. Is there any sentence or paragraph that does not say enough, that raises a question in your mind that you want answered, that tells you something that you want to know more about? If so, which sentences/paragraphs seem incomplete? What are the questions you want answered?

4. Do the sentences/paragraphs follow one another logically? If there are any non-sequiturs, cite them.

5. Is the writer specific enough, concrete enough, or does he/she approach his/her subject in a general, vague, abstract manner?

6. Are there any sweeping or too-broad statements that need support now missing? If so, cite them.

7. Can you find any extraneous language (verbal deadwood)? If so, put it in parentheses and write "delete" in the margin so the writer will know what you think unnecessary.

8. *Are there any statements so obvious that they need not be stated at all? If so, cite them.*
9. *On the whole, is the paper very interesting, fairly interesting, or only somewhat interesting?*
10. *Does the paper tell you something you didn't know (that the targeted audience doesn't know)? Is it all familiar or has it been presented in a new perspective, with a new twist that makes old material still interesting?*
11. *Is there anything else that might be done to bring this paper up to a grade of "A"? Be as specific as you can.*

The faculty at the writing workshop were asked to revise this instrument so that it might be used by faculty and students in specific disciplines.

II

One member of the faculty/staff writing workshop at Appalachian is Paul G. Kussrow, Professor of Leadership and Higher Education, who also serves as Director of the Center for Community Education. Kussrow regularly gives grant writing seminars. The author of two dozen articles and monographs in such publications as *Grants Magazines, Community Education Journal*, and *Community College Catalyst*, Kussrow first produced the following:

Workshopping Class For Community Leaders

Exchange implementation papers. Review your colleagues' papers and answer the following questions in writing on the margins of each paper you review. Your editorial suggestions should be given with the intent of helping the writer improve clarity and the possibility that this proposal can be implemented.

1. Is the concept clearly stated? Can the reader quickly determine what the concept-idea-strategy or approach is and how it is related to the writer's discipline, agency or institution?

2. Do the agency's stated or implied goals, mission or objectives complement the concept? If not, in what ways could the writer bridge a relationship for the reader?

3. Are the administrative steps, methods and timelines logically presented? Are all the bases covered in your mind? Is there something more you or someone else might want answered before buying into the concept? If so, where does the writer need to elaborate, add sentences or answer unanswered questions? Does the order and arrangement of the narrative follow a logical sequence?

4. Do projected resources (funds, space, people) match the administrative methodology? Are allocations reasonable? If not, cite other parallel and concrete examples.

5. What barriers to implementation are not addressed? Does the writer propose a well thought out system in dealing with implementation problems? Are strategies too vague? If so, suggest other approaches.

6. Once implemented, what are some not-so-obvious audiences that need to learn of the implementation of this concept?

7. Is the paper written at the professional level such that it is ready to be presented to a governing board or to your chief executive officer?

8. Does the paper hold the interest of the reader? Does it provide a new approach or response to an existing problem? Does the approach complement current organization support structures that are in place at your agency or institution?

9. In what ways would you suggest improvement either on the paper its content or approach?

At the following session of the workshop, Kussrow decided to revise his instrument, adding detail needed for his readers. In his revised instrument Kussrow added two criteria not found in the original:

2. Can the reader be directed to on-site applications of the concept? Does the writer refer to professional readings, research or literature that can support the concept?

Kussrow has unwittingly moved from Maxine Hairston's second to her third class of writing (444-45), from extended and somewhat complex writing wherein he knows his subject fairly well from years of professional practice to a more reflective writing wherein he develops both the proposal's form and the writing's conceptual basis by advocating that readers be provided with practical on-site experience. Here he moves even more strongly to reader-based prose than he had in his first draft sharing -- as Linda Flower put it -- professional "language" and "content" (19-20), in this case ones common to community leaders. Kussrow's revision has developed into an important guide for advanced students and professional writers, one which will bring writing center services into the classroom and/or a professional writing environment.

Kussrow also added:

> 8. *How will the concept and its implementation be evaluated and reported? Who are the primary and secondary audiences who need to know?*

He did this after discussing in the workshop Rorty's application of Kuhn's proposals about the way scientific communities demand evaluation in order to justify belief in each other's work. Seeing that varied audiences will read the piece for which the instrument is giving criteria, Kussrow reminds the writer to be aware of primary and secondary audiences, providing proof of research in order to give the reader appropriate experience and evidence of the writer's authority on the subject.

III

Leslie Anne Perry has had thirteen years public school teaching experience. She has served as a classroom teacher and a remedial reading specialist at the elementary and middle school levels. Currently, she is an adjunct assistant professor at Appalachian State University where she teaches reading education and language arts courses. Dr. Perry is the co-author of *Teaching the Reading Teachers, Teaching Basic Skills in Reading*, and *Fry's Instant Word Puzzles and Activities*, and is the author of *Primary Reading and Writing Activities for Every Month of the School Year*.

Perry revised the instrument so that she might use it herself when publishing and have her students use it when writing. Perry first wrote:

Peer Response To Writing: Writing Workshop Activity For Reading Education Faculty And Students

A. Exchange papers with a colleague/classmate. Carefully read the paper you receive. As you read, record your comments and suggestions on a separate sheet of paper. Additionally, number each paragraph in the margin of your friend's paper and mark any errors (including typos) directly on the paper.

The purpose of this activity is to help your colleague/ classmate produce a final product that best fulfills his/her purpose.You will do this by responding to the following questions in writing:
1. Is a clear, specific purpose stated at the beginning of the paper?
2. Are all sentences and paragraphs clear and easily understood?
If not, which ones are unclear?
3. Are there any sentences or paragraphs that seem incomplete or that leave unanswered questions in your mind? If so, which ones?
4. Are ideas presented in a logical order? If not, which statements seem out of order?
5. Do all the paragraphs contain a single focus? If not, which ones need rewriting?
6. Are transitions used effectively? If not, indicate places where improvement is needed.
7. Does the writer approach his/her topic in a specific and concrete manner, or is the information presented in a vague or abstract way?
8. What other changes could be made to this paper that would result in its overall improvement?

B. Return the paper to your colleague/classmate. Discuss the changes you have recommended and answer any questions he/ she may have regarding your suggestions.

Leslie Anne Perry's final instrument makes notable revisions on her first draft.

Peer Response To Writing: Writing Workshop Activity For Reading Education Faculty/Students

For faculty:
  The purpose of this activity is to help a colleague produce a final product that can be favorably considered by a journal that publishes material in the area of reading. You can do this service by following the steps suggested below.

For students:
  The purpose of this activity is to help another student to produce a final paper that will receive an excellent grade because it is virtually ready for publication. You can do this service by following the steps suggested below:

A. Exchange papers with your colleague or classmate. Number each paragraph in the margin of your colleague's /classmate's paper and mark any errors (including typos) directly on the paper. Then read the paper a second time very carefully. As you read, record your comments and suggestions on a separate sheet of paper. Please include responses to the following questions:

1. Is a clear, specific purpose stated at the beginning of the paper?
2. Are all sentences and paragraphs clear and easily understood?
If not, which ones are unclear?
3. Is the language specific and concrete and likely to be understood by reading professionals?
4. Is the active voice utilized?
5. Are there any sentences or paragraphs that seem incomplete or that leave unanswered questions in your mind? If so, which ones?
6. Are ideas presented in a logical order? If not, which statements seem out of order?
7. Does the paper contain any unnecessary words that do not contribute to the overall effectiveness of the paper? Indicate any words or phrases you feel should be deleted.

> *8. Do all the paragraphs contain a single focus? If not,which ones need rewriting?*
> *9. Are transitions used effectively? If not, indicate places where improvement is needed.*
> *10. Does the paper contribute new information to the field of reading (or offer a unique perspective to previous knowledge)?*
> *11. What evidence exists that previous research in reading/ language arts/literacy has been taken into account?*
> *12. If the paper is research based, are the reported results related to actual classroom practice?*
> *13. What other changes could be made to this paper that would increase its chances of being published/favorably evaluated?*
> *14. If writing for publication, has your colleague utilized specific submissions information (e.g. following APA format from the current edition of the <u>Contributor's Guide to Periodicals in Reading</u> (IRA) or from the journal where the article will be submitted?*
>
> *B. Return the paper to your colleague/classmate. Discuss the changes you have recommended and answer any questions he/she may have regarding your suggestions.*

In her last copy Perry gives evidence of her readers' need to know the purpose of the activity before being given directions on how to workshop the paper, and so she revises her first two paragraphs. She has intuited Cicero's conviction that the orator begins by swaying the audience with some "mental impulse" (*De Oratore* II, XLII), in this case a commitment to service. She takes her own advice from her sixth criterion: present materials in logical persuasive order. Then, in her directions, Perry supports the mode of the editor who writes directly on the pages of the manuscript, but also asks for notes that, in their expansiveness, need more room than margins provide.

Perry's first draft did not provide criteria three, four, seven, ten, eleven, twelve, and fourteen. In the last draft's number three, she exhorts her workshoppers to assure professional readers of the writer's competence because of the use of commonly held terms, thus following Rorty. Her new fourth criterion demands clarification of who or what is the grammatical subject of sentences, thus clarifying praise and blame -- as bureaucratic prose so often does not. Clarity is the focus for adding

criterion seven: specific details provide readers with sensory particulars
that anchor otherwise abstract concepts.

Criteria ten and fourteen of the revised instrument also direct
workshoppers to highly professional concerns. Readers should be
assured the writers have done their homework. Writers must know what
others have said about their topics, and provide that information to gain
credence and to remind readers of previous research and scholarship --
and do so in the format which the varied journals use.

IV

Dr. G. Creighton Frampton is an Associate Professor of Marketing
at the Philadelphia College of Textiles and Science. Currently the editor
of the *Journal of Economic and Financial Experts*, he has written
numerous articles in business and economics, and is a certified member
of the American Forensics Association.

Dr. Shah Mahmoud, who is Frampton's co-author for the
following instrument, is a Professor of Management at Appalachian
State University. His research interests over the years have been in the
areas of finance management and human resources, and he has
published widely in both professional and academic journals, such as
the noted *Journal of Management*.

Workshopping Class

*Workshop participants for business and economics papers
should make initial constructive contributions by
accomplishing the following: (1) quickly analyze mechanical
flaws (grammar, punctuation spelling); (2) see if thoughts are
presented in a flowing logical order; and (3) examine the text
for structural writing flaws when combining statistical and
business data with other facts and opinions.*

*Writing in management, marketing, accounting and other
related functional areas of business administration must be
salient and communicate effectively. Business writing must
have concise objectives, content and conclusions. Following
are some guidelines to observe:*

1. Introduction and Plan

Recognize the business audience, and give a brief statement of the purpose of the information presented.

Include a letter of transmittal, a title of the report, its date, its preparer's name and the audience for whom the report is intended.

Include a brief summary along with a description of the method used in the collection and analysis of the information.

Include a summary of findings and recommendations as well as solutions for anticipated problems that may be encountered in everyday business.

Focus on the interest of the reader, being professional in the use of precise business language and ideas.

2. Organization

Write in an organized fashion. Give a statement of the purpose of the manuscript. Be sure that paragraphs are succinct and contribute to the development of arguments.

Use an outline to enhance the flow of thought and control the structure.

Use visual aids, charts, graphs, maps, pictures, illustrations, tables, specialized formats, and fonts.

Stress clarity, conciseness, simple language, and logical construction.

Avoid the use of numbers in writing; instead use tables and graphs to indicate significant trends and critical points and findings, but make sure they are correct, understandable, and explained.

Provide simple, easy, informative and usable information.

Explain the sampling procedures and the analytical techniques that are used.

3. Conclusions

Present your conclusions in a usable format to a business owner, operator, or manager. Give basis and benefits for the recommendations.

Interpret statistical information and state how the information can benefit a business enterprise.

> *Write clearly and in the third person so that the business report is scannable because of the generous use of simple listings and enumerations.*
> *Follow a clear style manual such as Turabian.*

> *Return the report to your colleagues, with recommended changes and possible suggestions.*

Professors Mahmoud and Frampton have written a commentary on their instrument: *"The revisions between the first, second, and third papers presented by Professors G. Creighton Frampton and Shah Mahmoud were quite noticeable, both in content and organization. The final revisions encompassed a specialized approach to the writing of business English. Business calls for precise writing. The reader must be able to analyze the content quickly because time is usually limited.*

The orientation of the revised papers was primarily based on the business maxim, POC; plan, organize and control. Because writing presents significant data that concerns an objective, the information must be organized with utmost clarity. Although brevity is a key factor under consideration in business writing, it must not interfere with the clear flow of thought. Emphasis is placed on significant numbers and corresponding data and it is highly important that form must not be neglected or total meaning and interest will be lost. In the aspect of control and content, the focus of a paper must be usable. A solid focus will allow the writer to expound and control thoughts and ideas with correlation and clarity.

In the final analysis, mutually collaborative efforts are productive and efficient. Such efforts provide a useful and worthwhile experience. Teachers and students at the graduate and undergraduate levels are able to learn how to write correctly for the world of business where precision is highly valued."

V

David D. Phoenix, Jr. is Assistant Professor of Management and Assistant to the Vice Chancellor for Academic Affairs. Professor Phoenix has written an instrument to be used by undergraduate and graduate students of health care administration. He already delineates possible issues in that field, giving advice for papers about organizational phenomena, finances, policies, missions, strategic management and about evaluation. For each, Phoenix provides helpful, precise heuristics that insure collaborative learning between writer and workshop reader as well as planning for professional readers of the final product.

Workshopping Class For Health Care Administration Students And Practitioners

Exchange papers on health care organizations, financing, administration and policy analysis. Review each paper and respond in writing to organizational, financial, and policy issues presented. Your editing should help the writer to present the issue(s) in a clear and interesting fashion.

1. Is the issue clearly defined? Can the reader determine the nature of the problem? Is the writer's perspective clear on whether the problem is organizational, administrative, financial or policy related?

2. Does the writer provoke critical thought about the <u>organizational</u> phenomena presented? Are the ideas presented supported by the literature or recent research findings?

3. Does the writer present <u>financial issues</u> from practical micro-or macro-focused viewpoints? Are solutions presented from a variety of theories relevant to managerial accounting, managerial or public finance?

4. When <u>policy issues</u> are presented, does the writer present their impact on the multiple levels of health services delivery? Are criteria for choosing among several policy alternatives presented? Are problems in feasibility and implementation discussed?

5. Does the writer discuss the <u>organizational mission,</u> goals or objectives when a service marketing issue is presented? Is the target market identified? How is the market segmented? Is it clear what share of the market the organization wishes to capture with their service?

6. When <u>strategic management</u> is the topic, does the writer clearly present the current entrepreneurial position of the organization? Is an analysis of the organization's external environment presented? Is the desired market position presented as well as the steps to achieve it?

*7. Does the writer present and discuss information to
determine the relevance, progress, efficiency, effectiveness and
impact of health service activities or programs when
<u>evaluation is</u> the topic?
8. Is the paper written at the level of the writer's desired
audience?
9. How would you improve the paper, its content or
approach?*

Phoenix works by classifying the focuses of his discipline, health
care administration. For each he establishes specific proper modes of
analysis and of proof or evidence, leading his readers to think critically
about what they are reading. Like the other writing workshops
members, he reaffirms the need to review previous literature and
research, the relevance of theory to practice, and the force of practical
concerns. The importance of financial considerations, on the other hand,
emerges as a serious issue, as it had in the instruments of Kussrow as
well as Frampton and Mahmoud.

VI

Donald L. Clark is a professor of Psychology at Appalachian State
University.

Workshopping Class For Psychology

*Exchange papers and read them. Write your comments on
pages separate from the text. Make editorial suggestions that
will help the writers to improve their initial efforts during
revision.*

*Psychologists generally write empirical studies, review
articles, theoretical articles, or clinical reports. Determine
which type of writing you are reading.*

*1. For empirical studies, are the tests, measurements,
methods, and evaluations described in precise, perhaps even
statistical, terms? Is the language appropriate to the kind of
experiment performed? Is the problem clearly stated? Do the*

hypothesis and the experimental design relate closely and clearly to a stated problem?

2. For review articles, has the author provided a thorough synthesis of the latest research?

3. For theoretical papers, is there a clear and specific statement of purpose- -a thesis? Are clear definitions of terms provided?

4. For clinical reports, is there a fully detailed summary right up front? Does that summary provide sufficient descriptive detail to give you a feel for the real human being you are reading about? Are appropriate terms used for diagnosis and treatment?

5. Who is the audience? Imagine yourself as part of the audience. Does the author understand the audience? Can you cite a place where the writer shows or does not show an awareness of audience? Keep in mind that the paper before you is a piece of reading for you, not a piece of writing for the author.

6. Has the author reviewed previous literature on the subject in order to establish professional credibility and to serve readers' needs for understanding the piece's context?

7. As you read, do you understand exactly what the writer is saying in every sentence, every paragraph? Is each sentence maximally informative, especially the lead or final sentence of each paragraph? If not, which passages are unclear? Rewrite them. Are the words used the most precise terms? Can you think of more appropriate words?

8. Do the sentences/paragraphs follow one another logically? Is the author building a case step by step or does the author veer off course into extraneous matters?

9. Is the research cited pertinent to the specific issue being addressed or does it appear that the author is padding the report with tangential data? Is there a logical continuity between previous work and this present work? Where is that continuity presented? Does the author stick to some recognized format of presentation such as (1) a historical approach which should begin with the most important current research and work backward in time, or (2) a spiral approach building a case and inserting research findings to support each point?

10. Is the writer being specific enough, concrete enough, or instead does he or she approach the subject in a general, vague, abstract manner? Are there any sweeping generalizations that should be narrowed?
11. See if the writer has used proper coordinating and transitional terms appropriate to the relationship between the clauses?

relationships	possible terms
cause	because
effect	therefore
time	after, then, while
contraries	although
condition	if

12. Watch for overuse of passive verbs. Rewrite the passive sentences into an active form.
13. Correct unclear pronoun references. Rewrite sentences beginning with weak pronouns such as this, it is, that, and these.
14. Be sure the correct singular and plural are used, such as phenomenon, phenomena, datum, and data.
15. Correct sentences so that they have strong beginnings.

> *Weak: There are four men running into the museum.*
> *Strong: Four men have just run into the museum carefully holding packages that may be bombs.*

16. If the author is not sure of his or her audience, do you know of publications whose editors might be interested? Name them.
17. Suggest possible publication for the piece according to audience and style:

American Psychologist: prestigious, formal, academic
Psychology Today: reliable, but informal and popular

If different styles are mixed, suggest revision into two articles: one academic, one popular.

Clark's beginning not only gives clear and terse directions, it also explains some varied kinds of writing that psychologists engage in. Donald Clark prudently concerns his workshoppers with the relationship between audience and form. Knowing that professional psychologists will write for popular as well as academic readers, he asks in his last criterion that workshoppers give informed advice about appropriate forms for publication. But he is also aware of the various forms of discourse which psychologists need to compose. In his first draft of the workshopping he wrote briefly of several such forms:

1. For empirical studies and review articles, can you locate and understand the definition of the problem being addressed? For theoretical papers, is there a clear, specific statement of purpose--a thesis? Do you know in the beginning what the paper is about? For clinical reports, is there a good summary right up front and does the summary give you a feel for a real human being that you are about to read about?

His final copy provides the reader with more specific and individual guidance for each form covered, developing the details of his advice and expanding it from one criterion to four.

Criterion six guides workshoppers in aiding writers to present themselves as authorities. Clark presents advice similar to that of R. J. Light and D. B. Pillemer when he insists that psychologists first, know the major trends in the area (144); second, help readers interpret research with insight (147); third, examine different research in order to reveal the strengths and weaknesses of varied research forms and designs, sometimes resolving apparent contradictions (149); fourth, contribute to the understanding of generalized propositions (153). Including literature reviews may be seen, says Clark, as guiding our scholarship, our daily behavior and the direction of programs.

VII

Jane Vick Robinson is an administrative assistant and secretary in the Department of Communication Arts. She earned a B.S. in Elementary Education from Queens College (Charlotte), an M.Ed. in Early Childhood Education from Georgia State University, and an Ed.S.

in Developmental Education as well as Adult and Higher Education from Appalachian State University. Ms. Robinson taught kindergarten, developed an early childhood program for the state of Georgia, and developed an early learning center in North Carolina. Eventually she opted for dealing with older students.

Friends and colleagues have encouraged Ms. Robinson to write for the general public some stories she has told them for many years. The tales center around not only her life as the mother of two children--a physician and a scholar of Latin and Greek--but also as the daughter of a woman suffering from Alzheimer's disease. Ms. Robinson's recovery from an aneurysm is the focus of some of her most inspiring stories.

Her instrument will be valuable to teachers and students of creative writing because they show a growing sophistication in her literary art.

Workshopping Class For Faculty And Staff: Editing Fiction

Read the story and then answer the following questions in writing. Your answers- -and your purpose- -is to make editorial suggestions that will help the writer rewrite and improve his/her initial effort. If you find errors in spelling or punctuation, please mark them.

1. Does the story make you want to know what happens next? Comment on the story as a whole, its beginning, and its ending.

2. Do you understand exactly what the writer is saying in every sentence, every paragraph? If not, which passages are unclear?

3. Is there any sentence or paragraph that doesn't say enough . . . that raises a question in your mind that you wanted answered . . . that tells you something that you want to know more about? If so, which sentences, paragraphs seem incomplete? What are the questions you want answered?

4. Is there any word, sentence, or paragraph that is not important to the story or that distracts from the story? If so, put it in parenthesis and write "delete" in the margin. Write on your comment sheet your reasons for wanting the deletion.

5. Is there any character whose depiction is vague or whose motivation is obscure? If so, which characters and ideas need attention? What more do you want to know?

6. Does the writer reveal/show/illuminate the ideas and characters, bringing them to life? Cite passages which are flat and merely report.

7. Is the point of view clear? Consistent? Could the story be better told from another point of view?

8. Is active or passive voice used? Is it the most appropriate?

9. Now reread the story and reflect on the following.

> *A. Are there any allusions in this writing? If so, are they related to character?*

> *B. Are there any analogies, similes, or metaphors in this writing? Are comparisons and expressions appropriate to character and theme?*

> *C. Are there any examples of literary symbols in this writing? How appropriate to theme is the meaning suggested?*

> *D. Are there any uses of personification? Are representations appropriate?*

10. Do you have any further comments or suggestions that you wish to make? If so, please wax eloquent.

Robinson's instrument was originally written only from her own experience as a writer before and during the workshop. She then consulted H. Hugh Holman's *A Handbook to Literature* where she found references to point of view, so she added what is her ninth criterion. But she gives evidence of learning on her own some of the critical apparatus which Wayne C. Booth proposed in *The Rhetoric of Fiction.* In the workshop, her discussions of her stories were often couched in Booth's terms, such as telling and showing (3-22); realism and reality (23-36); and authorial silence (271-310). In other words, she learned her art personally and without academic instruction, but she developed language to talk about her art not far from or identical to Booth's terms. This extrapolation from experience to the guidance she gives in her instrument assure her authority to help others collaborate on the creation of literature.

VIII

Conclusions/Suggestions:

The workshop is a circle at which the avenues of many disciplines and staff orientations may convene, there to truly write across the disciplines. The mutual understanding arrived at in the workshop circle will be returned to the departmental milieu and from there to the classroom, to the students. Thus writing center services are brought to the full body of the academic institution not just by bringing students, but also faculty and staff, through the Center's services. The Center not only draws those it serves; it goes out to those it serves. Collaborative learning need not be just a buzz term; collaborative learning can become a reality.

First: Faculty and staff known to a writing center director will often need little persuasion to join a group writing in a cooperative and pleasant forum, and later they will enthusiastically recommend it to others. J. David Johnson of Michigan State University has proposed for the business world what is also true for the academic community:

> In persuading people to take part in innovation, personal channels are more likely to be effective than impersonal ones because they help to get questions raised and answered so that uncertainty is reduced and understanding increased about the innovation and its environment (19-20).

Second: Professionals in such institutions as business and education schools often function in and teach about worlds where competition, not cooperation, are the norm. But their exposure to a friendly world of cooperative learning generates effective writing in which they know the proposed criteria, especially when they help create them. The relaxed atmosphere provides for mutual understanding and improved writing.

Third: At a faculty/staff writing workshop, conversation leads first to personal development in a self-referential system, as Rorty's terms seem to mean. However it also leads to the Burkean ongoing conversation of mankind (110-11) when not only colleagues but also students become engaged in dialogue to become a part of the social construction of reality. (For discussion of Burke and Rorty, see Lentricchia 12-16). One

important subject of the dialogue should be, perforce, what Rachel
Spilka, of the University of Maine, calls "the role of interaction. . .in
multiple audience analysis and adaptation" (44). But John D. Beard,
from Wayne State University, proposes that "given the trend toward
assigning collaborative writing in professional-communication courses,
it is obvious that more research is needed in the area"(47), and Beard is
right.

Fourth: Writing centers need to offer services for faculty and staff for
several reasons:

> A. The services will improve faculty and staff writing and
> publication.

> B. The services will develop the faculty and staff's view of the
> thought and work going on among colleagues in their own and
> other disciplines.

> C. The services will help faculty bring to their classrooms
> more refined attitudes and skills in teaching writing, perhaps
> using collaborative learning.

> D. The services will develop instruments to be used by faculty
> and students in composing and revising writing in and across
> the disciplines.

> E. The services will bring to the classroom many of the
> activities now taking place in the Center.

> F. Therefore, the Center will be spared some of the time-
> consuming activities that will take place in the classroom.

> G. The faculty/staff services will allow the Center the time to
> provide more one-on-one tutoring and work in small groups.

> H. Finally, the Center will be able to create more new
> activities to advance the "conversation of mankind."

Works Cited

Beard, John D., Jone Rymer, and David L. Williams. "An Assessment System for Collaborative-Writing Groups: Theory and Empirical Evaluation." *Journal of Business and Technical Communication* 3 (1989): 29-51.

Booth, Wayne C. *The Rhetoric of Fiction*. Chicago: The University of Chicago Press, 1961.

Bruffee, Kenneth A. "The Brooklyn Plan: Attaining Intellectual Growth through Peer-Grouping Tutoring." *Liberal Education* 64 (1978): 447-68.

_____. "Liberal Education and the Social Justification of Belief." *Liberal Education* (1982): 8-20.

_____. "Peer Tutoring and the 'Conversation of Mankind.'" *Writing Centers: Theory and Administration*. Ed. Gary A. Olson. Urbana: NCTE, 1984. 77-84.

_____. *A Short Course in Writing* 2nd edition. Cambridge, MA: Winthrop, 1980.

_____. "Staffing and Operating Peer-Tutoring Writing Centers." In *Basic Writing: Essays for Teachers, Researchers, and Administrators*. Eds. Lawrence N. Kasden and Daniel R. Hoeger. Urbana: NCTE, 1980, 141-49.

_____. "Two Related Issues in Peer Tutoring: Program Structure and Tutoring Training." *College Composition and Communication,* 32 (1980): 76-80.

Burke, Kenneth. *The Philosophy of Literary Form*. 3rd ed. Berkeley: University of California Press, 1983.

Cicero, Marcus Tullius. *De Oratore*. Trans. E.W. Sutton and H. Rackham. Cambridge, MA: Harvard UP, 1959.

Cox, Bene Scanlon. "Priorities and Guidelines for the Development of Writing Centers: A Delphi Study." *Writing Centers: Theory and Administration*. Ed. Gary A. Olson. Urbana: NCTE, 1984. 77-84.

Fish, Stanley. *Is There a Text in This Class? The Authority of Interpretive Communities*. Cambridge, MA: Harvard UP, 1980.

Flower, Linda. "Writer-Based Prose: A Cognitive Basis for Problems in Writing." *College English* 41 (1979): 19-37.

Hairston, Maxine. "Different Products, Different Processes: A Theory About Writing." *College Composition and Communication* 37: (1986): 442-52.

Harris, Muriel. *Teaching One-to-One: The Writing Conference.* Urbana: NCTE, 1986.

_____. *Tutoring Writing: A Sourcebook for Writing Labs.* Glenview, IL: Scott, Foresman, 1982.

Holman, C. Hugh. *A Handbook to Literature.* 4th ed. Indianapolis: Bobbs-Merrill, 1980.

Johnson, J. David. "Effects of Communicative Factors on Participation in Innovations. " *The Journal of Business Communication,* 27.1 (1990): 7-23.

Lentricchia, Frank. *Criticism and Social Change.* Chicago: University of Chicago Press, 1983.

Light, R. J., and D. B. Pillemer. *Summing-up: The Science of Reviewing Research.* Cambridge, MA: Harvard UP, 1984.

McLeod, Susan H., and Laura Emery. "When Faculty Write: A Workshop for Colleagues." *College Composition and Communication,* 39 (1988): 65-67.

Oakeshott, Michael. "The Voice of Poetry in the Conversation of Mankind." *Rationalism in Politics.* New York: Basic Books, 1982.

Olson, Gary A., ed. *Writing Centers: Theory and Administration.* Urbana: NCTE, 1984.

Perry, William G., Jr. "Examsmanship and the Liberal Arts." *Examining in Harvard College: A Collection of Essays by Members of the Harvard Faculty.* Cambridge, MA: Harvard UP, 1963.

Rorty, Richard. *Philosophy and the Mirror of Nature.* Princeton, NJ: Princeton UP, 1979.

Spilka, Rachel. "Orality and Literacy in the Workplace: Process- and Text-Based Strategies for Multiple-Audience Adaptation." *Journal of Business and Technical Communication.* 4.1 (January 1990): 44-67.

Meeting the Needs of Graduate Students:
Writing Support Groups in the Center

Sallyanne Fitzgerald, Peggy Mulvihill, Ruth Dobson
University of Missouri-St. Louis

"I' m not sure that anyone will be able to understand the ideas in my paper since no one else is in my department," stated a graduate student while attending one of our first graduate writing support group meetings. Another student chimed in, "Well, I know my writing is so bad that it doesn't really matter what my ideas are since no one can understand what I've written." In spite of such fears, students have volunteered to join graduate writing groups organized and facilitated by our Writing Center. These groups meet approximately every two weeks to discuss any writing project the graduate students bring. A faculty member is compensated to facilitate the group's meetings. We started the groups in our drop-in Center because we thought they would attract more graduate students to our service and because we agreed with Di Pardo and Freedman whose review of research into writing groups indicated that groups provide an audience, support the process approach, provide a response, and enhance time allowed for the process of writing.

We also believed that groups offer a unique opportunity for collaborative writing. "Developing claims cooperatively, collectively, collaboratively, the members of such a community-within-a-community learn from one another, teach one another; they support and sustain one another" (859), declared Reither and Vipond when talking about the benefits of coauthoring and workshopping forms of collaborative writing. Bruffee and Elbow have previously voiced similar claims for collaborative writing.

When writing theorists speak in terms of collaborative writing, they mean a writing situation where two or more writers develop a product. Usually, collaborative writing is discussed in connection with the writing classroom, although it is also typical of the Writing Center. Gere mentions that all writing groups share similarities, but she distinguishes between volunteer groups, such as we have formed, and those that the teacher constructs in the classroom. Gere raises the issue of authority, also the concern of Tebo-Messina. In a truly collaborative situation, the authority is the students' not the teacher's. For such a writing group to happen, the Writing Center provides the ideal setting:

The writing center, then, can be, in certain ways, more flexible than the classroom to anticipate the special requirements of individuals; it is not a substitute for the writing course, but neither is it subordinate to, the classroom. It is an alternative resource, with its distinctive advantages, available whenever writers, at any level of competence, desire the focused attention of a discerning reader. (Brannon and Knoblauch 46)

In our Writing Center, we wanted to help graduate students discover the benefits of collaborative writing outside of their required courses as they pursued a writing project. Such an approach addresses several issues of importance to graduate students. First, graduate students frequently feel as if they are pawns in the academy where faculty members appear to be the authorities in control. In contrast, within the writing groups, the graduate students are the authorities since the group facilitator simply keeps the group on task and acts as a resource without playing the role of teacher/evaluator.

Then, in the collaborative setting, students have an opportunity to learn the language of the academy without abandoning their own speech community. The debate that currently rages about the importance of learning academic discourse in order to join the academic community is a very real issue for graduate students, most of whom are planning to join that community at least during the time that they spend pursuing at advanced degree. Joseph Harris explains that we need to help our students become part of the community while at the same time remaining part of their own. It is the social aspect that helps students to gain access to the discourse/speech community they are attempting to join. Di Pardo and Freedman trace the importance of the development of the social interaction in the acquisition of language and cite Vygotsky, Bruffee, Hairston, Emig, and Labov as supporting that social aspect.

This social approach to learning the language of the academy is particularly important for students whose native language is not English and who feel a loss of personal identity when asked to abandon their own discourse in favor of the English one they are entering. As Gere explains, "learning to write means learning to use the language of a given community, and writing groups provide a forum in which individuals can practice and internalize this language" (96). On our campus, the writing support groups are the only organized approach to helping graduate students whose native language is not English. So within the graduate writing support groups, non-native speakers can practice both written and oral communication in a non-threatening setting.

In order to develop graduate writing support groups with faculty facilitators, the Writing Lab staff had to consider the situation of our campus and the rationale for the groups. At UM-St. Louis, a commuter campus where most of our students go to classes and then go to work, we have a difficult time gathering students for any kind of voluntary meetings. Our first dilemma, then, in beginning the graduate groups, was to find out if there was a strong enough need for writing support to outweigh the tight schedules of most of our graduate students. Finding a common time slot was also an initial concern.

We began by targeting the teaching and research assistants, graduate students who worked on campus and who were, therefore, more likely to have times available for group work. We sent each of them a survey, which inquired about their current writing projects, their anticipated writing projects, their prior experience with the Writing Lab, their interest in the Writing Lab, and their interest in writing groups and workshops. Finally, we asked them to indicate times they were available to join a writing support group. (See the appendix for the questionnaire.)

To advertise the graduate groups further, we sent some of the surveys to graduate advisors in each department so that they could distribute them to students who were not teaching or research assistants. The responses started coming in a week after we sent them, and soon we began our first graduate writing support group. The Writing Center supervisor, who was the only faculty member involved during that first semester, worked with the Writing Center assistant, an exceptional undergraduate English major, who gave the group members some valuable feedback both as a competent writer and as a student.

The first ten graduate students who participated in the group represented many disciplines (psychology, political science, business, economics, chemistry and history). Because of the discipline variety, one of the first issues we dealt with was the issue of understanding content. The students were willing to trust that the group would work, but they wanted to discuss the issue and lay some ground rules. We decided as a group that, for the most part, their writing needed to be clear enough for everyone -- even those outside their disciplines -- to understand. All group members agreed to strive for clear writing, free of jargon and pompous vocabulary. The students also agreed that the content of their writing should be too important to hide behind muddled language and garbled syntax.

Having established the need for clear and valuable content, we conceded that there would inevitably be times when the group members from other graduate areas could not understand the content. In these instances, the writer would simply explain, if possible, the information that an expert audience would have available. When the content was unclear, the group members would challenge the writer to explain why the writing would be clear to the intended and final audience. Interestingly, this issue forced the writers into a constant awareness of their audiences and their purposes for every assignment. And as the group members became better editors, they seemed to improve their abilities to distinguish between unclear writing and uninformed reading.

Another concern we addressed from the start is one that virtually all writing groups have in common, at least for the first few times they meet. The students simply feared criticism of their writing. They experienced the same feelings of inadequacy that most writers have known at least once at some stage it their work. To make the group as comfortable as possible, the facilitator gave the students some tips on what to look for and how to respond to certain writing issues. We also agreed as a group on our purpose--to give constructive criticism to each writer so that each writer could improve the submitted draft. We took some time discussing our purpose in order that the group members understood and agreed that everyone was there to receive criticism. Positive comments from readers were encouraged, but our real goal was to focus on the areas that could be enhanced. Much of the initial fear was relieved as soon as members relaxed and agreed that they wanted the group's criticism. They also tended to relax when they understood that, for our group's purposes, "criticism" was not a series of negative comments, but rather, a series of honest comments and helpful suggestions.

Another way they allayed their fears was to go individually to the Writing Center supervisor/faculty facilitator for feedback on their writing. The facilitator learned quickly, though, that this kind of help can backfire when the goal is to establish trust in the group. One student, a psychology Ph.D. candidate, relied so heavily on the facilitator's personal help that she did not want to submit the drafts to the group. The facilitator had to stop helping her individually before she would again participate in the workshops. Also, the word of her coming to the facilitator for individual help spread to the rest of the group, and before the facilitator knew it, most of the members were requesting conference time to get feedback on their drafts. Eventually, the facilitator persuaded these students to rely on all the group members for criticism by refusing to help them individually.

The facilitator tried to remain sensitive to the group's fears throughout the meetings, and she found that the more they learned about workshopping one another's writing, the more their fears about sharing their material waned. She gave the group some practical advice as they went along because it soon became clear that many of them needed the same types of writing advice. The tips she shared with them seemed to give them more confidence both as writers and as editors. They were eager to hear any advice she or the assistant could give them to improve their writing. Concrete advice, such as how to use strong verbs and active voice, gave the members a starting place when they were blocked as editors, and it gave them more confidence as writers.

When she saw that the group would have ten members, she first thought that she needed to divide the ten into two groups. Her first inclination was to assign same disciplines to same groups because she thought it only natural to move toward a homogeneous group that would share understanding and interests. But the students told her, almost unanimously, that they preferred to be in groups with people from other disciplines. They said they wanted the groups to be free of competition, something that was inevitable in the other aspects of their graduate programs. Working with individuals from other areas, they explained, gave them some freedom to experiment with their writing styles and to relax when they shared their writing. They were predisposed to compete with other graduate students in their own areas, and for many of them, the competition had dwindled some of their confidence. They didn't want to have to worry about "presentable" writing before bringing their drafts to the group.

They also indicated that they were reluctant to share their ideas with students from their own disciplines because they feared prematurely putting their ideas in the public domain. They explained that even in their seminars they didn't share ideas for papers, fearing that someone might decide to use the same ideas. Sometimes the ideas appear in someone else's paper unintentionally, but the result is nonetheless disheartening for the idea's originator. In other words, they trusted students outside their own disciplines more than they trusted students in their same programs.

The students ended up working in a mixed group anyway, because we could not find two common times for the members. We decided to run one large group. Rarely did all ten of the students show up for every session, and rarely did those in the same discipline sit in on the same session. In fact, we averaged six or seven students per meeting, which worked as a manageable group. Each time we met as a group we workshopped one or two drafts, and it seemed that those who knew they would soon need our services, because of an anticipated due date, felt obliged to show up and give as much feedback as possible so that they might in turn receive the same helpful input. Their sense of obligation to one another, even though they hadn't known each other before the group was formed, kept the group meeting. Our fear that a mixed group would lack cohesiveness and loyalty turned out to be unnecessary.

In fact, the mixture of represented disciplines served these graduate students quite well. It removed the element of competition, the fear of losing original ideas and some of the fear of inadequacy, just as the students hoped it would. And because they knew very little about one another's fields, they had to read and listen carefully as each writer took a turn in the group. Consequently, they had a relatively easy time respecting one another as "experts" in their given fields. This mutual respect bolstered the writers' confidence and created a proper atmosphere for collaborative work.

Since that first semester, we have found that the writing groups appeal to a special graduate population--English as a Second Language (ESL) graduate students. ESL graduate students also benefit from the audience, the process approach, and the response time of writing support groups, and they, too, began to learn the language of the academy. In fact, one of the greatest benefits to the ESL graduate students is the opportunity to practice both speaking and writing in the writing support groups. Two types of production inaccuracies, errors and mistakes, are found in interlanguage, the step between starting to learn a language and its full acquisition. Peer group members may easily teach the correct form of errors, those linguistic missteps which occur because the student has not yet acquired the knowledge required for accurate production, and the group can also assist each other in eliminating mistakes, inconsistent inaccuracies in the production of the second language which occur when the writer has learned the rules but doesn't always remember them.

Some of the same problems occur for the ESL groups as for the other graduate support writing groups. For example, arranging times

and locations for the ESL graduate writing support groups is
particularly difficult, and just as with the first groups, ESL students
may seek individual attention using the schedule conflicts as an excuse.
We have found that with these students, in particular, the best way to
handle the request for individual conferences is to encourage students to
analyze each other's papers as one of the steps in the writing process.
This approach has the advantage of developing student metalinguistic
awareness sufficiently for them to know where the problems lie in the
written discourse they are examining. An additional advantage to using
this approach is that it makes students aware of the problems they are
also having, and since the groups consist of students from various first
language backgrounds and levels of development, error analysis can be
very effective.

While the problem of students seeking individual attention instead
of participating in the group is not restricted to the ESL groups, other
issues, such as cultural ones, are unique. For example, since some
cultural groups tend to revere the teacher, they may find it hard to value
their own opinions enough to express them. Other cultures value
themselves so highly that they have difficulty accepting critical analysis
even from a teacher and certainly from a fellow student. For these
reasons, we have found it is useful to have a facilitator continuously
ready to offer not only judgment, but also explanations.

Other aspects of culture play an important part in helping ESL
graduate students benefit from a writing group. One of these aspects
seems to relate to the responsibility for understanding the discourse.
English writers generally are expected to take the responsibility to write
clearly enough so the reader is not left with questions. Some cultures,
such as the Japanese, are sufficiently homogeneous that the writers in
that culture feel that the background material is commonly known, or
should be, so that they do not need to give it to the reader. Explaining
the differences between cultures in terms of reader and writer
responsibility becomes easier in a multi-cultural group setting.

Aside from addressing the issues typical of all writing groups and
those unique to ESL groups, we have found several procedures
particularly useful in ESL groups. We began by engaging the entire
group in analyzing one paper which has been either copied so that they
can comment directly on the paper or transferred to an overhead
transparency so the group can look at the paper together. This procedure
gives the group a clear idea of what to look for so they are better able to

analyze the other group papers, and it also helps members of different cultures understand that this sort of analysis is acceptable and useful.

Another technique that may be particularly useful for ESL groups is contrastive analysis, the comparison between the student's native language and English. Contrastive analysis was originally intended to concentrate upon phonology and syntax. However, most graduate students are able to separate their oral phonological errors from their written discourse while they may have difficulty with syntactic errors, which can persist for years. In fact, non-native speakers can take six to eight years of living in this country to learn how native English speakers use something such as articles. The logic behind the sentences may also prove difficult for ESL students. For example, in Chinese and sometimes in Japanese, the writer may start with old information and proceed to comment on it with new information rather that produce the English S-V-O (subject/verb/object) structure. Writing in English, these students may, therefore, leave out the subject and object required by English, but not by their native language.

Contrastive analysis is also useful in comparing the discourse styles of different cultures, perhaps using Kaplan's doodles as a guideline (410). Since in English we expect to see writing samples, particularly exposition, which follow a straight line of thinking, anything which deviates from this style seems to us to be unclear, disorganized, or even random; other cultures do not, however, conceive of discourse in this fashion. We have found that it is important to use the information about discourse styles carefully: because many ESL graduate students are planning to return to their own countries, they often see this insight into their style as a reason to find an editor for their papers rather than to learn how to write clear and concise English or to participate in a writing group. One such student from an Arabic background who teaches in a Middle Eastern university and was temporarily in the United States earning a doctorate became discouraged about his ability to produce acceptable papers for one of his professors. The facilitator shared information on discourse styles with the student who decided that since he was returning to his native country after receiving his degree he just needed at editor to fix his papers after he had written them. Six months later he still did not understand why it had been impossible to find an editor who could both understand his papers and edit them in the twenty-four hours he expected.

Two other problems may be related to discourse style. First, ESL students may have learned that English style expects explanations and definitions and yet may not be able to employ these effectively, failing to write concisely. Then, the student may have come from a culture where writing instruction ended at the age of puberty. Such students tend to write using the same styles and patterns they find acceptable for oral language, creating many circumlocutions and incomplete information. Both of these problems benefit from the writing group assistance. Perhaps one of the strengths of these groups is that various disciplines and cultures are usually represented. Because of this the students ask questions that usually only arise when the reader does not share the writer's background and hence cannot know without being told what the writer means.

Since we began our graduate support writing groups, we have learned that our writing groups offer benefits cited by most of the literature, but in addition, there are unique benefits as well as problems for such groups. Especially in the case of English as a Second Language graduate writing support groups, we have found that collaborative writing has special benefits while at the same time such groups are faced with issues related to culture and to language learning in general.

QUESTIONNAIRE

Name:_____

Dept.:_____

Campus Address:_____

Phone:_____

1. Are you currently working on a thesis or dissertation?
   yes_____   no_____

2. If not, do you plan to begin work on one soon?
   yes_____   no_____

3. Would you be interested in participating in a writer's support group with other graduate students?
   yes_____   no_____

4. If the Writing Lab offered workshops for graduate students, would you be likely to attend?
   yes_____   no_____

5. If so, please check or write in the topics that interest you.

   ____Clarity/Wordiness
   ____Documentation
   ____Grammar
   ____Sentence Structure
   ____Punctuation
   ____Revising/Proofreading
   ____Transitions
   ____Other(s), please list:

6. Have you used the Writing Center's services? yes____ no____

7. If so, please write a brief description of your experience.

8. If not, why not?

9. When would you be most likely to attend workshops or support group meetings? Please be specific about times.
   Morning_____ Afternoon_____ Evening_____

10. Which would you prefer: a writing group from your own discipline_____ or a multidisciplinary group_____?

Thank you for your time. Your input will help us to provide better services to the graduate community.

Works Cited

Brannon, Lil, and C.H. Knoblauch. "A Philosophical Perspective on Writing Centers and the Teaching of Writing." *Writing Centers: Theory and Administration*. Ed. Gary A. Olson. Urbana: NCTE, 1984. 36-47.

Bruffee, Kenneth. "Writing and Reading as Collaborative or Social Acts." *The Writer's Mind: Writing as a Mode of Thinking*. Eds. Janice N. Hays, Phyllis A. Roth, Jon R. Ramsey, and Robert D. Foulke. Urbana: NCTE, 1983, 159-169.

Di Pardo, Anne, and Sarah Warshauer Freedman. *Historical Overview: Groups in the Writing Classroom*. Technical Report No. 4. Berkeley and Pittsburgh: Center for the Study of Writing, May 1987.

Elbow, Peter. *Writing Without Teachers*. New York: Oxford UP, 1973.

Gere, Anne Ruggles. *Writing Groups: History, Theory, and Implications*. Carbondale, IL: Southern Illinois UP, 1987.

Harris, Joseph. "The Idea of Community in the Study of Writing." *College Composition and Communication* 40 (1989): 11-22.

Kaplan, Robert B. "Cultural Thought Patterns in Inter-cultural Education." *Readings on English as a Second Language*. Ed. Kenneth Croft. Cambridge, MA: Winthrop, 1980, 399-418.

Reither, James, and Douglas Vipond. "Writing as Collaboration." *College English* 51 (1989): 855-867.

Tebo-Messina, Margaret. "Authority and Models of the Writing Workshop: All Collaborative Learning is not Equal." *Writing Instructor* 8 (1989): 86-92.

A Lot of Pleasure, A Bit of Agony:
Producing a Newsletter for the Faculty

Richard Leahy
Boise State University

Getting people outside the English Department (and sometimes inside it) to know about the writing center and understand what it does is a continuing challenge. Each year a new crop of students and faculty must be reached, to say nothing of the old ones who still haven't caught on. At Boise State we have discovered a powerful ally in our struggle: we publish a newsletter on writing, distributed to all faculty and staff, which we call *Word Works*[1].

Word Works (simply called *WW* on campus notes and memos) does more than publicize; it establishes the Writing Center in many people's minds as the prime campus resource center for writing across the curriculum. It is also instrumental in bringing students to the writing center with their assignments and drafts. It has succeeded, we think, because it is a newsletter with a difference. I will try to explain that difference, and describe how we produce the newsletter, with a bit of agony but a large measure of fun and profit.

Reaching The Faculty

As Writing Center Director, I co-edit the newsletter with Roy Fox, the Director of Writing. We also take turns writing the copy for the majority of issues. Our original motive in starting the newsletter was to invigorate a writing-across-the-curriculum effort that was in danger of fading away. The two of us taught summer seminars for 36 of our faculty under an NEH grant in 1983 and 84, but when the grant ran out, so did the administration's support for further development of WAC on campus. Roy, as director of the NEH project, worked hard to keep in touch with the 36, but with no funds for follow-up activities we were not advancing; if anything, we were slipping back, as some of the 36 retired or left for other jobs.

As an attempt to get WAC moving again, *WW* has succeeded, because it has influenced our administration to support a proposal for a comprehensive WAC program for all Boise State students. But more

---

[1]Anyone interested in sample copies of <u>Word Works</u> may write to me at the Department of English, Boise State University, Boise, Idaho 83725.

145

importantly, from my point of view, it has brought the Writing Center into the limelight as the true center of writing on campus, bringing increased cooperation with faculty and a solid increase in clientele. Much of the success, we believe, comes from the unique character of our newsletter.

WW is not a newsletter in the traditional sense. It contains precious little news in the form of notices, announcements, or other fare typical of campus newsletters. This was not a deliberate choice. When we started out four years ago we intended to publish mainly short items, quick teaching ideas, brief profiles of faculty, etc. But in the actual writing, *WW* began to evolve in a different direction. Now we devote most issues to single long articles, up to 2000 words each. We have even published some articles of 4000 words, spread over two issues. We have found that, the more we've worked on the newsletter, the more we have to say. The format grew from a letter-size sheet to legal size, and has just grown again to four pages on a folded 11 X 17 sheet. That is probably as big as we will allow it to get. The single-article issue will likely remain the standard. We are now convinced that if we want to sell our faculty on writing-for-learning, we need to write fully enough to help them understand the theory and purpose behind the ideas we are suggesting they try.

In a sense, we're producing a textbook for our campus in serial installments, teaching the basics about writing processes and writing-for-learning, besides educating faculty about the writing center. We do present practical tips for using writing in the classroom, but always in conjunction with the principles of good writing and teaching. We also address our readers as teachers who not only use writing in their classes but are writers themselves. We're capitalizing on the fact that our faculty are feeling increased pressure to publish, but more importantly, we believe teachers must understand their own writing processes in order to help their students use writing productively.

With our longer articles we've gambled on the notion that our readers will be more likely to use our ideas if we publish them one at a time, and in some depth. Traditional newsletters, which publish four or five short items in each issue, might be less effective for some readers. Short items can fragment the reader's attention, with the net result that not much substance sticks in the mind after the reader puts the newsletter down. A long article does run greater risk of going unread, but readers who stay with it get more in-depth treatment of the subject.

To estimate the effectiveness of *WW*, we recently ran a readership survey. Out of 600 surveys sent to all faculty, office personnel, and administrators, we received 48 replies representing 28 different departments and offices -- a pretty decent response. Of those responding, 29 said they had used ideas from *WW* in their teaching, and 25 said they had applied ideas to their own writing. This response pleased us most of all; we frankly did not expect so many to use our ideas in their own writing. We think it's reasonable to guess that about half the people we have actually reached with *WW* took the time to answer the survey. We didn't, for instance, receive responses from a dozen or so faculty who have sent us fan mail at other times. That means we may well be reaching about 100 faculty and staff, a number that makes us feel our newsletter is well worth the effort.

Since we do not yet conduct regular WAC workshops, *WW* helps fill in that gap. Until our formal WAC program is fully under way it's our best means of reaching a large audience. At present, our WAC is still in its fledgling stage, with a few writing-emphasis courses and a few writing assistants from the Writing Center working with some of the courses. Certainly there is no way a newsletter can deliver the power of a face-to-face workshop, but even so, it has advantages. The newsletter brings the education directly to the faculty without their having to leave their offices. We reach some instructors who might not give up the time to attend a live workshop. A second advantage is that the newsletter provides a permanent, accurate record of information that instructors can refer back to. Whereas the ideas conveyed in a workshop can fade, the ideas in a newsletter remain. We also print plenty of extra copies so that we can send back issues on request. (We were pleased by a frequent complaint on our survey, that people were finding the legal-size pages hard to file and put in binders. Several readers are saving every issue.) As our WAC program develops, we see *WW* as still serving as a supplement to faculty workshops.

By focusing on student writing and the Writing Center, the newsletter emphasizes teaching. These days, when the pressure on faculty to publish has reached down into smaller state colleges and universities like BSU, faculty have to devote more time to research and writing. In addition, our enrollment has grown without a proportionate increase in faculty positions. Classes are bigger. The English Department, for instance, has for the first time begun to fill most of its upper-division classes and turn people away. Faculty in my department and all across campus are feeling the pressure from both sides. They are expected to publish more articles and to teach more students.

Consequently, *WW*'s mission to focus on teaching becomes more important all the time.

That *WW* emphasizes teaching is nothing new; ultimately this is what all WAC efforts are about. And it is what makes faculty begin to understand what the Writing Center can offer. I saw an illustration of this just recently. Roy is leading a seminar for 13 faculty, preparing them to teach writing-emphasis courses. One member of the seminar, a Communication professor, told me, "You know, I went into this thinking I was just going to learn how to use writing. Now I find I've started to re-think my whole approach to teaching." He went on to say that, now that he was thinking hard about his students' writing, he was also thinking about ways to coordinate his efforts with the Writing Center. To help more of our faculty think the same way, we publish at least one major article about the Writing Center each year, plus a number of short reminders and hints dropped into articles on other subjects. We are trying to convey the message that the Writing Center is not just a place to send students with writing problems; it's a support facility for students and faculty alike in our mutual effort to improve teaching and learning.

The Content Of *Word Works*

Over the years *WW* has covered a wide range of topics. We don't plan topics very far ahead, but usually write what comes to us. The effect is one of variety and surprise (as one reader put it on the survey). I suppose, if we have a strategy, it is to make each issue as different as possible from the previous one.

Two articles on writing the long research paper gave detailed steps, from selecting a topic, to thinking about and organizing the material, to incorporating source material in the text. This series has been widely recopied by faculty and distributed to classes, and it is also used as a Writing Center handout. A second, equally popular series described the research report for sciences and social sciences. One article (which was heavily theoretical but nonetheless received several grateful memos and phone calls) explained James Britton's ideas on the writer's and reader's roles in poetic, expressive, and transactional writing.

We know from talking with some of our readers that they received a rather traditional education in writing and grammar and need be made aware of current knowledge about how people learn to write. For that reason, we devote many articles to debunking entrenched myths. In one article on research papers, we cautioned instructors not to insist on note cards, because they contribute to meaningless cut-and-paste products. In an article on paragraphs, we tried to brush away the cobwebs of traditional teaching by pointing out that paragraphs are not deliberately planned structures (essays in miniature, topic sentence plus support, inductive vs. deductive development, etc.) Citing work by Braddock, Stern, Berthoff, and Bruffee, we argued that paragraphs are largely intuitive divisions of a text, more useful as handles on revision than as building blocks for constructing a draft.

In a two-part essay on journals, we listed several ways journals are used in various disciplines, but we also examined what journals can and cannot be expected to do, and detailed the ways in which journal assignments, if they are to succeed, have to be nurtured and integrated into the overall purpose and design of a course. In our readership survey, a surprising number of faculty said they were planning to use journals, even though we made no attempt to sell the idea. Quite the contrary, we tried to lay out realistically all the effort and planning that must go into a good journal assignment. We may have discouraged some instructors from using journals, but I believe we gave others the confidence to try them, once they saw how journal assignments can be designed to aid learning.

We try to range over just about any subject related to writing. One article, taking off from William Stafford's famous advice, "Lower your standards," described ways to get started writing and ways to keep the writing from bogging down. Another gave an inside view of the 13 participants in Roy's seminar attempting to write their way through a problem -- a lively, often hilarious illustration of how different people think on paper. Other articles have dealt with responding to student writing, responding to ESL writers, and fostering critical thinking.

Production And Distribution

Physical production of *WW* has not been exactly high tech. Roy and I both have Apple II computers at home and therefore can trade disks back and forth. Up to now the final copy has been produced on my Apple IIc using a MultiScribe word processor, which is mouse-driven, has Mac-like pull-down menus, and sports a wide variety of type fonts. The final copy has been printed on a small home dot-matrix printer, pasted up, and delivered camera-ready to the print shop. Soon we hope to convert to desktop publishing and a laser printer. This will be less convenient than working on production at home. The days of dining-table paste-ups will come to an end. But the change will please some readers, particularly a chemistry professor who called recently to suggest, "You really should consider that a lot of us aren't getting any younger, and your print is a little hard on the eyes."

Funding, fortunately, has not been a problem. Since we deliver camera-ready copy to the print shop, printing costs are kept down. For a typical run of 700 copies, the cost is around $50-60, depending on the paper and color of ink we choose. The English Department chair willingly pays the bill for the printing, and for mailing out 70 copies to WAC coordinators and writing-center directors at other campuses. It was not hard to persuade the department chair to fund us, considering the exposure our newsletter gives the English Department and the Writing Center.

In addition to the details of production, we've had to make sure the newsletter gets into the right hands. We discovered that some department secretaries do not place bulk mailings in faculty mailboxes, but instead leave them in piles to be picked up by those who want them. To keep *WW* from ending up in these junk-mail stacks, we've created mailing labels for all faculty and staff-- 600 altogether -- which we update each semester. We feel pretty sure that department secretaries are more inclined to distribute the newsletter in the mailboxes when each copy has an individual's name on it. Department secretaries receive the newsletter, too, and some of them tell us they post their copies on departmental bulletin boards, giving us a little extra visibility (some of the secretaries are also among our most faithful readers).

We are always looking for places around campus where the newsletter should be visible. We noticed, for instance, that the outer office in the university Executive Offices did not display the newsletter prominently; a word with the office manager corrected the oversight.

Putting Writing At The Center

An important reason for reaching the faculty directly is that, through them, we reach more students. Our Writing Center statistics show that far more of our clients learn about the center from their teachers than from any other source. At least once a year we use *WW* to publicize the Writing Center and explain the kind of help it offers. Several *WW* articles have been written by Writing Center tutors, providing an inside perspective on what goes on in a writing conference.

After publishing several short notices reminding faculty to recommend the writing center to their students, and urging them to invite us to speak to their classes, we were eventually inspired to devote a full issue to explaining what the Writing Center is all about. The first such article was called "Seven Myth-Understandings about the Writing Center." In a full issue, we explored the many reasons people avoid or ignore the writing center, or try to use it in the wrong way:

1. The Writing Center is a remedial service for poor writers.
2. The Writing Center is mainly concerned with competency exams.
3. The Writing Center is only for students in English classes.
4. The Writing Center does work for students that they should be doing on their own.
5. Faculty should require students to visit the Writing Center.
6. The Writing Center only helps with essays and term papers.
7. The Writing Center is only for students.

So far we have published two full-length pieces in attempts to wipe out the pockets of ignorance concerning the Writing Center that still linger on our campus, as on many others. I have included the complete text of one of these issues as an appendix to this article. It picks up where the myth-understandings article left off, going further into an explanation of the writing process and the collaborative nature of writing. It also explains who works in the Writing Center and what a typical writing consultation is like. It concludes with a not-so-subtle call to action: a list of suggestions on how faculty might use the Writing Center to the benefit of their students and to their own benefit. We believe that such a detailed description of what the writing center is all about is at least as effective with some faculty, much more so than brief notices, handouts, posters, and even visits to classes. We use those, too, our most effective being a printing of 15,000 bookmarks which the bookstore distributes for us each fall with textbook purchases. This second article about the Writing Center appears to have been more effective than the first -- at least, judging by the response afterward, where several faculty called to find out more about our services or to invite us to visit their classes. We've timed the writing-center articles to appear fairly early in the semester, about the time instructors are giving out their first writing assignments.

Fun And Profit
Our colleagues on other campuses ask how we find time to put out a newsletter. There is no magic way to create time. As Writing Center Director and Director of Writing, we have enough to do, besides teaching and spending time working with people outside our

department. The writing gets done evenings, weekends, on airplanes, during semester breaks and summer vacations, and while our students are writing in class. We also do our share of writing for professional publication. There are times when producing *WW* interferes, but there are times when our other writing makes writing for *WW* easier. The momentum carries us, and also the ideas carry over. An article for a professional journal will spin off a newsletter article, and vice versa. Recently I found an irrelevant paragraph in the draft of a *WW* piece I was working on. That paragraph turned out to be the germ of a separate article, which was later published in the regional language arts journal. In many ways such as these, our writing for *WW* has nourished our writing lives.

WW keeps us writing, and so, since we are writing teachers, it keeps us honest. I'm reminded of a note a woman wrote me at the end of an Advanced Composition course, in which she had struggled and suffered but produced some fine work: "Loved the class! (and hated it some, too)." Her few words capture the pleasure and agony we find in writing *WW* - - and in any writing we do.

It seems to me the relative freedom and flexibility of writing center work -- even for those of us who are busy with many other responsibilities -- lends itself ideally to the production of a newsletter. It can become a community effort, with director and writing assistants all chipping in. Another payoff, besides increased visibility for the writing center, can be the strengthening of the university by drawing others, students and faculty, into the writing community.

Appendix - - A Sample *Word Works* Issue

The text of Word Works Number 33, January 1990

WORD WORKS

WHAT IS THIS PLACE CALLED THE WRITING CENTER?

Hesitantly, the young woman poked her head in the door of the Writing Center. "I need help with this history paper," she said, but I don't know if this is the right place. Do you help other people besides students in English classes? We assured her that we did, and in a few seconds she was seated at a table with a cup of coffee. A member of our staff sat down with her, and together they got to work on her draft, talking out the problems she was having with it and looking for solutions. Some time ago, WORD WORKS published a piece called "Seven Myth-Understandings about the Writing Center" (Number 21, September 1988), in which we tried to dispel the main myths that cause people either to avoid the Writing Center or try to use it for the wrong reasons. People like this history student remind us that, despite all the posters we put up and the bookmarks we give away, we must keep working to make our real mission understood.

What Is the Writing Center the Center of?

The Writing Center is most visible, at least to faculty, through WORD WORKS. Since our job is to support writing on campus, we see this newsletter as one of the most important things we do. We also visit classes to conduct workshops and promote our services. But the real center of our mission is the one-to-one consultation we offer on writing. We are here to consult with anyone on campus who wants to bring a project or assignment to try out on a sympathetic, helpful audience. Indeed, we are most grateful when people show up at our door and simply say, "Help!" We are the central resource for writing support on campus -- the place where anyone can seek assistance.

The Writing Center and the nature of writing

The best way to get at the essentials of what the Writing Center is all about is to look at how people go about writing.

Writing is a highly complex activity -- more

complex than it is often given credit for. Not many years ago, writing instructors usually taught that the whole process was simple if you just did one thing at a time: first plan and collect ideas, then write the draft, then reread and revise, then correct for grammar, punctuation, and spelling -- et voila! A finished piece of writing, produced by a simple linear process.

Now, this advice is basically sound, and it can benefit many writers who are confused about how to proceed, but anyone who has struggled with writing knows it is much too simple for what really happens. Writers work recursively, circling back over early stages of the writing process during the middle or later stages. Different writers work in different ways. Some pretty much rehearse a whole piece in their heads before writing anything down. Others do all their thinking on paper, writing multiple drafts, gradually working toward "getting it right." Not only that, but different writers use different processes from one writing task to the next. It's impossible to say that any method is better than any other. The ultimate advice to any writer is, do what works for you, but be open to other methods you haven't tried. Many writing courses today focus on introducing writers to a variety of options and strategies for getting the writing done.

Writing is nearly always collaborative. Hardly anyone writes completely alone -- or

should. True, everyone needs plenty of time alone in order to think. But at some point, everyone also needs an audience to respond to the writing and offer assistance. The essential principle underlying all writing-center work is this: To some degree, every writing task is collaborative. This does not mean that everything is co-authored, because in our society we insist on individual ownership of our work. It does mean that nearly all writers call on trusted readers for help at one or more stages in the writing process.

In emphasizing collaborative learning, the Writing Center promotes what writers actually do. In business and industry, writers work together all the time to produce letters and reports. College professors write with abundant help from colleagues, as we can see on the acknowledgements pages of their books and in the notes to their articles. Even novelists, essayists, and poets -- especially poets, working in what is often considered the most personal and creative medium -- share their drafts with friends and ask for help. Several members of the BSU English Department have formed writing groups, to which they can bring their own writing for help and feedback. They freely suggest to each other ways to develop, organize, and even word their drafts. When they finally work out the kinks in an article or a poem, the whole group glows with delight and self-congratulation. The poet Donald Hall, speaking on campus recently, said, "I have lines in poems by leading poets all over the country, and they have lines in mine."

The Writing Center, then, offers this realistic kind of collaborative work, which everyone needs, from the beginners to the most experienced writers in the university community.

Who makes up the Writing Center staff?

The staff of the BSU Writing Center is made up of upper-division and graduate students. Most are majors in English, though we've also had majors in history, education, music, biology, communication, and math. (As BSU becomes more involved in writing-across-the-curriculum, we will be seeking a wider diversity of majors.) They are hand-picked, usually by faculty nomination, as people who are strong writers and good listeners and who work well one-to-one with other students.

Everyone working in the Writing Center takes part in an ongoing training program. Each week, the entire staff meets to update their training by studying professional literature on writing and by sharing their own experiences and ideas.

What goes on in a writing conference?

When a client comes to the writing center seeking help, we first try to determine exactly what the assignment is. (It is far preferable if the instructor has given out the assignment in writing.) We start up a dialogue by asking questions like "How do you usually go about a writing task? What sort of planning have you done on this paper so far? How did you go about writing this draft?" Often a writer who has run into trouble needs to try a different strategy. If the writer has become confused trying to compose an outline, we might demonstrate alternative methods for organizing, methods such as clustering and diagramming. If the writer is having trouble putting a difficult idea down on paper, we may run the writer through a short brainstorming or freewriting exercise to break through the block, or demonstrate how to write through the difficult passage in short, simple sentences, to be re-edited into more sophisticated prose later, after the idea becomes clear.

One of the most powerful strategies, we find, is simply to listen and encourage. We often help our clients deal with muddled drafts by asking them to put aside the paper and just tell us what they want to say. Almost invariably, the writer will tell it orally in a straightforward, clear manner. We reply, "Then write it down the way you just said it," and we wait while the writer does so.

What about writing in different disciplines?

Some instructors have expressed misgivings about recommending the Writing Center to their students because their assignments require specialized knowledge that a lay person might not understand. However, when we've worked with faculty we have always found that different bodies of knowledge present no major problem. Often, in fact, the "naive" reader is the most helpful because she can report back to the writer just where the writing is not clear, where he is assuming too much knowledge on the reader's part. As Sue Hubbuch of Lewis and Clark College argues, the very ignorance of the writing consultant "forces the student to take responsibility for his/her paper.... I find that I am in an excellent position to help students see that many of their questions do not have simple right and wrong answers, but raise issues that the student must make decisions about, based on their conception of the purpose, context, and audience of the specific paper they are writing." We have observed that BSU instructors generally prefer their students to write in a form and style that will be understood by the general reader, avoiding specialized formats and jargon when possible. But we are always eager to work with new, unfamiliar, and specialized assignments; they provide opportunities for us to learn and grow, just as they do for the students who are assigned them.

How the Writing Center can work with you and your students?

The BSU Writing Center is eager to reach out across campus and work with faculty in all departments. If you are assigning a writing project for your students, here are some ways the center might be able to assist you.

* By all means, tell your students about the Writing Center. Our statistics show that word of mouth from instructors is more powerful than any other means of attracting students to the center. But please advise them that it's best to make appointments one or two days ahead of time, because our calendar fills up quickly.

* Bring copies of the assignment and, if possible, two or three papers from previous terms that fulfill the assignment well. With this material, we will know what you expect of your students.

* Invite someone from the Writing Center to visit your classes. You might give us just a few minutes to deliver our sales pitch, or you might have us spend more time working with the class on a specific assignment.

* Arrange for your students to meet with a member of the Writing Center staff in small "support groups" to go over each other's drafts.

* Bring your draft of a new assignment to the center for feedback on its clarity and feasibility.

Changing The Ways We Teach:
The Role Of The Writing Center In Professional Development; Or, The Virtue Of Selfishness

Jay Jacoby and Stan Patten
The University of North Carolina, Charlotte

An idealized but nonetheless popular image of the writing center is that of a place where crack teams of beleaguered tutors work selflessly, with little thanks and no extrinsic reward, to ensure the academic safety and survival of students. For writers struggling to incubate a thesis, resuscitate their syntax, or "revive [sic] an essay," writing centers function as on-campus Emergency Rooms. Many even have their own versions of 911: Writing Center Hotlines (at UNC Charlotte, ours is 547-HELP!). Tutors serve as the Emergency Medical Technicians of the university. Sometimes trained in the "paramedic method" that Richard Lanham advocates in his *Revising Prose*, they specialize in "Crisis Intervention in the Writing Center" (Ware 5-8) and "Triage Tutoring" (Haynes 12-13). The immediate rewards for students who avail themselves of a writing center's services are better papers. Putting it more realistically, and perhaps less cynically, those students become better writers -- their writing attitudes and practices improve.

If tutors function to save the academic lives of their student clientele, they may also act to preserve the mental health of faculty. The writing which results from tutor-student consultation is often more focused, better organized and developed, and clearer than writing that students do alone. Student writing which has been somehow overseen by tutors grants faculty more access to what student writers want to say, and permits them to attend less to the surface and more to the substance of students' arguments. Moreover, tutors often have specialized training in how to teach writing and how to intervene in the writing processes of others. This training is neither required nor available as part of most faculty members' graduate school education. Even when faculty (trained or not) do include writing instruction as part of their curriculum--and more and more faculty are doing so--tutors can extend, supplement, and complement such instruction. This is especially true by virtue of the fact that tutors are not classroom teachers; tutors are often more effective *because* they are separate from any assignment-making, grade-giving power structure (see Jacoby, "Shall We Talk" 1). Finally, and most importantly, tutors provide the kind of one-on-one conferencing that is frequently essential in the development of writing abilities but impossible to provide for in large classroom settings, or when faculty have large numbers of students to teach.

The writing center services we have been reviewing here are by now commonplace. Indeed, at many institutions, the writing center is seen as a primary site for campus altruism: selfless tutors aid in university efforts to rescue and retain hundreds of at-risk students and permit university instructors to maintain higher writing standards within their classrooms. And it is on this service-to-students-and-faculty platform that many writing center budgets are fought for and won.

As most writing center administrators know, the best way to get, maintain, or increase funding is to leave a conspicuous trail of paper- - including student and faculty testimonials, case studies of at-risk students, and statistical data on writing center use -- from the writing center to the offices of whomever holds the institutional purse strings. What has been kept secret, or at least has not been sufficiently acknowledged, is that the primary beneficiaries of the writing center are often those who work there and those they go on to serve outside of the writing center. When funding formulae are established, administrators should be cautioned not to look solely at the grades and careers of students who came to the writing center for help, or to the expressions of satisfaction by faculty who referred them. Administrators should also look at the grades and careers of writing center tutors. Funding should be based in part -- and in large part, we would argue -- on the short- and long-term benefits accruing to those who serve in writing centers. Our position is based on the fact that service in a writing center is the best possible method of professional development in writing instruction.

Diana George's "Who Teaches the Teacher? A Note on the Craft of Teaching College Composition" made explicit what many of us involved in writing centers have long known: tutoring in a writing center is an excellent preparation for classroom teaching. In her review of three texts aimed at teaching teachers how to teach writing, George focuses on two texts which come out of the writing center experience: *Teaching One-to-One* by Muriel Harris and *The Practical Tutor* by Emily Meyer and Louise Z. Smith. George clearly recognizes a reality of teaching writing, especially freshman composition: "Although we are learning more and more about teaching writing, most of the writing that is being taught in colleges and universities is still being taught by teaching assistants, part-time faculty, and even undergraduates who serve as peer tutors in writing centers" (419). Turning her attention to *The Practical Tutor,* George observes that a "book on training writing tutors might seem an odd one for a review on books designed to train classroom teachers. Still, the writing center experience has much to teach us about training teachers of writing" (420).

Because the average tutor is inexperienced in both composition theory and actual teaching experience, time in any training program must be spent presenting new tutors with a background in composition theory and practice. People with teaching backgrounds but no tutorial experience may or may not have this background; regardless, these tutors frequently need to "unlearn" their teaching practice in order to become effective tutors. Combining composition theory and research with teaching practice, Muriel Harris brings "the lessons of the writing center into the world of classroom instruction" (422). George continues:

> Harris has learned through her writing center experience that teaching writing is not a matter of understanding the writing process; it is a matter of understanding the writing processes, especially as they occur for inexperienced writers. Further, the writing center teaches us that written response is strongest when it is coupled with conferencing and that conferencing is most useful when it is understood as coaching rather than as judging. (422)

These are but some of the lessons we learn from the writing center experience which helps prepare teachers to enter or return to the classroom environment.

Over fifteen years ago, the Writing Resources Center at the University of North Carolina at Charlotte was conceived selfishly, without much regard for the services it would offer to the institution. Several students in an expository writing class found that they worked especially well together in pairs and in writing groups. They found that their writing products improved when they were given an interested, trained, private audience through whom their writing effectiveness could be measured. And they found that their own writing processes improved when they were expected to talk intelligently about other people's writing (i.e. we learn more about a subject by first teaching it). As many of us who use writing groups might imagine, however, these students made these discoveries in about the twelfth week of a fifteen-week semester. They sought some way to continue working and learning together -- and so the rather formally named Practicum in Teaching Composition was born.

The addition of a three-credit hour Practicum to the English curriculum was justified on the ground that 1) it would offer training in the theory and practice of composition to prospective English teachers (it became a pre-requisite for student teaching in junior and senior high schools) and others with a professional interest in writing (journalists, technical editors, etc.); and 2) it would offer members of the UNC Charlotte community help with their writing. Students who enrolled in the Practicum would be required to tutor each other on various writing projects, and they would also be required to tutor others in a writing center.

Initially, at least, we thought that work in a writing center was a small price to pay for the establishment of an advanced workshop in expository writing. What we rapidly found out, however, was just how much those who enrolled in the Practicum learned to write not only by writing but also by tutoring writers. And then, as we added graduate assistants, who were required to tutor for a year before teaching Freshman Composition, and some full- and part-time faculty to our writing center staff, we began to discover how much tutoring contributed to our pre-service and in-service education as classroom writing teachers.

Through the Practicum and other ongoing support services, all tutors are trained, with particular attention paid to methods of intervening in the writing processes of others, to the dynamics (psychological, pedagogical, and political) of one-to-one tutoring, to the interactive dimensions of teaching writing, and to the implications of transferring tutorial pedagogy to the classroom environment. Central to this professional development is the belief that tutorial practice transfers more readily to the classroom than teaching practice does to the tutorial situation. We agree with Annette Rottenberg who stated:

> most of the lessons derived from tutoring are relevant to the whole teaching experience, however organized. Tutors learn at first hand about the anxieties of the student writer (which may not always be visible in the structured environment of the classroom), about the evolution of process to product, and about the relationship between author and critic -- knowledge that they will later acquire in the classroom but at a somewhat greater cost. Learning will take longer and will often be sacrificed to the exigencies of classroom administration. (*WLN* 11)

Despite the rapid growth of client services and population since 1974 (the number of tutoring appointments has increased twenty-fold), UNC Charlotte's Practicum and Writing Resources Center has continued to serve primarily as a source of professional development for staff who will go on to teach writing and/or write professionally. As we indicate to students in the Practicum's Course Objectives: "the emphasis will fall not only on those you serve, but also on you, on what you have learned and how you are applying what you have learned to your own writing and/or teaching." While we certainly do not wish to minimize our service role to students and faculty who avail themselves of the writing center, we also cannot deny that serving others is the best way of advancing our own writing and teaching abilities. Former tutors who go into teaching or into the corporate world where collaborative and/or individual writing is an essential component of the job offer ample evidence of the value of this cornerstone of the Practicum/Writing Center experience. Their testimony falls into two basic categories: specific practical advice for writing teachers, and more theoretical advice on teacher-student relations.

One example of practical advice grows out of strategies tutors learned for conducting writing conferences (including such details as positioning and who holds pen and paper). Dottie Howell, after a year of teaching Freshman Composition wherein writing conferences formed a central part of her method, notes, "I don't like to think about the kind of teacher I might have been had I not experienced one-to-one tutoring sessions." More specifically, she observes:

> *In our training to work in the writing center, we were taught*
> *that sitting beside the student is essential to the tutoring process--*
> *not standing over, not sitting across from with a table between, but*
> *sitting down together, as two people would do in a non-threatening*
> *manner when addressing a paper together. This positioning sets up*
> *a co-learning attitude. The focus is on the paper, and there are two*
> *minds at work. One of the cardinal rules we were taught as tutors*
> *was, "You don't write on the student's paper." This tactic says*
> *something important to the student. It says, "This paper is yours."*

Prior to their year of teaching Freshman English (one section of 101 in the fall and two sections of 102 in the spring), students who are selected to be graduate teaching assistants at UNC Charlotte must take the Practicum in Teaching Composition, which focuses closely on one-to-one teaching, and another course, Teaching College English, which focuses more broadly on current issues of pedagogical theory and practice. In addition, they must tutor between twelve and fifteen hours a week during each semester of their first year. It is the latter work, which graduate assistant Judy Lassiter calls "the best pre-teaching experience I could have had," that contributes further practical knowledge to another important area of teaching: assignment design. Lassiter goes on, "More than anything, I've had the opportunity to see the kinds of assignments used by faculty here. I've had the chance to observe students' reactions and responses to those assignments." Nan Budd, another first year graduate assistant, wrote at length about some of the bad assignments that, as a tutor, she had to work on with students -- assignments that were either too general, or too personal and artificial ("I always wonder how many people would write, 'The most significant moment in my life happened in the backseat of a black Camaro' if they were writing only for themselves."). Budd concludes her detailed analyses of several varieties of bad assignments with the following observation:

What I have learned from all of these experiences with bad
assignments . . . is that students do take their writing seriously and
they do not work in a vacuum. "Garbage in, garbage out" is the
general relationship of assignment to student work. . . . the more
work the instructor has done in anticipating possible responses to
assignments and tailoring the assignment to enable the student to
concentrate on what the instructor is looking for, the less time the
student has to spend second guessing (and at entry levels guessing
wrong) what the instructor wants. . . . Whether or not the
instructor takes into account cultural constraints that the student
feels, they are operative. It is rare to see students given a choice of
major assignments, but such a policy might eliminate possible
conflict in this area. We need "student-friendly" assignments.
Most importantly, perhaps, I have witnessed how easily student-
instructor relationships can become adversarial instead of
cooperative. Having spent a year clearly on the student's side and
understanding how many of their complaints are truly valid, I hope
I can manage to avoid falling into this trap when I teach.

Contributing to Nan Budd's conclusion was also her observation of
the grading and response practices of writing teachers, a third area for
would-be teachers' practical consideration. On this subject Barb West
notes

At the very least, working in the writing center helps you
see teacher reactions to student work from a freshman point
of view. . . . What's also very interesting is to hear what
students think of teachers who were fellow students with me and
who I personally know are dedicated to helping students. I think
students (young ones at least) often see teacher as adversary no
matter what the teacher does. I do think it would help any future
teacher to spend time tutoring in a writing center if only for the
experience of seeing things through the battered students' eyes.

Kim Whittington, one of Barb West's classmates, concurs: "It's been
fun trying to decipher faculty comments on a student's paper, which has

helped me to realize how important a faculty's comments can be.
Hopefully, I will remember to make my comments legible,
understandable, and clear."

What Kim, perhaps in her pre-service naivete, has labeled "fun,"
was viewed as a more humbling experience for one of the authors of the
present chapter. At the time he taught the Practicum, Jay Jacoby argued
against having faculty tutors in the writing center on the grounds that
"college-age writers are often more receptive to the opinions of their
peers than to the remarks made by faculty tutors" ("What a Peer Tutor
Is Not," 5). On the other hand, in order to convince writing center staff
that he had more than a nodding acquaintance with the tutorial problems
they faced, Jacoby did consent to work in the writing center himself.
At the time, he was also teaching two sections of Freshman
Composition in addition to the Practicum. It was his custom, in
responding to student papers, to use standard marginal notations --
AWK, FRAG, REF, etc. -- keyed to a handbook. It *was* his custom,
that is, until a student he was tutoring in the writing center said, "I
can't figure out my instructor. No matter what I write, I can't get higher
than a 'D,' but my instructor keeps writing that she agrees with me
[i.e., the notation AGR] all over my paper." It was on that occasion
that Jacoby began to pay much closer attention to how those he tutored
interpreted their teachers' comments rather than interpreting them for
those students.

And it was on that occasion that Jacoby reversed his position on
the use of faculty tutors in the writing center. The following semester,
he began to request, as often as he could, one-course reductions for full-
and part-time writing faculty who worked regularly in the writing
center. As a result of such in-service training, many faculty improved
their teaching practices. For example, a semester of tutoring students
who were overwhelmed by the multiple demands of their teachers for
improvement in *all* areas of writing caused many experienced
instructors to adopt a mode of "minimal marking" and seriously reduce
the demands they themselves made on students. First-hand knowledge of
how students reacted to sarcasm (especially when directed toward writing
to which the faculty tutors had contributed) caused a remarkable
reduction of sarcasm from those tutors' responses to their own students'

writing. It is now felt that the insights gained from working closely with students *other than those whose work one assigns and grades* should far outweigh any reservations we once had about writing center clients working with non-peers as tutors.

While certainly reinforced by service in a writing center, the kinds of practical teaching methods so far discussed -- conferencing strategies, assignment design, and techniques of responding to student writing -- can also be learned from a good text on writing instruction such as Barbara Walvoord's *Helping Students Write Well*. On the other hand, there is some pedagogy for which reading a text is no substitute. Students who have worked in the writing center before going on to teach -- either at the college or secondary level -- repeatedly expressed the notion that, more than anything else, a year spent in tutoring writers helped to humanize the learning process. After a year of teaching, Janet Smith notes, "Taking on the role of teacher was much easier for me than it might have been otherwise because I feel I had a dress rehearsal all last year. " With those sentiments Janet's classmate, David Teague, concurs, adding, "Tutoring blunts the emotional shock of confronting twenty peers suddenly, disguised as 'an authority.' The process of demystification experienced when going from student to teacher is more humane before a congregation of one."

For Judy Lassiter, this humanizing process affected her attitudes toward students' work: "Above all, working in the writing center has made me a more generous, less censorious human being. I no longer believe there's a right and wrong way to write, to punctuate, to choose words, to order sentences." For Janet Smith, the process affected the role she took in the classroom: "I also became very adept at saying, 'I don't know, but I'll find out.'" For Barb West, a non-traditional, older graduate student, the humanizing experience in the writing center altered her attitudes toward the student-teacher relationship: "What has been a surprise and a comfort to me has been having my suggestions ignored. I was encouraged to see that my age and experience didn't influence students into thinking that my ideas must surely be better than theirs. They had minds of their own."

West identifies what is probably the most valuable benefit of writing center experience for prospective teachers: seeing students as individuals. As Paul Price put it following a very successful first year of teaching, "After tutoring for a year, I began to see that teaching is not a different beast entirely, but rather it is a stylized format of tutoring twenty people at once. Tutoring taught me to see a class not as an amorphous group, but as individuals sharing space and time to learn." Dottie Howell echoes these notions when she claims, "When I face a classroom of students I don't see them as a class. I see them as individuals. They each have opinions, unique abilities, feelings that are important to them, and a wealth of living behind and before them." Howell's comments were prompted, at least in part, by her experiences tutoring a student for whom English was a second language:

> *Her English was halting, but she was patient with me as I often asked her to repeat things, and I had come to appreciate her persistence long before she brought in the paper that described her terrifying escape from Vietnam as one of the boat people. This young lady is alone in Charlotte, working the afternoon shift in a factory in order to support herself, and attending UNC Charlotte full-time in an effort to get her education. Her family is still in Vietnam and she is saving money to sponsor them and bring them to America. I felt privileged to sit beside her and share in her struggle.*

In our experience of thinking of the writing center first and foremost as a means of professional development for teachers and those who will write or intervene in the writing processes of others, we have discovered what we think may be the most important function of any center, the one that most merits institutional funding and support: tutors become sensitized to the pluralism evident in any cross-section of writers. They develop the essential critical awareness that writers range in ability; they are multi-cultural; they are multi-ethnic; they are male and female; they write about a wide range of topics (some which interest them greatly, some not at all); they present a highly divergent set of writing anxieties (process and product); and they fall anywhere from the highly committed to the less than enthusiastic. Whereas a classroom instructor might see a group of students, the writing center

tutor is exposed to the variety of <u>individual</u> writers. The comments of
tutor Barb West provide fitting closing testimony to our own
discoveries:

> *Standing in front of a bunch of faces is not the same thing
> as sitting close together in one of those cubicles, smelling
> bad breath, looking at bad skin, and sometimes seeing
> desperation or even gratitude in eyes. What I'm saying is
> that tutoring is up close and personal and cannot be
> impersonal. Maybe it's easier to realize that there are
> consequences to your actions as "prof" when you're looking
> into these eyes. I wouldn't trade my experiences in the writing
> center for anything.*

Works Cited

George, Diana. "Who Teaches the Teacher? A Note on the Craft of Teaching College Composition." *College English.* 51 (1989): 418-423.

Haynes, Jane. "Triage Tutoring: The Least You Can Do." *Writing Lab Newsletter,* June 1989: 12-13.

Jacoby, Jay. "Shall We Talk to Them in 'English': The Contributions of Sociolinguistics to Training Writing Center Personnel." *The Writing Center Journal.* 4 (1983): 1-14.

--------. "What A Peer Tutor Is Not," *Writing Lab Newsletter,* May 1983: 5-7.

Rottenberg, Annette T. "Learning to Teach by Tutoring." *Writing Lab Newsletter,* June 1988: 11-12.

Ware, Elaine. "Crisis Intervention in the Writing Center." *The Writing Lab Newsletter,* June 1986: 5-8.

Tutor-Teachers: An Examination Of How Writing Center And Classroom Environments Inform Each Other

Robert Child
Purdue University

Writing centers have been around long enough that we have begun to see a cadre of teachers developing who were first tested not at the lectern but at the table -- not by a class "capped" at twenty-five students but by one student who *chose* to visit the center. As someone who works in both tutor training and teacher training, I've been intrigued by this new group's arrival, especially since my informal observations led me to believe that these tutor-trained teachers prove to be very effective classroom instructors.

Rather than simply accepting that writing center training enhances classroom teaching, however, I scrutinized the activities of two classroom instructors: one who had received tutor-training before he taught in the classroom and one who had received tutor-training after he taught in the classroom. I also interviewed four other instructors, two each who fit the above profiles (i.e., two with writing center experience before classroom experience and two with classroom experience before writing center experience). I invited particular participants who matched these profiles and who had been trained in various writing centers rather than all having been trained by a particular person or within a particular program.

Benefits Of Tutor Training: An Overview

An examination of the literature concerning tutor training and its benefits reveals an historic progression, a coming of age of writing centers, in which tutoring moves from being quietly -- almost sheepishly -- justified to being vilified. This coming of age can be classified using three categories: "Justifying Tutoring," "Authorizing Tutoring," and "Integrating Tutoring."

Works from category number one, "Justifying Tutoring," attempt to show that even though tutees might not show improvement as a result of having been involved in tutorials, tutors do improve. These studies, largely empirical and largely focused on variations of peer tutoring, generally ignore examinations of tutoring as teaching; instead, they focus on measuring learning of both instructor and instructed (primarily by means of pre- and post-tests of content knowledge).

169

Works in category number two, "Authorizing Tutoring," attempt to define writing centers and writing tutors and to validate our activities not by lauding our own improvement but by focusing on how our practices differ from "generic" classroom practice. These works stem from the assumption that one-to-one teaching differs essentially from classroom teaching. Because so many of these works focus on this inherent difference and stress how writing centers and one-to-one instruction are unique and distinct from other teaching environments and approaches, they are largely directed at the writing center community rather than at the larger community of composition instructors, and they generally emphasize training, offering advice on how to institute training programs not only as part of our in-house, daily concerns but also as a major professional concern; in fact, fully 35% of the 500 writing center articles reviewed by Child and Adams focused on tutor training, most of them providing specific and detailed discussions of programs.

Conscious moves toward training, then, constitute one way in which the college writing center differs from the college classroom, but the important item here is that such a distinction is predicated upon the base concept that the two teaching arenas -- the writing center and the classroom--radically differ. In fact, most of our early attempts at defining ourselves -- at establishing ourselves as viable teachers and researchers within the professional community -- focused on what Louise Smith, in her discussion concerning decentralizing writing centers, described as the idea that "Intellectual and political movements often seem to require an early phase of separatism, of gathering their self-definitions into a fist." Yet after establishing themselves as distinct and viable, "these movements outgrow their fierce need for separatism. The fist begins to open, to relax its grip on authority, and to welcome collaboration with other, sometimes quite variously dextrous and differently motivated, hands" (3).

In effect, then, we are no longer posturing; we have a position--and a viable one -- within our departments, our schools, and our institutions, and we have determined (and made sure that others were privy to our determination) that providing services does not equate to being servile. From this authorized position, then, we can integrate ourselves into the larger community. Hence, the materials in category number three, "Integrating Tutoring," acknowledge that our goal of providing quality composition instruction holds true in both the writing center and the classroom. Works in this category focus not so much on the differences between the two types of teaching as upon the similarities, attempting to show that the inherent difference is between the teaching situations/environments rather than among the various teaching strategies/principles. These articles generally support a hypothesis that writing center training enhances classroom teaching and that there is a connectedness, a similarity between the two types of teaching, which allows us to focus on how these teaching environments can inform each other. Premiere among this group are Peggy Broder's discussion concerning tutors who have entered the classroom, which defines specific classroom activities that are informed by tutoring experience, and Kate Gadbow's discussion concerning teachers who have entered the writing center, which establishes categories of writing center practice that can inform classroom teaching.[1]

Design of the Study

The concerns of category three--of integrating tutoring, of breaking the barriers between tutoring and teaching and focusing upon how these arenas can and do inform each other--are the concerns which drive this examination. Therefore, I chose to study, with a qualitative rather than a quantitative eye, the activities of a writing center tutor adjusting to teaching in the classroom and the activities of a classroom teacher readjusting to teaching in the classroom after having tutored in the writing center.

In gathering data for this study, I observed and took notes as the tutor/teachers taught their classes; I recorded their responses to a general prompt ("How has the experience of tutoring either enhanced or hindered your classroom teaching; in effect, to what extent do you think that it has informed or failed to inform your classroom practices?"); and I recorded their responses to five categorical prompts established after coding the data gleaned from my observations and their general responses.

---

[1]Among others who have contributed to the idea of the relationship between writing center tutoring and classroom teaching are Irene Lurkis Clark, "Preparing Future Composition Teachers in the Writing Center," *College Composition and Communication* 39.3 (1988): 347-350; Muriel Harris, *Teaching One-to-One: The Writing Conference* (Urbana, IL: NCTE, 1986); and Robin Magnuson, "Preventing Writing Wrecks: The Role of the Writing Lab in Teacher Preparation," *The Writing Lab Newsletter* 10.8 (1986): 11-14.

Tutorial Influences: Mode Of Analysis

The purpose of this section -- and indeed the entire study -- is to delineate dimensions of classroom teaching influenced by one-to-one teaching experiences, in effect to identify and operationally define arenas of classroom teaching altered or influenced by arenas of writing center teaching. Since the teaching strategies found in college writing classrooms do not necessarily match the guidelines that one finds in educational methods texts and since both guidelines and practices prove too diverse to categorize in specific manners, I chose not to establish specific categories for observations and interviews; instead, I conducted the initial investigation free from any governing taxonomy. After the first round of interviews, however, certain categories began to become evident as overriding concerns: establishing agendas, dissuading authority, presenting material, questioning, modeling, and testing performance. These six categories of general response held true not only for the interviews; they also held true for coding the observations, and they held true for coding the responses of the four other tutor-teachers.

Establishing Agendas: In general, agendas for tutorials are highly personalized and situation specific; they are seldom if ever written out. Agendas for the classroom, on the other hand, tend to be rather generic and are often little more than filing cabinet documents. In addition to the expected agendas (e.g., documents such as syllabi, unit plans, and daily lesson plans or teaching notes), this category includes the tutor-teachers' insights into motives, intentionality, and goal-setting.
Dissuading Authority: Although the idea of teacher as authority figure is firmly entrenched within every level of the educational system, the tutor's advantage of not wielding the power of the grade allows him/her to play the advocate role more than the classroom teacher. And, of course, the extent to which either the instructor or the student accepts or denies authoritarian roles without question influences the dynamic of both the tutorial and the classroom.
Presenting Materials: Since lecture is the presentational mode traditionally associated with the classroom and since many of our moves toward an interventionist pedagogy have targeted teacher-talk and particularly teacher dominant discussion as something to avoid, it is extremely interesting to see how much tutors limit or avoid such practice in the classroom.
Questioning: In the tutorial setting, much of what we learn about a writer and her/his writing processes is a result of our questioning and

our ability to offer open-ended questions which encourage the writer to disclose her/his ideas rather than leading questions which encourage parroting or guessing games in attempt to determine the "correct" response. Questioning strategies, then, provide inroads through which instructors can gain insight into writers' composing processes.

Modeling: Most students seeking assistance in writing centers have been "taught" the material before, but for some reason it hasn't "taken"; therefore, much of what goes on in the tutorial is either an attempt to focus the student's attention on one aspect of the process or to present material in a way that sheds new light. As a result, modeling --showing rather than telling -- is a strategy applied in many tutorials, yet most texts and classroom manuals encourage modeling only in the sense of reading essays.

Testing Performance: Within the tutorial setting, virtually everyone performs some form of quality control testing, checking to see that a writer in fact can do what s/he claims to be able to do after the tutorial. Of the six categories of response, this was the one category that held universally for every tutor-teacher; each of the six tutor-teachers indicated that due to his/her experiences as a tutor s/he continually asked students in the classroom to demonstrate knowledge through both written and oral response. Since the responses for this category were virtually identical for each tutor-teacher, I have dropped it from the discussion sections that follow.

Greg And John: Profiles Of Tutor-Teachers

Beyond the fact that Greg and John are both graduate students working as classroom teachers and writing center tutors at a large, midwestern university, there are very few general statements that can be made about them as a pair. They do both have a strong commitment to teaching composition, but Greg sees it as his career and is pursuing it as a course of study while John sees it as part of his career -- as something he will do along with his work in British literature -- and only concerns himself with what he sees as the practical side, leaving the theoretical issues to others.

Like many other tutor-teachers entering the classroom, Greg started out as an undergraduate peer tutor. As part of his training at a mid-sized, southern university, Greg participated in a for-credit practicum, a course in which he studied theories and practices of composition and one-to-one instruction. Greg describes the course as "approximately one part theory, two parts practice" and recalls being highly motivated by the class "mainly because classroom participation took on a whole new meaning. Instead of arguing with my classmates about some author's ideas, I was talking with writers about their writing."

Although the mid-sized, midwestern university which John attended has a writing center and provides opportunities for peer tutoring, John was never encouraged to work as a tutor; in fact, as John puts it, "If anyone had asked me to work with writing and writers, I probably wouldn't have seen it as being related to my career. I thought I was going to teach literature; I thought that was what English teachers did."

And it's not surprising that John didn't really think of college English teachers as instructors of writing; both he and Greg had received Advanced Placement credit and subsequently been exempt from their freshman composition requirement.[2] Of course when John began his stint as a Graduate Instructor, he found out what English teachers did. Arriving just one week before his students, he first registered for his own courses; then he was given a text and a syllabus and assigned to a teaching group in which he underwent three days of orientation before he started teaching two sections of freshman composition. Obviously then, John did not move into composition instruction either as early or as gently as did Greg. Greg had learned what composition instructors do by conferring with their students for several years before he ever walked into the classroom. In fact, Greg had been tutoring and working within a community of tutors for three years before he was called upon to move into the classroom. Having discussed issues of writing instruction--both practical and theoretical--for such a lengthy period of time, Greg's major job upon entering the classroom was not to learn how to perceive of himself as a writing teacher but to perceive of himself as a classroom teacher of writing; John, on the other hand, had to learn how to perceive of himself as both.

John: Moving Back To The Classroom

John believes that tutoring in the writing center has "radically improved" his classroom teaching, that he is much more comfortable in the classroom as a result of his writing center experience, and that rather than conducting a class he now promotes an interactive classroom.

---

[2]Interestingly enough, none of the six subjects of this study had ever been in an "average" freshman composition class until they taught in one. Of the six, three had received CLEP or AP credit, and the other three had been placed in accelerated courses of various design.

Ultimately, he believes that his writing center experiences have "come closer to transforming than informing his classroom teaching."

Establishing Agendas: John says that before he tutored in the writing center and worked one-to-one his classes were text-driven and plan-driven, that he was task-oriented. After tutoring, however, he feels that he has replaced his task orientation with a skills orientation which allows him to focus on student understanding rather than adherence to a tight schedule. The drawbacks to this are that he sometimes falls considerably behind his syllabus and that because he is "more willing to drop things that don't work and move on" his teaching occasionally looks sloppy and disorganized, possibly even unprepared.

John also believes that his students appreciate his new approach to establishing agendas because they know more about what they're doing. According to John, "I'm now very conscious of forecasting and explaining what we will do. I used to do this for goals only, but now I emphasize the procedures as well." Ultimately, John feels that he is more flexible and that his syllabus and his daily lessons are more student oriented as a result of his having worked in the writing center.

Dissuading authority: Although John's response to the direct question concerning how his work as a tutor might have changed his ideas concerning authority in the classroom was that he saw no change, his general response indicated something entirely different. In the general discussion, John stated that "one of the more important things that you get out of the writing lab experience is a sense that you can go into the classroom and be yourself." He continued by saying that prior to working in the center he had thought of having "a classroom face or a classroom persona" but he no longer felt that he had "to go into the classroom and be a pleasant little automaton or a Mr. Tibbs."

Presenting Materials: Because of the training he received in his teaching group, John used peer groups in his classes prior to working in the writing center, but he claims to have felt more comfortable lecturing; subsequently, he figures that about 80% of his class time used to be spent in lecture and text analysis. Now he spends approximately 10% of class time on such activities, preferring instead to focus on peer groups and question and answer sessions. John says that as a result of tutoring, he "do[es] group work for different reasons," that it is now purposeful and that he is much more willing to intervene.

Questioning: John says that before working in the writing center he rarely asked a student what s/he thought about her/his own writing, yet now, as a result of his tutoring experience, "variations of the question, 'What do you think?'" drive much of his teaching -- both in class and in conferences. John attributes much of his skill in questioning to his writing center work, saying that it taught him how to continually rephrase and modify his questions, and -- more important -- it taught him to be willing to wait for answers, to be willing to accept long periods of silence. Ultimately, John feels that his newly found questioning skills allow him to establish a livelier classroom where students play an active role.

Modeling: Of all the things that John feels that he learned in the writing center, he believes modeling concepts to be the most important. According to John, "People who have not tutored simply can't understand the importance of modeling." John says that he uses the overhead projector "at least three times as much as before," often putting four or five versions of a paragraph on a transparency and offering it up for discussion. The real value that he see in modeling, however, is that he can "actually show rather than tell." John now plans, composes, revises, and edits with his class.

Greg: Moving To The Classroom

Greg fears that he will never feel as comfortable in the classroom as he does in the tutorial, and he says that he never feels good about a particular class until he has met with the individual students in conferences. Ultimately, he feels that his writing center training and experience have greatly informed his teaching, but he also feels that these experiences have made him "not so much a better classroom teacher as a more frustrated classroom teacher."

Establishing Agendas: When making the move into the classroom, Greg felt that establishing agendas for anything except conferences was the single most difficult adjustment for him to make. In fact, Greg still sees the idea of planning a semester and establishing a syllabus before meeting classes and determining the needs of individual students as "patently absurd." To highlight the absurdity of such practice, he draws a direct comparison between the writing center and the classroom: "Tutoring is reacting. You don't plan to tutor, yet you plan to teach." In effect, Greg believes plans for a tutorial are constantly negotiated and adjusted during the tutorial. According to Greg, agendas for tutorials cannot be planned, in part because "Students don't know what a tutorial is. Therefore, an agenda is determined by arbitration and need rather than by socialized prescription or syllabus." He sees agendas in the writing center as infinitely more sensible because they are arbitrated among three parties -- the writer, the tutor, and the absent instructor. As a classroom teacher, however, Greg says that he sees the "lamb-like qualities of students" who expect him to provide agendas rather than presenting their own for consideration/arbitration.

Dissuading authority: Overall, Greg feels that he has "lost the credibility that was part and parcel of being a peer tutor," and he believes that his students are afraid to be honest with him in the way that those students he tutors are. When Greg bottom-lines the entire authority issue, he drops it all in the gradebook: "Now that I've got the grade, they question me according to the assignment instead of according to the writing process." Ultimately, he feels that his students are afraid to be honest with him because as long as he has a gradebook they can't perceive him as an advocate.

Presenting Materials: As a result of his experiences as a tutor, Greg says that he knew that he could not dominate the classroom, that he had to get his students involved through peer group and individual activities, whole-class discussions, and question and answer sessions. While he picks and chooses from among these presentational modes, Greg "believe[s] that group work is the way to translate what goes on in the writing center and get it to work in the classroom." But he gets frustrated by group work because he "can't get it to a tutorial level where there is someone who can see the problem from a slightly-more-than-peer perspective." Greg totally avoids lecturing, and although he continues to try group work, his most productive class time comes during question and answer sessions.

Questioning: Greg is superb at questioning, and he attributes his skills to his writing center experiences. As he puts it, "I was trained by a Rogerian, and I threw enough of it away that people didn't think I was obnoxious." Greg believes that his training as an English major focused on analysis but that his work as a tutor showed him that such a "focus on the text and the product provided virtually no insight into why something was on the page"; subsequently, he claims that he learned "to put faith in questioning and dialogue." Greg believes that tutoring allowed him to learn how to use open-ended questions effectively, but he also feels that it taught him how to ask follow-up questions and how to focus his questions by knowing when he was "asking for a definition versus an extrapolation." Finally, as did John, Greg attributes his willingness to rephrase his questions and his ability to deal with silences to his tutoring experience.

Modeling: In both his classroom and his conferences, Greg uses modeling extensively. He attributes his comfort with modeling to his work in the writing center, but he doesn't see modeling as a writing center or tutoring phenomenon. In fact, he quickly points out that many people involved in writing centers "fear modeling because someone might think that a tutor has crossed the line and given text to the writer."

Mini-Profiles: Four Other Teachers
To provide additional information for coding data and to ensure that if one of the tutor-teachers was providing idiosyncratic information that I would recognize it as such, I interviewed four additional instructors who fit the profiles: two who tutored before going into the classroom and two who tutored after having taught in the classroom.

Moving to the Classroom
Linda and Scott both worked as peer tutors before entering the classroom. Linda went on as a teaching assistant at a large, midwestern university, and Scott went on as a teaching assistant at a small, southern university. As with Greg, both Linda and Scott felt that establishing an agenda was restrictive. Scott's comments were virtually identical to Greg's; he saw no sense in establishing generic agendas. Linda, on the other hand, said that she saw both semester-long and daily agendas as "good organizational tools, but only if you don't take them too seriously."

Both Linda and Scott echoed Greg's concerns over losing their "credibility" when making the move from tutor to teacher and from peer to "authority figure." They too felt that much of the distancing could be attributed to their owning the grade. Linda indicated that at least part of the distancing could be attributed to her rather than to her students because she was "so worried that [she] wouldn't be objective about assigning grades."

As with Greg, Linda and Scott never considered lecture as a dominant presentational approach, but each of them privileges a particular style of presenting materials. Linda prefers to have her classes do a lot of in-class writing, and she "move[s] around the room, running very brief little tutorials." Scott devotes much of his class time to peer group work, but like Greg, he doesn't feel that the students are giving each other the kind of advice that he could provide, so he moves "in and out of the groups, offering advice."

Linda feels that her writing center experience shows most in her ability to question, and like Greg, she describes her ability to pose different types of questions. Scott, on the other hand, says that classroom questioning is very frustrating because he "can't ask the sorts of questions [he] would ask in a tutorial: either writer/text specific or so global as to be vague."

Scott and Linda also differ on the issue of modeling, with Linda's attitude being similar to Greg's; she writes with her class, using both the board and the overhead projector, and she brings in "lots of student examples to show everything from how to write an introduction to how to establish a subordinate clause." Additionally, Linda tries to model strategies, showing how she uses a cluster diagram, how she revises, and how she edits. Scott limits his modeling to the examples in the text and says that he was trained not to provide students with models because they would perceive them as formulas.

Moving Back to the Classroom

Judy and Sharon each spent two years as teaching assistants before working as writing center tutors, both in small midwestern universities. They, like John, believed that working in the writing center improved their classroom teaching.

Both Judy and Sharon said that their work in the writing center had taught them to be more flexible concerning establishing agendas. Likewise both Judy and Sharon talked about trying to determine what their students' agendas were, an idea that Sharon says she "would have rolled [her] eyes at before having tutored." Judy goes so far as to say that the most important thing she took back to the classroom was the knowledge of "when to push paper, pencil, text, and syllabus aside and just talk."

Before she worked as a tutor, Judy claims that she began her classes by establishing a distance between her and her students. After tutoring, she says that she feels comfortable with her classes and attempts to "put them at ease." Sharon, too, says that she feels more comfortable with her students, and like John, she states that she no longer feels as if she's required "to put on a teacherly face."

As with John, both Judy and Sharon say that they spend much less time lecturing, both estimating that they have cut their lecture time in half. Sharon now spends much more time in whole-class discussions and question and answer sessions, and Judy says that she "learned early that the benefits of tutoring were weighted toward the tutor rather than the tutee"; therefore, she places more emphasis on peer group work as a result of her tutoring experience.

Both Judy and Sharon feel that their work with individualized instruction has helped them to improve their questioning strategies. Judy says that for the sake of inquiry, she is willing to pose questions that she can't answer. Sharon, like John, points to her willingness to accept silence and to her understanding of the need to rephrase a question to make it more accessible to the class.

Neither Judy nor Sharon models strategies by composing with their classes; however, they both feel that they are more willing to incorporate models and to model specific strategies than before having tutored. Judy, in particular, emphasizes modelling specific strategies for proofreading and editing, something she claims "never gets taught."

Findings

Both Greg and John -- in fact all six of the tutor-teachers in the study--felt that they had benefitted by teaching in the different environments and that their work in one-to-one instruction had informed their classroom teaching. John, in particular, felt that he had learned a tremendous amount as a result of having worked in a writing center. Likewise, the other two teacher-tutors who came to the center after having already gained teaching experience in the composition classroom felt that their teaching practices had been greatly informed by their writing center experiences.

What I found most interesting, however, was that Greg felt debilitated in the classroom. Although he had three years experience as a writing instructor, he walked into the classroom and felt that he had lost his edge, his advantage, and that he couldn't gain control of the environment, that he had much to offer but no place appropriate for offering it. The importance of this is enhanced by the fact that the two other tutor-teachers who had gained experience as tutors before going into the classroom felt similar anxiety and frustration.

In effect the teacher-tutors who came to the center after having taught in the classroom found a sense of freedom when establishing agendas; they found that diminishing authoritarian roles opened up their classrooms; they found new, comfortable ways of presenting material; they found various ways and degrees of posing questions; and they found that modeling was a productive pedagogical practice. The teacher-tutors who went from the writing center to the classroom didn't fare as well, however: they found classroom agendas to be restrictive and prescriptive; they found that their students vested them with authority that they didn't desire; and they found that presenting materials to large groups rather than to individuals didn't produce the results that they desired. On the up side, however, they found that their questioning strategies paid off well and that their modeling strategies fared well also.

Implications

As with any study of this sort, findings cannot be bandied about as universal truths which can be dropped upon any population, in any situation, at any time. Nevertheless, we can take away new awarenesses and concerns as to how our practices might help or hinder the tutor teachers in our programs. Clearly the three tutor-teachers in this group who came to the writing center from the classroom felt that the experience had informed -- and in fact transformed -- their classroom teaching practices by providing them with diverse and important philosophical and practical considerations. Furthermore, these classroom teachers saw the strategies they found in the writing center as flexible and portable, as capable of adjusting to different environments. The tutor-trained instructors, on the other hand, seemed to see the environments as barriers which undermined the flexibility and portability of the strategies. Although the writing center had informed their classroom practices, these tutor-teachers felt, to varying extents, a sense of frustration resulting from their inability to adjust their strategies from one environment to the other.

My original, informal observation -- that the tutor-trained teacher makes a very effective classroom teacher -- held up under scrutiny, but that same scrutiny brought other, important issues to bear: To what extent does experience in one-to-one teaching frustrate the new classroom teacher of composition? Can composition teachers be "livened up" and become better classroom teachers through exposure to teaching in a one-to-one environment?

Given these questions, I am certainly going to be more attuned to the opportunities that writing center tutoring can provide to "loosen up" classroom teachers. Likewise, as we train more and more future teachers of composition, I will be concerned about how much a focus on one-to-one instruction might cause our peer tutors difficulty in adapting to other teaching environments, concerned about how much our attempts at "authorizing tutoring" may have taken too well and concerned that

our past closed-fisted attempts at defining and separating ourselves
might not be far enough in our past.

Works Cited

Broder, Peggy F. "Writing Centers and Teacher Training." *Writing Program Administration* 13.3 (1990): 37-45.

Child, Robert D. and Ronald J. Adams. "Publications and Writing Labs: What Have We Done?" Annual Meeting of the Southeastern Writing Centers Association. Atlanta, GA, April 1985.

Gadbow, Kate. "Teachers as Writing Center Tutors: Release from the Red Pen." *The Writing Lab Newsletter* 14.4 (1989): 13-15.

Smith, Louise Z. "Independence and Collaboration: Why We Should Decentralize Writing Centers." *The Writing Center Journal* 7.1 (1986): 3-10.

The Gift of Insight:
Personality Type, Tutoring, and Learning

Maurice Scharton and Janice Neuleib
Illinois State University

Verily great grace may go
With a little gift; and precious are all things that come from friends.

Theocritus, Idylls

We are nominally the directors of a large writing, reading, and study skills center. We say "nominally" because we abhor most administrative duties. We are often neglectful about phone messages, absent-minded with details, and truant from meetings. One of our two fulltime assistant directors, a writing specialist, loves meetings of the most painful duration, will schedule them with remorseless regularity, and will travel enormous distances and be absent for weeks at a time to inflict meetings on people she doesn't know. Our other assistant, a reading specialist, happily spends stupefying amounts of time organizing study skills programs, small group activities, and tutor training sessions with a personal style reminiscent of George Patton. While we admire and rely on the orderly efficiency with which our assistants oversee the day to day operation of the center, we have neither the least desire to emulate their behavior nor the least twinge of guilt about letting them do most of the hands-on administrative work of the center.

Do we seem to be making lurid confessions about dereliction of our duties? We hasten to add that we worked tirelessly to design and set up the center several years ago, and we step in when policy decisions need to be made or when responsibility needs to be taken. It's just that now that the center is running efficiently -- with a civil service secretary, two full-time assistant directors, five receptionists, fifteen computers, a seventy hour operating week, 120 tutors, and over 2400 contact hours annually -- our gifts aren't as useful as they were a few years ago. Accordingly, our duties now resemble those which Diana and Philip Mountbatten discharge for the British government. We appear in public on state occasions, gesturing ceremoniously and speaking in an epideictic vein. We try to dress and live well, and to let others give their gifts.

184

Of course we aren't quite serious in our description of our behavior, but we are quite serious in our belief that each person working for us has preferences and that those preferences represent the person's gifts. The delightful consequence of recognizing the gifts of others is that we are allowed to do more of what we want to do and to cease pretending to be competent at everything. But we have not always done, or even known, exactly what we wanted to do. A person who has administrative responsibility is subject to all sorts of pressures -- to schedule and run meetings, to spend time chatting with staff and writing memos, to soothe ruffled feelings, to become mired in the dullest sorts of tiny details. Although we do these things when necessary, we have learned that they are not our gifts.

We began to understand the idea of gifts when a friend, a psychological counselor, gave us the Myers-Briggs Type Indicator (MBTI), a personality inventory which poses 126 questions to measure eight different personality traits and thereby to categorize respondents as one of sixteen personality types, each with its own gifts. In this essay, we will explore the significance to tutoring of the eight MBTI traits: extraversion, introversion, sensing, intuition, thinking, feeling, judging and perceiving. Although space will not permit us to explain how all eight traits produce the sixteen types, we will broadly outline how the last four traits interact to produce four **temperaments.** We hope thereby to give some hint of the rich store of wisdom about human motivation found in type theory.

The Gift of Energy: Extraversion and Introversion

One of the MBTI questions asks respondents to characterize themselves as either "good mixers" or "quiet and reserved." While we feel quite able, thank you, to hold our own at a cocktail party, we could not bear to describe ourselves as "good mixers," a phrase which brings to our minds an undignified person who tells off-color stories or a pixilated chatterbox flitting dizzily about. One can be quite good at an activity, yet not have a gift -- that is a preference -- for the activity. In the categories of the MBTI, the difference between the good mixer and the quiet and reserved person produces one of several questions which help determine the degree to which a respondent is either "extraverted" or "introverted." Among the other extravert-introvert choices are "hearty" versus "quiet" and "breadth" versus "depth" in friendships.

The Swiss psychologist, C. G. Jung, coined the terms *extravert* and *introvert* in his book, *Psychological Types*, which is the theoretical basis for the MBTI. Extraverts, according to Jung, experience surges of energy in contact with the external environment of people and things, whereas introverts experience energy in contact with the internal world of people and ideas. Thus differences in the experience of energy lead to differences in behavior. An extravert who put energy into dealing with varieties of people and activities would probably feel that he or she was getting energy back. An introvert might put energy into such extraverted activities without feeling much of a return on the investment.

While the direction of psychological health and personal development for an introvert would be away from the external world, job pressure might not allow the introvert the luxury of private time for reflection. Introverts who were part of a group dominated by extraverts might even try to persuade themselves that they <u>should</u> want to go to meetings and that they <u>ought</u> to feel the same about their duties as extraverts do. These "shoulds" and "oughts" might send an introvert down a personally costly path of chronic fatigue and anxiety at work which could easily spill over into the rest of life.

In fact, this is exactly our experience with administrative responsibility. We can do it, and do it well, but it takes energy without giving any back, and it does not make us better people. So we are distant and non-directive: we defer to our extraverted assistant directors' love of meetings and management.

Of course extraverts have their problems as well. Under pressure to write, extraverts must endure isolation from the people and things which are their energy sources, making it very difficult for them to get published. Even extraverts who are intellectuals would rather talk about ideas than write about them, and would rather act on ideas than talk about them. One of our assistants found the job of writing her dissertation arduous almost beyond endurance. She sought and received support from her friends in toiling through the experience and has not tackled a major writing task since finishing several months ago. If circumstances conspire to force her into this work, she may do some more sustained writing, but she will need a good deal of support from us to make up for the energy that such work costs her.

Some traits often found in extraverts are tendencies to prefer oral to written communication, action to reflection, interaction to concentration, and breadth of relationship to depth. Introverts reverse extraverted preferences, and we can add that introverts tend to be more territorial than social, more likely to conserve than to expend energy (Myers, 56). Few extraverts or introverts exhibit all these traits to a great degree. Ronald Reagan and John Kennedy are representative examples of strong extraverts. Woodrow Wilson and Calvin Coolidge are representative examples of strong introverts.

As you read over the list of traits and people, you may have said to yourself, "What sort of person would rather have a lot of surface relationships with different people instead of a few really intimate ones?" If you experienced such a reaction, you can suspect that you may have introverted tendencies, and you can be sure that another, more extraverted reader of this essay would respond with "No one person can be everything to another person, so of course you have to know a lot of people to get what you need." The most valuable insight that personality type provides is the knowledge that one's own preferences are not universal, that people are different for good reasons, and that differences run deep.

Personal difference implies personal gifts, and a belief in one's own gifts implies a belief in the gifts of others. Thus it becomes reasonable to accept the idea that jobs ought to go to those who have the greatest natural predisposition to do the jobs. While an introvert cannot rely on extraverts to do all the extraverting, a humane principle of Conservation of Energy would dictate that the more extraverted person in a work or personal relationship take the greater share of the responsibility for dealing with the outside world and the introvert the greater share for the inner world. At times, the introvert will want to meet people, answer phones, run meetings, and so forth, just as the extravert will need to do some occasional navel-gazing. Trading roles is healthy so long as people choose their roles and recognize the cost.

Inevitably, the personal preference of the director of a writing center will acquire the force of law in the ways that tutors and others deal with clients. Thus a strongly extraverted director might tutor with a gregarious style, tending to deal with a large number of clients through short appointments and group activities. This person, unaware of type preferences, might naturally accumulate a staff who shared those preferences, and the center would develop a style which attracted those who shared the preference and repelled those who did not.

On the other hand, an introverted director might tend to emphasize long-term commitments to fewer clients who were tutored in greater depth. While an introverted client would thrive on this sort of attention, an extravert might find it dull, even exhausting. We have learned to withhold judgment a bit when we see an extraverted tutor burbling away with a rather quiet client; the tutor may not be dominating the client. We recognize that extraverts tend to think with their mouths open, processing information that an introvert might process inwardly. Both styles represent thought and interaction: extraverts simply make more noise when they think.

We teach tutors the difference between extraversion and introversion by way of group activity. We give them the MBTI so that we know their types. Before we tell tutors how they came out on the MBTI, we divide them into groups, extraverts on one side and introverts on another. We then ask them to imagine that it is Friday afternoon and they have encountered a client who is worn out from studying and attending review sessions. They are to list the activities they would suggest to help the client refresh herself before taking an exam on Monday. Their answers reveal their differing views of how to renew energy.

Both groups tend to suggest sleeping late, but extraverts suggest seeing friends, playing team sports, going to parties, and visiting family members while introverts suggest reading a book, taking a walk, working in the garden, or having an intimate dinner with a close friend. If a group of extraverts lists reading a book, for example, questioning will often reveal that that activity will be reserved for late in the day as a prelude to getting a good night's sleep. If introverts list attending a party, questioning will often reveal that they too plan to use the activity to tap off surplus energy in order to relax.

We point out the differences in how the two groups' processes work, how noisy and exuberant the extraverts seem by comparison with the introverts' dignified concentration, and yet how each group accomplishes the assigned task. The differences lend credence and substance to the ideas, and the groups help people to see themselves more clearly. Introverts are usually in the minority, so the groups help them to give themselves permission, if need be, to exercise their preferences. We can explore and explode prejudices based on type. We teach tutors that extraverts are not thoughtless--they simply think out loud. Nor are introverts tongue-tied--they simply speak in thesis statements and topic sentences.

In earlier years our center staff was mostly introverts, but the center now employs a preponderance of extraverted tutors since we have surrendered the central administrative role to extraverts. In recruiting tutors, we have for years relied on written applications and letters of recommendation, both rather introverted methods. Our extraverted assistants have recently developed a system of group interviews to begin socializing next year's new tutors to the center. While we acknowledge that the additional contact may strengthen the commitment of some tutors to the center, the get-acquainted activities remind us unpleasantly of a mixer sponsored by the Pan-Hellenic Council. We worry that introverted tutors will find these extraverted interviews appalling, so we try to spot the introverts and to connect with them to show them that the center has introverts as well. During the year, we plan some training activities, such as keeping journals, that draw on the introverts' gifts for learning through intense concentration.

The Gift of Perception: Sensing and Intuition

A second aspect of type theory, preferred mode of perception, also bears strongly on learning preferences. Jung categorized people as either sensing or intuitive in the way they gather information. The MBTI gets at this difference by way of questions such as whether one would prefer to be considered "practical" or "ingenious." Practical sensing types prefer to take in information through their senses in linear, objective ways. They like facts, details, particulars, examples, illustrations, clarifications, and elaborations of an idea. Sensors may prefer the sciences to the humanities. They may tend to prefer fact-oriented courses like accounting to theory-oriented courses like economics. If they enter a humanities discipline such as English and become teachers, sensors may emphasize facts about literature -- the names of characters and the details of the plot -- and the facts about writing--spelling and punctuation will count and the five paragraph theme, or for the more modern, the three draft essay, may be required.

The ingenious intuitives, more theoretical as a group, prefer to look at the big picture, always leaping to generalizations, associating facts with ideas and other facts, inventing metaphors and analogies, perceiving information in structures and gestalts, and losing track of details and facts. In a lecture class an intuitive is likely to be thinking ahead of or around the points the speaker is making, wondering why the speaker does not hurry on to the next interesting theory or speculation. A sensor in the same class is likely to be wishing the speaker would slow down, give some more examples, and go into a bit more detail.

A simple way to get hold of the difference is to remember that sensors like to focus on one bit of information and intuitives like to compare two bits of information. Thus sensors tend to concretize and intuitives tend to abstract. Where a sensor would see a fork and a spoon, an intuitive would see silverware. It's easy to understand why an intuitive, preferring to see one bit of information in the context of another, would be given to abstraction and inference, would be comfortable with teachers who emphasized theory, and would be impatient with teachers who focused on facts instead of relationships.

Once again we introduce tutors to these ideas through group activities. We divide them into sensors and intuitives without telling them the basis of the division. This creates a mix different from the groups of extraverts and introverts, for there is no necessary connection between being an extravert, say, and being a sensor. We send the new groups off to do some perceiving--by gathering information about the building they are in or activities on the quad.

If we give them twenty minutes to perform the task, we can usually count on seeing the first group of intuitives back in ten minutes. The very short list of what they have perceived will contain items like "ideas," "learning," "relationships," and "trees in an irregular pattern." The intuitives will sit down and begin making profound (so they think) theoretical and symbolic meaning and pattern from their observations, giving far more time to processing the information than to gathering it. Some time later, the sensors will return bearing a much longer list rich in concrete detail -- the colors of the tiles in the floor, the smell in the hallway, the texture of the clothes people are wearing, the names of the trees on the quad. The sensors may not have time to begin organizing the information because they have spent all their time gathering it. Observers of these workshops see quickly that each information processing style carries its strengths and its limitations.

Writing instruction on our campus and, we believe, on most campuses, comes in both sensing and intuitive orientations. Our business college, for example, offers writing instruction in a sensing style. It is focused on genres -- the memo, the proposal, the technical report -- which may be composed according to linear procedures and about which facts may be taught and learned. English department faculty condemn this sort of instruction as product-oriented. The associative, holistic messiness of the process approach to writing seems more "right" to our writing faculty, who are without exception intuitives. We cannot generalize about the type of the teachers of business writing, but research into type and profession tells us that sensing types are drawn in far greater numbers to business related occupations than to the abstract concerns of the liberal arts (Myers & McCaulley, 246-248).

In the natural course of events, we are accustomed to seeing clients from both business and academic writing courses. Occasionally students will cross from one discipline to another. We know many English majors who have taken business writing courses as a hedge against unemployment and who have found the slow, deliberate, linear instructional style infuriating. We also deal frequently with students whose sensing preferences make them experience process-oriented instruction as oppressive.

For example, a few years ago we worked with an extraverted sensing-type woman who was enrolled in an advanced writing course. Our involvement came too early in our acquaintance with type theory for us to help her much, but we did learn from the experience. A successful writer, teacher and student with an outgoing and practical nature, our client, Sandra, had enrolled in an advanced writing course to motivate herself to work on her master's thesis. Her introverted and highly intuitive instructor worked without a book or a set syllabus, loosely structuring the course around a sequence of peer review sessions to which students were to bring independently conceived and executed work for criticism. Lacking a textbook, prescribed subjects, or a series of genres to master, our client developed a writer's block which grew more and more debilitating as the semester wore on. Her teacher sent a strong message that facts and procedures had nothing to do with the writing process (an intuitive assumption) and that writers in advanced writing courses ought to work independently (an introverted assumption). Since her writing was governed by a set procedure and since she relied on guidance in the external world to set agendas and make judgments, she felt unable to contribute to the group. Silence seemed safer than self-incrimination, and, eventually, absence less painful than interaction.

We knew it was not a good sign when an extravert began choosing to avoid social contact, but we were uncertain what to do with our knowledge, other than urge the writer to talk to the teacher. The teacher and writer frustrated each other, and neither was able to communicate across the gulf of their differing views of the writing process. The writer eventually wrote and defended a very successful thesis, but not for that teacher. She temporized all term, eventually just dashed off a few papers at the last moment, and took the inevitable C.

Had we been more conversant with type theory, we might have been able to mediate their interaction. We should have tactfully informed the teacher that his introverted tendencies to process everything inwardly made him difficult and frightening for an extravert to deal with and that the writer's sensing preferences for practical and sequential learning were colliding with his intellectual and free-wheeling approach to writing. Had the student been given permission to ask for the kind of instruction she needed, the instructor might have been willing to provide it for her, but they would have needed our continuing intervention to assist them to appreciate each other's perspectives since strong sensing types miss the forest for the trees, and strong intuitives miss the trees for the forest.

The sensing-intuitive difference is difficult to perceive because it is, in Emily Dickinson's phrase,"an internal Difference/Where the meanings are." Whereas extraverts often behave in ways visibly different from introverts, no one can observe the processes which transform information into meanings. One of the few obvious differences is speed: intuitives tend to write and think faster because they work from hunch, guesswork, and association instead of the methodical accumulation of facts and details. Sensors will often slow down the pace of a discussion and want to get facts and details (such as length requirements and deadlines) in order before beginning to compose a paper.

The Gift of Judgment: Thinking and Feeling

The composition of a paper brings us to the next set of internal differences, the ways people make judgments about information. We do not mean Judgment in the Biblical sense, though we will get around to talking about shame and guilt in this context. In Jungian type theory, judging is a way of responding to information. After people take in information in their preferred mode of sensing or intuition, type theory suggests that their reactions to information are governed by a process of thinking or a process of feeling. The MBTI measures these preferences by way of questions which pose dichotomies such as head and heart, logic and sentiment, reason and feeling. Though thinking types feel and feeling types reason, each type tends to prefer one or the other as the basis of decision making. Thinking types rely on relatively objective and logical methods such as cause-effect reasoning, classification, flow charting, cost-benefits analysis and so on. Feeling types work through information using more subjective and humane methods such as persuasion, appreciation, values clarification, and empathy. As you might guess, feeling types are well represented in the arts and in the helping professions as counselors, ministers, personnel people, social workers, sales people. Thinking types predominate in the hard sciences, in business, and the law (Myers & McCaulley, 248-251).

We illustrate the judging functions through an exercise which divides tutors into thinking and feeling groups, and asks them to define the term *love*. This assignment produces loud groans, mostly emanating from the thinking group. The thinkers give abstract definitions from dictionaries, philosophers, and theologians, or refuse to give a definition at all, observing that love is indefinable. Feeling types can go on for hours on this topic elaborating on the warmth and caring involved in love, quoting poetry, and illuminating the margins of their lists with hearts and flowers, birds and bees. Both types produce existential statements. Usually one of the feeling types will jokingly quote Charles Schulz's "Love is a warm puppy." A few years ago one of our thinking tutors amused his compatriots and dismayed the feeling group with "Love means never having to say you're horny."

In tutoring, thinking-feeling differences are played out via the style of relationship between tutor and client. The two types bring different agendas to a personal encounter. For the thinking type, learning is a matter of seeing what needs to be done and doing it. Nothing else is logical, and nothing illogical is permitted to interfere with getting the work done. A feeling type sees tutoring in the context of a human relationship which is at least as important as the learning, so that the relationship and the learning mutually reinforce or inhibit each other. The strong thinking type tutor wants to get the forms filled out and the session underway, while the strong feeling tutor wants to take time to experience the client's values and needs before negotiating what they are to do together.

During the spring term of 1989, we tutored an extraverted intuitive feeling type in grammar. No, we were not so retrograde as to suppose that grammar would improve her writing. She was taking a course in traditional grammar, and we were simply trying to help her take hold of the material. The intuitive thinking type who taught her course laid out language systematically through lectures, some group activities, and many exercises. The exams were based on the exercises, so she called on us for four sessions after she had done rather badly on the first exam.

The instructor's classroom presentation was scrupulously logical, as a thinking instructor would make it. It was also rather linear, proceeding from parts of speech to phrases to sentence grammar to some applications of traditional grammar in punctuation and style. In teaching the course over a period of years, the instructor's methods had evolved from an intuitive approach featuring theoretical lectures and readings to a more sensing approach through exercises and experiential activities. He had discovered that intuitive types could find the structure in a sensing presentation more readily than sensing types could sort the facts out of an intuitive presentation.

Our client, Ellen, was bright, cooperative, and very verbal, qualities which made her easy and pleasant to tutor. Her extraversion made it fun for her to supply us with an oral protocol of her thinking processes in doing the grammar exercises. She would simply think out loud as we went over the exercises with her. Hearing her reasoning out loud we immediately found out, for example, that she tended to drop details she considered unimportant in the exercises. When the task was to bracket clauses in a set of sentences and to draw a line under finite verbs, she made a value (feeling) judgment that dependent clauses were less important than independent clauses and therefore not to be marked. Of course, the instructor intended for her to make a logical (thinking) judgment that both independent and dependent clauses contained the elements definitive of clauses.

Simple Gifts: How Thinking and Feeling Focus Intuition

We can further clarify Ellen's case using **temperament** theory (Keirsey & Bates), an outgrowth of type theory which suggests that the eight traits of the MBTI interact to form four temperaments. According to the theory, people who share a temperament develop some similar basic goals, strengths, and weaknesses. *Intuitive thinking* types form one of the temperaments, and *intuitive feeling* types form another. Of course both temperaments use intuition to gather information in associative and holistic ways.

The intuitive thinking types -- Ellen's instructor was one -- process information using objective, logical principles. Their drive to analyze and systematize information gives them a gift for learning new ideas and skills. Thus acquiring competence at an ever-widening series of activities becomes an important general life goal for intuitive thinking types. These people constantly strive to gain new skills and to think deep thoughts in order to better their personal bests. *Star Trek's* immensely competent and rational Mr. Spock is a representative intuitive thinking type.

Intuitive feeling types like Ellen prefer to process intuitively acquired information by getting subjectively involved, using non-logical methods such as appreciation and empathy. Their tendency to personalize information leads them to an interest in people issues: who they are; what it means to be human, or an artist, or a writer, or a doctor; and how they can have harmonious relations with people in their environment. For Ellen, taking a grammar class was a personal challenge, a venture into a subject better suited to the preferences of a thinking type.

Although Ellen shared only the intuitive preference with her instructor, she liked and admired him. When she received her score on the first test, a 57%, she was horrified not only because it represented a poor grade but also because she felt that she had not been paying enough attention to the class and, by implication, to her instructor. The instructor's feelings would be hurt. She felt guilty, as if she ought to do some penance, but she was afraid to approach him for forgiveness.

Her intuitive thinking instructor had a different interpretation. From his perspective, a low grade was a sign of her incompetence, not of any bad feelings toward him. While it would be appropriate to experience guilt if one had harmed someone else, falling short at a task would summon a different emotion--shame. Thus rather than thinking of himself as a person wronged, the instructor thought that he had caused Ellen to shame herself. He was careful not to reveal her "secret" and would not discuss it with her unless she brought it up. Reasonable guilt and shame are healthy reactions to failure, but they need to be acted on or else they can block growth. Penance and forgiveness, which would resolve Ellen's guilt feelings, were in the hands of the teacher in this case. Ellen could not give herself conferences or extra homework in order to make up for having done poorly on the test. Since the teacher supposed that she felt shame, he waited for her to approach him to ask for help and meanwhile behaved "normally" toward her so she could see that he accepted her even though she had failed. They were blocked, each assuming it was the other's part to initiate contact. When we told the teacher how Ellen felt, he immediately invited her to a conference and took over the tutoring duties. Like us he found it quite pleasant to work with so forthcoming a person as Ellen, and she loved the personal attention from someone she admired. She eventually earned a B in the course.

We do not mean to imply that only feeling types or only women have emotional reactions to learning. We have found, however, that many thinking types are so accustomed to suppressing their feelings and doing what is logical that they have little ability to name or deal with emotions, and may therefore react emotionally to a life or learning situation without being aware of that reaction. We framed Ellen's problem to her instructor logically as a conflict in interpretations of the situation in order to make it as comfortable as possible for him to deal with her. Not that all thinking types are ruthless logic machines. Most of the thinking types we know quickly lose their detachment and dignity in a pet store. Nor are all feeling types as warm and caring as Ellen. One intuitive feeling type we know acknowledges that he has no trouble feeling how other people feel, but that appreciating others' feelings doesn't necessarily require doing anything about them. He has his own feelings to worry about.

We can think of temperament as a way of framing situations. For example, to someone of the intuitive feeling temperament, the B Ellen earned would mean that her relationship with her mentor had given her the support she needed. To someone with this intuitive thinking temperament, the B would mean that she had worked hard and proven her competence. Of course both are valid interpretations of the sequence of events, but they represent different ways of framing the outcome, and the two participants would carry those interpretations with them into future situations.

Of all the personality traits we have so far discussed, thinking and feeling are probably the least available for inspection by outside observers since they represent the assumptions people use to make decisions from the heart or the head, using sentiment or logic, being sympathetic or reasonable. Since the issues are complex and the evidence scarce, awareness of the thinking-feeling difference may be as far as most tutors will be able to go.

The Gift of Perspective: Judging and Perceiving

A much more accessible set of differences, the last two traits the MBTI measures, proceeds from preferences about the sensing-intuiting (perceiving) and thinking-feeling (judging) functions themselves. Katherine Briggs and Isabel Briggs Myers, who developed the MBTI, went beyond Jung's three polarities -- extraversion-introversion, sensation-intuition, and thinking-feeling -- to extrapolate a fourth factor from Jungian type theory, calling it "attitude," meaning something like "perspective," the habitual way a person interacts with experience.

The developers of the MBTI reasoned that a person would have a preference for either perceiving information or judging it. For example, a person who was both intuitive and feeling might prefer intuition, and would therefore tend to remain open and continue intuiting information. Or the person might happen to prefer feeling and therefore tend to close off the flow of information to use feeling to judge the information. A person who preferred to remain open to information and delay judgment as long as possible was called a perceiving type, and one who preferred to close off the flow of information to arrive at quick judgments was called a judging type. Many of the MBTI questions which measure the judging-perceiving polarity inquire whether one likes or dislikes such information-processing tools as lists and schedules.

We illustrate this difference to tutors with an activity based on planning. Dividing them into judging and perceiving groups, we ask them to tell us how they prepare to begin a semester at school. The judging types produce a virtually infinite list of articles to pick, purchase, pack, and arrange; classes, study groups, extracurricular activities, and part-time jobs to schedule; and parents, friends, and significant others to call and trade addresses and schedules with. Even the introverts talk happily about their lists and have to be silenced eventually. The perceiving types agree after a moment of conference that they pack their stereo, their credit cards, and then find some sort of adventure.

These preferences often produce observable differences in tutoring behavior. Take lists for example. A judging tutor is likely to come to closure about a tutoring session before it begins. The judging tutor will arrive with an agenda, probably written out like a shopping list to be worked through item by item. Once the agenda has been established, a judging type is unlikely to deviate from it, which makes the person extremely reliable and therefore likely to acquire responsibility.

A perceiving type is less likely to make lists of agenda items in the first place, but having made a list or having encountered a judging client with a list, the perceiving tutor is likely to treat the list as if it were a menu, choosing a few interesting items from the list or disregarding it entirely if the client seems to have a more important problem to solve at the moment. The differences in behavior result from the perceiving type's preference to continue perceiving, to continue to sense or intuit the flow of information until the last possible moment, as opposed to the judging type's preference to make judgments, to think or feel about the information in order to gain the satisfaction of making a decision.

The judging type has gifts for management: discipline, organization, and follow-through. We believe that most study skills programs were developed by judging types. Our perceiving tutors and clients tend to agree that the neat time charts and lists of activities leave them cold and uninterested. The same is true of the organizational plans for doing research. Perceivers do not go to the library and take notes or Xerox pages, then make outlines, and finally write up the data. A perceiver is likely to read much more comprehensively than a judger and still be reading the night the paper is due, not wanting to miss that last bit of information. Judging tutors have to learn to understand that orderly planning and note-taking annoy perceiving types and deprive them of the fun of bringing the paper in just under the deadline. The tightly organized, orderly study skills activities are just right for judging types. Probably, no one needs to tell judging types about schedules and lists. They were likely born with a clear agenda.

In our center, we, our assistant directors, our secretary, and our two graduate assistants are all judging types. We all make lists of jobs to accomplish, and we all treat our lists like shopping lists, experiencing pleasure in crossing the items off our lists, one by one, until we get to the bottom. The majority of our tutors are perceiving types, which works because perceiving types can use their gifts for problem-solving-- flexibility, responsiveness to new data, and agility of thought--to stay open to new clients and new problems.

These differences can cause immense friction on the wheels of the administrative machinery. Extreme judging types can be bossy, opinionated, inflexible, compulsive micro-managers of their own and everyone else's lives. If the judging types are also thinking, they can be insensitive and infuriatingly logical; if they are feeling, they can probe for guilt and shame to manipulate other people. Extreme perceiving types can be unreliable, irresponsible, indecisive, uncommitted saboteurs of their own and everyone else's plans. If the perceiving types are thinking, they can constantly produce hare-brained ideas which are never developed; if they are feeling, they can flit impulsively from one mood and personality to another.

In order to lower the level of friction, judging directors need to learn to offer or seem to offer choices to perceiving types. Telling tutors that the appointment record forms must be in by Friday afternoon will produce immediate compliance from judging tutors, who didn't need to be reminded anyway, but is likelier to produce antagonism or indifference on the part of perceiving tutors. The key is to leave the issue open to some degree, telling the tutors that they may turn in their record forms on Friday if they want the secretary to enter the data on their time-cards, or they may turn the forms in on Monday if they do not mind entering the data themselves and possibly receiving their paychecks late.

The perceivers' key for dealing with judging types is to give them enough lead time to adjust their expectations. A judging director who learns that a tutor cannot keep an appointment will be annoyed at first but will calm down if the perceiving type has covered the appointment and notified everyone involved. The director will eventually work the change into the schedule, and eventually come to believe that it was her idea all along.

Simple Gifts: How Judging and Perceiving Focus Sensing

The judging and perceiving preferences also play a role in temperament theory, where they combine with the sensing preference to produce the *sensing-judging* and the *sensing-perceiving* temperaments. Recall that temperaments imply common basic life goals and ways of interpreting events. The factual orientation of the sensor when combined with the orderly attitude of the judger produces a person who believes in the social order as a fact of life and who wants to play a part in that order. These down-to-earth, practical, conventional and trustworthy people are the bulwarks of the families, churches, schools, and corporations in which they take on responsibilities as parents, deacons, principals, and middle managers.

A good writing center director, or any successful executive, needs to be or find a sensing judging person to handle details. Our secretary provides the stability and dependability that tutors need. She always knows where everyone is, whose time card needs to be signed, who needs to be reminded of a meeting or an appointment. She attends to detail with a patience that bespeaks the true gift of the responsible and loyal sensing judging person.

Sensing-perceiving types, on the other hand, are free spirits. Their practical sensing orientation combines with an open perceiving attitude to create a gift for living in the present and a consequent drive for independence: *freedom* is a word with magical connotations for those with the sensing-perceiving temperament. They are rare in higher education because they have a low tolerance for theory (which frustrates sensing) and routine (which dulls perception). They become fire fighters, police detectives, military pilots, and, the patient ones, surgeons. Ingenious at creating and solving problems, they make exciting but rather temporary company, for they leave as soon as the excitement is over. They see rules as something to be manipulated or ignored and commitment as a trap. We recently dealt with a case of a sensing-perceiving high school student who ran afoul of a sensing-judging math teacher. The student, a second-semester senior, had enrolled in a pre-calculus course for which he was not really prepared, having earned Cs in previous math courses. Unfortunately he needed the credit hours to achieve the minimum number required for graduation from high school. He rapidly floundered in the course and, being an introvert, he kept his problems to himself.

His teacher routinely assigned him extra homework to make up for his problems. From her sensing-judging perspective, the extra homework meant that he was being given an opportunity to stay with the group. Since belief and membership in social institutions is a strong positive drive for sensing judging types, and fear of exclusion or abandonment is an equally strong negative drive, she thought she was doing the right thing, saving him from the worst possible fate. Unfortunately, the sensing-perceiving student had little desire to be part of a social institution. He interpreted the extra work as punishment. With his strong drive for independent action, he wanted only to flee from the imprisonment of the extra work, and eventually he stopped doing work and attending class.

We encountered him after he had failed the class and missed being graduated from high school. He had abandoned his vague plans of college, had moved out of his parents' house, had gotten into money difficulties, and was quite distraught. He felt imprisoned by his problems and could see no attractive courses of action. To a sensing-perceiver, the inability to see choices betokens despair. We helped him to perceive that he still had choices. He could return to his high school or take the GED; he could take a less expensive apartment or return to his parents' house. He took the GED and achieved a near-perfect score, returned to his parents' house and then moved with them to another state, and has begun to revive his college plans.

This conflict in temperament between sensing-judging types, who naturally gravitate toward conventional roles like that of teacher, and sensing-perceiving types, who according to some estimates represent over nine-tenths of high school dropouts, seems basic to the school situation (McCaulley and Natter). Temperament theory provides a way of explaining how people of good will can do great harm to each other while trying to help. This is painful knowledge, but it is knowledge we would not be without.

Giving Our Gifts

Before we can give our gifts, we must know them. We feel strongly that every writing center staff should include someone who is qualified to administer the MBTI. Week-long qualifying workshops are available in major cities all across the country through the Association for Psychological Type, 2720 N. W. 6th Street, Gainesville, FL 32609. We took our training from Otto Kroeger, at his training center in Fairfax, Virginia.

For directors who cannot presently afford the time and money to take a qualifying workshop, many college counseling centers will administer the MBTI as well, and directors can gain valuable personal contacts in such interactions. When we do workshops on type and tutoring, we especially recommend two books as introductions to type. Lawrence's *People Types and Tiger Stripes* offers a simple checklist of questions for relating learning preference to type, and Keirsey and Bates's *Please Understand Me* begins with a short questionnaire similar to the MBTI. Of course the simpler methods are also less reliable, so anyone using the information from them would have to be especially careful to maintain an open mind about type.

It may seem that guessing about type is dangerous, and it is, but so is tutoring without knowledge of type. We would echo Martin Luther's famous advice to "sin boldly." Every course of action produces both good and evil, so we should feel free to follow our consciences. We would only suggest that tutors who are working from guesses act out rather than talk about type to the client. If the client seems to be an intuitive, it will not do much harm to offer unstructured learning experiences with lots of time for following up hunches and speculating theoretically. It might do some harm to tell a client that he or she is an intuitive when no reliable measurement of the client's preferences has been taken; a client who took the tutor's judgment seriously might experience confusion and anxiety trying to live out something other than true type.

Jung saw personal differences as inborn and believed that the goal of life was to live out those differences. Jung's typology helps to elaborate people's reasons for their differences, affording both analyst and patient a clearer view of the preferences which motivate people's behavior and a language for discussing those differences. Ideally, type theory would enable people to live out the unique life implied by their personal gifts lead them and to avoid self-defeating behavior.

Although Jungian analysts make much clinical use of type theory and empirical research has partly confirmed Jung's hunch about the biological basis of type, we cannot doubt that behaviorists, cognitivists, neo-Freudians, social constructionists, and a host of other theoretical schools would take sharp issue with many of Jung's preconceptions and conclusions. Fortunately, we do not need a theorist's permission to try to understand people. Whether we agree with Jung that the mind is genetically programmed or with behaviorists that there is no such thing as mind, we can use type theory as a starting point from which to begin learning about how people are motivated, how they take in information, how they make decisions, how they relate to the environment, and how, through all of these functions, they deal with the ideas they discover and the emotions they feel. We know that the questions people bring us are embedded in lives extending far beyond books, classrooms, and whispered conversations with a tutor. We are persuaded that the answers we give have effects we cannot imagine. Since we cannot be sure that we are giving enough, we must be satisfied with giving the best gifts we have.

Works Cited

This list includes both works cited and introductory sources on type theory.

Bates, Marilyn, and David Keirsey. *Please Understand Me.* Del Mar, CA: Prometheus Nemesis Book Co., 1978.

Eysenck, H. J. *The Inequality of Man.* San Diego: Edits Publishers, 1975.

Jensen, George, and John K. DiTiberio. "Personality and Individual Writing Processes," *College Composition and Communication* 35 (October 1984): 285-300.

--------, and John K. Di Tiberio. *Personality and the Teaching of Composition.* Norwood, NJ: Ablex Publishing Corp., 1989.

Jung, Carl G. *Psychological Types.* New York: Harcourt, Brace, 1923.

Kroeger, Otto, and Janet Thuesen. *Type Talk.* New York: Delacorte Press, 1988.

Lawrence, Gordon. *People Types and Tiger Stripes.* Gainesville, FL: Center for Applications of Psychological Type, Inc., 1982.

Maid, Barry, Sally Crisp, and Suzanne Norton. "On Gaining Insight into Ourselves as Writers and as Tutors: Our Use of the Myers-Briggs Type Indicator." *Writing Lab Newsletter* 13 (June 1989): 1-5.

McCaulley, Mary H. and Frank L. Natter. *Psychological (Myers-Briggs) Type Differences in Education.* Gainesville, FL: Center for Applications of Psychological Type, Inc., 1980.

Myers, Isabel Briggs. *Gifts Differing.* Palo Alto, CA: Consulting Psychologists Press, 1980.

_____, and Mary H. McCaulley. Manual: *A Guide to the Development and Use of the Myers-Briggs Type Indicator.* Palo Alto, CA: Consulting Psychologists Press, 1985.

von Franz, Marie-Louise, and James Hillman. *Lectures on Jung's Typology.* Irving, TX: Spring Publications, 1971.

The Writing Center and the Research Paper: Computers and Collaboration

Irene Lurkis Clark
University of Southern California

Writing Center instruction has traditionally focused on helping students develop an effective writing "process," including prewriting, drafting, and editing; however, it has devoted little attention to the related "process" students engage in when they locate, evaluate, and work with outside information for a research paper. In fact, despite recent pedagogical interest in the benefits of collaborative learning, the "research process" is one which students still usually undertake alone, wandering ineffectively around the library, spending more time attempting to locate information than actually thinking about it or working with it. At the University of Southern California, however, the Writing Center has developed a collaborative computer assisted approach to teaching the research process, one which is also likely to foster greater understanding of that process. This essay describes Project Jefferson[1], a hypertext instructional program available in the Writing Center, which enables Writing Center tutors to assist students in developing an effective model of conducting research, one which can then be replicated in subsequent research projects involving the library.

Problems Associated With the Research Paper in the Composition Course

It is generally acknowledged that the traditional "research paper," which has long been a component of the composition course, frequently generates less than sparkling results. As many weary composition instructors can attest, student research papers are usually uninspired, pointless, unfocused, and occasionally plagiarized, problems which are compounded by confusion concerning purpose, form, and length, as well as by difficulties students often encounter in accessing information from the library. In fact, because research papers have caused so many

---

[1] See Irene Lurkis Clark, "Project Jefferson: A Hypertext Application For Teaching Students Research Skills," *Research in Word Processing Newsletter* (December 1988): 2-7.

problems, many composition instructors over the past twenty years
have avoided assigning them altogether (Ford and Perry).

Despite these difficulties, however, many composition programs,
including ours at the University of Southern California, feel that
providing students with opportunities to learn research skills should be
an integral part of the composition course. Research skills have long
been considered an essential component of undergraduate education--they
are important for students to broaden their knowledge and awareness on
their own and can have tremendous impact on students' academic and
professional achievement. As Jeff Jeske points out, the research paper
may be considered "a microcosm of education itself, inasmuch as it
requires first finding information . . .and then evaluating. . . what is
relevant and when it is valid" (63). Given the importance of research
skills, it seems preferable not to eliminate the research paper, but rather
to create a new method of teaching it, one which could be implemented
through the process approach characteristic of Writing Center pedagogy.

The Researched Paper: A New Approach to the Research Paper

Recognizing the importance of rethinking how the research paper
can be incorporated into the composition course, the Freshman Writing
Program at the University of Southern California has developed a new
model, designated the "researched" paper, to distinguish it from the
traditional approach, with all its attendant difficulties. The "researched"
paper, which also may be termed a "documented" paper, is a relatively
short paper (5-8 pages) concerned with a substantive, multi-faceted
content issue, which may originate with personal experience but is
ultimately text based. It requires students to acquire research related
skills by immersing themselves in a topic, examining key issues,
locating background information, and critically evaluating and using
secondary sources. Students undertake research in order to formulate an
informed position on a complex topic.

Staged Acquisition and the Writing Center

Moreover, the "researched" paper also implies a sequenced pedagogy
termed "staged acquisition," which is implemented through a series of
research oriented writing activities undertaken in the Writing Center,
often under the guidance of a Writing Center tutor. These activities
include locating key terms in an assignment, examining pertinent
background information and definitions, identifying critical issues in the

topic, locating and evaluating outside opinions concerned with the topic, and, ultimately, formulating a position to be developed in a documented paper.

Actually, one might perceive the concept of the researched paper simply as one which thoughtful instructors have always adhered to, and argue that such instructors have always chosen appropriate topics, clarified purpose and sequenced assignments. However, whether or not one perceives this model as "new" or simply as a workable adaptation of a previous model, is not important. What is important is that developing and working with this approach has enabled us to incorporate Writing Center pedagogy into the teaching of research skills.

The Researched Paper and Project Jefferson

The concepts of the researched paper and staged acquisition have been implemented in "Project Jefferson," a topic specific on-line information retrieval system located in the Writing Center, which enables students to access information, and secondary sources for their assignments. Utilizing Hypercard running on Macintosh computers , Project Jefferson establishes links between chunks of information, which can be accessed alphabetically, hierarchically, and associatively. The program thus simulates several models of information access characteristic of the research process which students can adapt to their own needs and apply to subsequent research tasks. Project Jefferson also contains a database of articles specifically concerned with the assigned topics, accessed through key terms or descriptors, enabling students to locate bibliographic information and abstracts of the articles. The articles, themselves, are located in three places: in a file cabinet in the Macintosh room, where they can be read but not removed, on reserve in the College Library, where they can be photocopied, or at a nearby copy center, where they can be purchased.

Another component of Project Jefferson is a word processor (Microsoft Word) which enables students to write responses to prewriting questions associated with their assignment, take notes, outline, and word process their papers. Ultimately, the system will provide access to the library on-line catalogue and to specialized on-line databases (magazine and newspaper indexes, etc.) so that students will be able to work with information from the library directly from within the Writing Center. Thus, through Project Jefferson, students are able to receive assistance not only in the writing process, but in the research process as well.

Project Jefferson received its name because it was formulated during the bicentennial year of the constitution and because its content is concerned with problematic ethical and social issues deriving from the constitution. These issues were selected because they were both controversial and complex, personally as well as socially relevant, and thus are well suited for an argumentative paper. In working with these topics, students have to formulate an arguable position; they cannot simply collect information and loosely paste it together, as was often the case in research papers in the past.

It must be qualified, however, that a variety of topics would be suitable for inclusion in Project Jefferson, and, in fact, that a new authoring version now enables various academic departments to create topic specific versions of the software to be used in their own courses. Recently, a professor in the School of Gerontology has compiled materials concerned with the topic of "death and dying," a topic for which we, in the Freshman Writing Program, will soon develop "researched paper" assignments.

A View Of Project Jefferson (Figure 1)

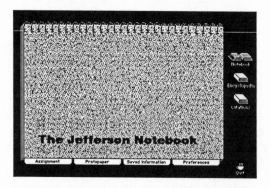

Figure 1 presents the opening screen which students see when they begin work on Project Jefferson. The three icons on the right represent the three components of the program, **Notebook, Encyclopedia,** and **Citations**. "Notebook" consists of prewriting questions, assignments, an outliner (Protopaper), and a place to store saved information (Saved Information). In figure 1, the Notebook is open, because students are placed in that section when they begin work. The other "books" open when students enter those sections. The

"**Encyclopedia**" consists of background information and definitions which can be accessed either alphabetically, hierarchically, or associatively. Figure 2 illustrates the alphabetic index in the Encyclopedia.

Figure 2

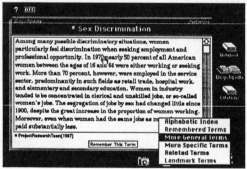

Figure 3

Figure 3 illustrates how the Encyclopedia enables students to find additional pieces of information. The term "sex discrimination" can lead them either back to the alphabetic index, to more general or specific terms, or to related terms.

"Citations" consists of bibliographic information including abstracts of articles pertinent to the topic. Figure 4 illustrates the Query screen, into which student has put the descriptor "affirmative action," a term which the system indicates is relevant to sixty-eight articles. In Figure 5, the student has narrowed the search by including the term "sex discrimination"; the system indicates that twenty articles pertain to these two terms. Thus the student is learning about using descriptors in computerized data bases, a method which libraries are using with increasing frequency.

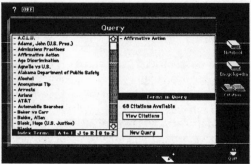

Figure 4

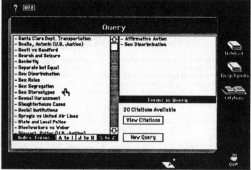

Figure 5

When students click on "View Citations," they are provided with bibliographic information (Figure 6) including an abstract (Figure 7). If they click on "Citations Index Terms," they obtain related terms which leads them to additional information (Figure 8).

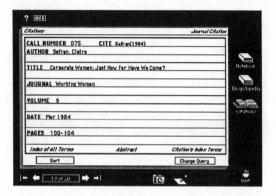

Figure 6

Figure 7

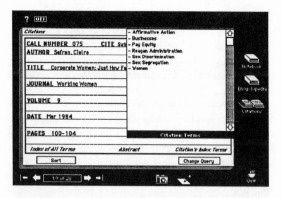

Figure 8

The Writing Center and the Research Process: An Illustrative Sequence

To illustrate how Project Jefferson works within the Writing Center, I will discuss a typical assignment sequence. Before students engage in research, they are required to learn to use Macintosh computers (easily learned through a "Mac Tour") and be comfortable using the wordprocessor (also not difficult to learn). They then come to the Macintosh Lab, sometimes as a class, to work through prewriting questions, which enables them to become preliminarily acquainted with the topic and examine their own feelings about it. An example of a topic which has worked quite successfully concerns the issue of equal opportunity and the social and legal issues associated with the policy of affirmative action. Therefore, students might respond to a preliminary question such as "What do you think is meant by the term 'equal opportunity'?" A second might be "Do you think it is the role of government to insure that everyone has equal opportunity?" A third might be "Do you consider yourself a liberal or a conservative on social issues? What do these terms mean to you?" These preliminary responses help students begin to think about the topic and can also serve as the subject of class discussion or of small group discussions within the Writing Center. Moreover, the computer setting within the supportive Writing Center environment has the effect of removing the isolation which often characterizes in-class writing. Students will often look at one another's screens and assist one another with the technical aspects of text-inputting. Such exchanges also facilitate the sharing of ideas between students and between tutors and students, interaction less easily achieved in the classroom.

After students have completed pre-writing activities, they are then given their assignment, which, requires them to formulate a position on a complex, controversial topic. In developing their position, they must indicate their awareness of the problematic nature of this controversy, demonstrate their understanding of key issues and concepts, including relevant background material, and refer to significant outside opinion.

A student may work with a tutor at any stage of the research process. A student may sit with a tutor at the computer and read through the assignment together, clarifying its purpose and selecting and defining key terms about which to locate additional information and background. Terms such as "equal opportunity," "affirmative action," "discrimination" and "reverse discrimination," can be easily located through Project Jefferson, and students and tutors might discuss which terms are relevant, how they might be used to generate a position, and what related terms and background material might be important to locate.

Tutors might also work with students on evaluating the quality and relevance of the articles listed under Citations. They might discuss the relative merit of one publication over another, compare two positions on the topic, or decide to search under different descriptors for additional perspectives. After a preliminary draft has been written, students can then consult with tutors on the necessity of finding further information, an easily undertaken task, since the information is right there on the computer. Without having to leave the Writing Center, the student can access additional information, incorporate it into the paper, and, if necessary, consult with the tutor once again. Thus, the Writing Center can be used to help students with all facets of the research process, without the long time lapse usually necessary when students have to return to the library.

Of course, one might question whether Project Jefferson and the assistance provided by the Writing Center really does prepare students for other, perhaps more complicated, research tasks which would require familiarity with library resources.Given the recognition that research processes differ from field to field, can students develop a model of the "research process" by working with simulated materials under the guidance of a tutor? Of course, my response to such questions must be qualified, since the project is relatively new. However, because the Project involves concepts which, we believe, are central to any research task (locating key terms and background information, defining controversy, and accessing critical opinion), it seems likely that students will be able to apply what they have learned through Project Jefferson when they engage in additional research assignments.

Moreover, some instructors are using the assignments and materials in Project Jefferson as a stepping stone toward further research assignments within the composition class. After students have completed a Project Jefferson "researched" paper, they are then assigned an additional paper involving outside research on a topic related to one included in Project Jefferson. Instructors who have tried this sequence find that once students have written about a topic and accessed relevant materials through Project Jefferson, they have not only acquired a "research process"; they have also developed a knowledge base on the topic from which to initiate a more successful library search. In other words, once students have written one "researched" paper on a particular topic, they now have a much better idea of the key concepts and critical conflicts within that topic, insight which enables them to work with outside information more effectively. Also, since Project Jefferson will soon include on-line access to the full range of library resources, including the library catalogue and on-line magazine and news indexes, students will be able to work with the library directly from the Writing Center.

Project Jefferson has enabled the Writing Center at the university of Southern California to utilize a "hands-on" approach to teaching research skills, an approach which we are still in the process of developing. Unlike the educational cassettes which were once a staple of Writing Center instruction, Project Jefferson fosters, rather than inhibits collaboration; the accessibility of the computer enables students and tutors to work together in accessing and compiling information through all stages of the writing process. The computer has thus provided us not only with a valuable teaching tool, but also with exciting possibilities for exploring different models of the research process.

Works Cited

Clark, Irene Lurkis. "Project Jefferson: A Hypertext Application for Teaching Students Research Skills." *Research in Word Processing Newsletter*. (December 1988): 2-7.

Ford, James E. and Dennis R. Perry. "Research Paper Instruction in the Undergraduate Writing Program." *College English* 44 (1982): 825-832.

Jeske, Jeff. "Borrowing From the Sciences: A Model Freshman Research Paper." *The Writing Instructor* 6 (Winter 1987): 62-72.

Portfolio Evaluation: Implications for Writing Centers

Nadene A. Keene
Indiana University at Kokomo

A Writing Center's fortunes often rise or fall in response to various assessment issues being explored, debated, extended, revised, or evaluated on a campus. I still vividly remember the look on the face of one Writing Center Director at a conference session when someone in the group suggested that all the portfolios for the school's 14,000 students be kept in the Writing Center. "Pain" doesn't half describe it. Fortunately for him, others in the room were sensitive to the struggle for space that his center had been waging and the idea was quickly dismissed. What's exhibited here is the natural concern of Writing Center Directors about how this new aspect of a writing program, portfolio evaluation, will affect their constituencies (clients, tutors, and faculty), their responsibilities, and their territory (both physical and pedagogical). The ways and the extent to which a Writing Center will be affected by a system of portfolio evaluation are dependent, to a great extent, on the type of portfolio system to be implemented.

Portfolio assessment is difficult to define because it has so many permutations. In the simplest sense, a portfolio system of evaluating writing involves collecting various materials which document a student's writing skills. Even this simple definition has various interpretations, however, for the purpose of the portfolio may be to document students' writing skills as evidenced by various products (essays, research papers, poetry, etc.) or as evidenced by various stages of the writing process (prewriting notes, drafts, peer-responses). Several portfolio systems are designed to assess a student's performance or writing within a particular class. Other systems are devised to collect a student's work so that the student can be placed in an appropriate writing course on the basis of an evaluation of past writing (i.e., placement portfolio). Still other systems are designed to be the culminating feature of a student's college career, a kind of capstone experience that collects writing from a period of years, from a variety of courses -- and thus a variety of disciplines -- perhaps even from extra-collegiate writing situations: e.g., work, volunteer responsibilities, or private pleasure.

Whether the portfolio is designed for a class, for placement, or for a capstone experience, the purposes may also vary. Sometimes the purpose of the portfolio is to present a range of the student's writing, from struggling abbreviated drafts to polished successful pieces. Other times the purpose of the portfolio is to present a record of the student's progress in writing. Sometimes the portfolio's purpose is to present the best of the student's writing. And sometimes (especially in the capstone portfolio) the purpose of the portfolio is left to the decision of the student.

Some portfolio systems, for example, require students to include various drafts of a document while other systems want only final drafts. Some systems encourage students to revise documents after they receive feedback from an instructor while other systems, usually placement designs, evaluate the student's writing as done without the benefit of the college instructor's response. (Placement portfolios seldom become the concern of Writing Centers, however, unless the portfolio is designated as deficient and the student is sent to the Writing Center for remediation.) Some portfolio systems want only documents written for college, or for particular courses (often designated as writing intensive courses, i.e., those courses which meet the school's writing across the disciplines guidelines), or for the student's major. Other portfolio systems allow students complete latitude as to what is to be included in the portfolio. (Note: Those systems which allow the most latitude in paper selection also often require the student to write a cover document which explains the underlying principle in the selection of materials within the portfolio.)

Whatever the configuration of portfolio that is adopted by an institution, the Writing Center constituencies -- students, tutors, and faculty -- will be most directly affected by the adoption of this new assessment procedure. Before I examine the effect of portfolios, let me present the portfolio system initially used at Indiana University-Kokomo.

Portfolios At IUK

A portfolio system of writing assessment was begun at Indiana University-Kokomo on a pilot-study basis in Spring of 1989. A second-semester freshman writing course focusing on researched writing across the curriculum (W132) was to be offered for the first time. The IUK English faculty met this challenge by setting up a committee to write a course description, devise a standard course syllabus, establish grading standards, and define assessment procedures. We elected to use a portfolio system of evaluation as part of the final semester grade. We chose a portfolio system because of six principles that we believe underlie portfolio assessment:

1) that assessment is necessary
2) that a one-time assessment instrument is not the best way to assess a student's skills or experience
3) that assessment of process as well as product is appropriate (and necessary given recent writing process theory)
4) that having students select, analyze, and evaluate their writing contributes to their self-knowledge and to a fuller development of their writing abilities
5) that evaluation of a portfolio by a committee or a committee-of-the-whole (i.e., all W132 instructors) helps to establish more consistent grading standards.

Those of us teaching the course comprised a subcommittee which agreed to meet weekly to discuss the problems and progress of the portfolio system. We also agreed that each instructor would do a mid-semester evaluation of each student's portfolio-in-progress. At the end of the semester, each student would prepare a portfolio of selected documents to submit to an outside evaluator, i.e., one of the other two W132 instructors.

This final portfolio was to be holistically evaluated by an outside evaluator as either satisfactory (C level or above) or unsatisfactory. Any portfolio judged to be unsatisfactory by the outside evaluator but judged satisfactory by the instructor would be submitted to a third and deciding evaluator. Any student's portfolio judged to be unsatisfactory by two outside evaluators could not receive a grade higher than C-. The instructor determined the grade (A-F) for any portfolio evaluated as satisfactory by two outside evaluators.

Thus, at IUK the portfolio system of evaluation was designed to assess student's writing abilities in two ways. First, it functioned as a kind of gate. To successfully complete W132, students had to produce a portfolio containing both documented and undocumented writing, both formal and informal writing which met departmental standards. Thus, writing standards were enforced. This portfolio system also functioned to emphasize writing as a process. Students were encouraged continually to evaluate and revise their writing throughout the semester. Several conferences were scheduled with the instructor and numerous class sessions were devoted to peer-evaluation and response, or to workshop. And the mid-semester evaluation was based on various drafts rather than on final products.

The pilot study was a success. All W132 instructors chose to continue using portfolio evaluation in that course, and they, as well as other members of the English faculty, expanded the use of portfolios to other courses. In addition, the Division of Education is adding portfolio assessment to their program evaluation. In this division, students will be asked to collect samples of their writing from various courses on a computer disk. This diskette will document student growth and development in professional studies. Thus, in various ways, students at IUK will continue to encounter the pleasures (and problems) of portfolio evaluation for some time.

And, if the number of papers being presented at conferences and the number of articles being published on portfolios is an indication (see the attached selected bibliography), more and more students at various colleges will have similar experiences. What does this mean for Writing Centers?

Implications For Writing Centers

For Writing Centers, the instigation of portfolio evaluation means both a continuation and an extension of services already being provided, of skills already being used. In terms of new responsibilities, it may mean a longer period of working with a particular student. (This most naturally would occur if a portfolio system is being used to collect materials over several semesters or years.) Specifically, it means continuing to act as interpreter of requirements with the student, continuing to be sensitive to the students' apprehension, continuing to increase students' ability to critically read, judge, and revise their writing--continuing to act as coach for the student.

Requirements

Writing Centers can help students interpret portfolio guidelines. Tutors need to know the purpose of the portfolio system being implemented in order to help students meet the requirements and make intelligent decisions on what to include in the portfolio. How can this be accomplished? First, Writing Center Directors need to know when a portfolio system of evaluation is to be implemented. Ideally, the Writing Center Director is included in all those decision-making processes involving writing or the assessment of writing. However, we do not live in an ideal world. As a Director, you need to read those multiple pieces of paper that float over your desk. Look for any bits of information regarding departmental or individual actions that may affect clients who visit the center. As you read, ask yourself how this action will affect students or the center itself. Become informed so that you can be prepared. Tutors surprised by a new system can do what tutors do well anyway--ask questions of the student, or use handouts, college catalogues, or other reference sources to seek out information. And, of course, they should discuss their findings with the Writing Center Director. Again ideally, a copy of portfolio guidelines and a discussion of potential student concerns would be included in tutor-training sessions before the portfolio system is introduced.

Apprehensiveness

Once students know what the portfolio system requires of them, the tutor's next concern may well be to alleviate the client's apprehension. Many clients at Writing Centers are highly apprehensive about writing. These clients, when confronted with the task of compiling a portfolio, sometimes panic. Their initial reaction may be that they have enough trouble tackling one paper at a time, let alone confronting the task of compiling multiple documents. Thus, writing apprehension may be intensified. The increased level of apprehension is reduced for some students, however, when they realize that their portfolio system allows them to revise their papers -- they don't have to worry about "getting it all right" the first time. Unfortunately, for other students apprehension about "getting it all right" is replaced with apprehension about having sufficient time to revise everything. Being faced not only with having to produce multiple documents, but also with multiple drafts of these documents seems insurmountable. Many may have no experience with revision. These clients need guidance through various revision procedures. Tutors can assure clients that just as there is no "one right way" to draft a paper, revising too can be achieved by a variety of means. (Tutors may find Donald Murray's article "The Maker's Eye: Revising Your Own Manuscript" helpful in providing a framework for one revising process. In addition, most textbooks provide some guidelines that tutors will find helpful.)

Whether the apprehensiveness stems from "getting it all right" or "getting it all done," Writing Center tutors can be, and often are already, trained to cope with and assuage writing and grade apprehension. One primary way of alleviating apprehension is through knowledge--the more information the student has about the system, the better the student can deal with it. If your school begins to use a portfolio system of evaluation, it may help both tutors and clients to see the parallel between this new system and the old system of evaluation. Tutors and students need to be aware of the instructions regarding the contents of the portfolio (just as they need to be aware of the instructor's assignments), they need to be aware of the criteria for evaluation of the portfolio (just as they need to be aware of the instructor's grading system), and they need to be aware of who will be evaluating the portfolio (just as they need to know who the intended reader of a document is to be or what pet peeves the instructor may have). Once they have this information, then both short-term and long-term goals can be set by the tutor and client for the individual paper or the portfolio as a whole. The goals that are set may well be similar to those that a client and tutor usually devise -- e.g., ample development, organization, sentence structure, comma use. The difference is that because the portfolio is not due until near the end of the semester, both tutor and client have more time to develop the needed skills.

In systems of portfolio evaluation in which the final portfolio is read by an "outside evaluator," the prospect of having their writing read by an "outside evaluator" may intimidate some students. Some students, especially highly apprehensive students or students who have often been told by instructors that they can't write or that they write poorly, may have just begun to trust one instructor when they must confront the possibility of having their writing evaluated by another, an unknown other. Thus, writing apprehension that may have begun to abate might return to high levels. Tutors need to be aware of this possible source of increased apprehension and to deal with it. Tutors can stress that such evaluators have usually been selected because they share common characteristics and/or knowledge with the student's trusted instructor. If the outside evaluator is from a field which differs from that of the instructor, the tutor and student can do an audience analysis that explores what that discipline commonly values in writing, what the common forms are, and what the preferred stylistic features are within that discipline. Once the unknown becomes more familiar, or at least verbalized, the apprehension should be somewhat lessened. The apprehension can be even further addressed, if need be, by the tutor and client designing specific ways of addressing the expectations of the outside evaluator in the texts to be written or revised and edited. As a last resort, tutors can discuss a worst case scenario with clients and take preventative measures to ensure that the worst case never occurs. I encourage tutors to use this only as a last resort, however, because its negativity may increase the client's fear and apprehension, rather than serve to reduce it.

Critical Thinking

A new portfolio system of evaluation may also mean that tutors need to be trained in some additional skills to encourage critical thinking skills among their clients. Tutors often work to have their clients become independent diagnosticians and learners, but the decisions usually focus on writing particular documents. With portfolio assessment, the concerns and the decisions are broader-based. Student clients need to be encouraged to approach their writing with what has been termed in psychology as "amiable skepticism." They need to question their text. The questioning of a text is often easier if distance from the text can be achieved. Sometimes a portfolio system enhances the achievement of this distance by its very nature, i.e., the collection of materials over a period of time. In some portfolio systems, however, students are required to submit a text for initial evaluation before it can become part of the portfolio. Achieving the distance necessary for the initial evaluation of the text under these circumstances is a problem that tutors already frequently encounter. Acting as a questioning reader for the client is already a valued technique in tutor training (see, for example, *The Practical Tutor* by Meyer and Smith or "Using Interviewing Techniques" by Malbec). Tutors need to be made aware of the increased need for questioning and evaluating in a portfolio situation. To examine this issue from an educational standpoint, tutors need to emphasize the evaluation level of Bloom's taxonomy. Keep in mind, however, that for clients to evaluate their text most effectively, the criteria for judging must be clear. This is why it is so vital to obtain as much information as possible regarding guidelines for portfolio evaluation.

Even given the guidelines, however, tutors and Writing Center Directors need to look beyond what's given on the page to the assumptions and principles underlying the portfolio guidelines. For example, inherent in most portfolios which are collected over several years or courses is the concept of appealing to and satisfying multiple audiences. A student will write a paper for a course, for a particular instructor. When that paper becomes part of a portfolio, however, the document is often then read by others. Ideally, evaluators other than the original instructor will be sensitive to the intended audience of the piece. All readers bring their own experience and assumptions to a text, however, and thus have their reading of that text influenced by these factors. Thus, tutors and clients need an increased awareness of audience.

Thus, with the introduction of a portfolio system, there may be a greater need for increased sensitivity to audience, both on the part of the tutor and the client. In a semester portfolio system, the documents are read by the instructor when they are first submitted for evaluation during the semester. Then the documents selected for inclusion in the portfolio are read again when the portfolio is submitted for evaluation at the end of the semester. If the portfolio is evaluated by the instructor, the student/client and the tutor need to be aware the instructor may well remember the piece and may or may not remember the comments made on the earlier draft. If an instructor remembers the draft and her comments, she may consciously or unconsciously evaluate the final document on how well the student followed the guidance provided earlier. Some instructors consciously compare the drafts; other instructors try to focus only on the merits of the final version of the document. Thus, both client and tutor need to be cognizant of this possible influence upon the final evaluation as decisions are made about revising the papers.

Territory

Physical

Fortunately, the physical territory of a Writing Center isn't endangered by the institution of a portfolio system of evaluation, unless its space is designated as the portfolio storage area. A Center might, I suppose, be the location for the portfolio evaluation to be done, but this would be a temporary displacement, as it is when Centers are the locales for placement evaluation. A Writing Center Director might even use these two circumstances to gain other advantages for the Center. For example, if the storage of the portfolios also involves locating and handing the portfolios to students who wish to add materials to their file, the Director can use this opportunity to show these students what the Center can offer them. Similarly, if the Center is to be the location of portfolio evaluation, the Director could subtly use this opportunity to show the faculty involved in the evaluation process some of what the Writing Center has to offer them and their students. In exchange for being the portfolio storage area, the Director might legitimately ask for additional budget. This additional budget might be used to pay for the extra time that the Center receptionist would spend answering questions or distributing and filing portfolios. Because additional storage space would be needed, the Director might also legitimately request a larger space for the center.

Another implication of portfolio evaluation for Writing Centers is a possible increased need for more specific record keeping. Some resistance to portfolio evaluation comes from those faculty who resist such a system of assessment because they see it as increasing the likelihood of plagiarism. If this occurs, Writing Centers may be called upon to keep more specific records of which papers students bring to the center for assistance and what specific aspect of writing are addressed during a tutoring session. For example, individual clients could be encouraged to keep a log listing the various stages in the evolution of a paper--what prewriting was done, who participated,
when the various sections of the paper were written and revised, what steps of the revision process took place, where the various writing steps took place, and what the student writer's thoughts/responses were during each writing phase--a kind of writing protocol in log form. Writing Center tutors also might wish initially to keep their own log of this information for those clients who are involved in a portfolio assessment program. (In essence, whenever a new course, new program, or new system of evaluation that affects writing is introduced on a campus, it behooves the Center to collect relevant data concerning this change. Often this data can become the persuasive basis of a request for additional funds or staffing for the Center.)

Pedagogical

A portfolio system of evaluation is most often a collaborative endeavor. Teachers work with students to help the students during the process of writing and revising. Students work with other students in both formal classroom procedures and informal study situations. Several authors of reports on portfolio assessment have commented on the increased collaboration between students, between student and teacher, and between teachers when a portfolio system of evaluation is introduced. (See especially Elbow and Belanoff; Burnham; Martin; and Ford and Larkin.) Does this mean that Writing Centers, those bastions of conferencing and collaboration, will soon become extinct, replaced by the very system which first clamored for their existence? No.

It is in terms of pedagogical territory that Writing Centers may most benefit from the adoption of a portfolio system of evaluation.

Lisa Ede's recent article "Writing as A Social Process: A Theoretical Foundation for Writing Centers?" describes a philosophy of Writing Centers that closely aligns with the underlying philosophy of portfolio evaluation--learning writing by constant interaction with others. Writing Centers, according to Ede, ". . .can build not only on theories of collaborative learning, as articulated by Bruffee, Hawkins, and others, but on the work of those who have recently challenged us to view writing as a social, rather than a solitary and individual, process" (5). This closely matches Peter Elbow's and Pat Belanoff's analysis that portfolio evaluation sends a "message to students . . .that thinking and writing are enhanced by conversation with peers and teachers" (104). Thus, portfolio evaluation can be a boon to Writing Centers because it encourages and enhances collaborative writing.

A portfolio approach to assessment often encourages collaborative learning. Students enrolled in courses where portfolio evaluation provides the basis of assessment are encouraged to confer with instructors and often at least some proportion of class time is spent workshopping students' writing, responding to each other's work, revising, or consulting with the instructor. Because of this emphasis on the collaboration, is it the case that the Writing Center will be phased out? That the collaborative classroom encouraged by portfolio evaluation will cause the demise of peer-response by trained tutors? On the contrary, because portfolio evaluation encourages collaboration, there may well be an even greater need for Writing Centers.

Conclusion

Writing Centers serve a variety of courses and disciplines. The use of portfolios within a college will probably supply the Center with even more clients. First, students who use collaborative techniques in the courses using the portfolio system of evaluation may well seek out additional opportunities (i.e., at the Center) to work with peers on their writing. This search for additional response may even continue when this particular course or set of courses ends. Second, students who are initially uncomfortable with the nature of portfolios (especially those who are distrustful of their instructors) may well seek further explanation of the system and reassurance from their peers in the center. Third, faculty who are new to portfolio evaluation may well seek out the advice and assistance of the Writing Center Director as someone who has more experience than they in the quick reading and diagnosing of writing.

Writing Centers can also provide assistance in another area of their expertise, conferencing. Because some instructors within the portfolio system will be new to conferencing, they can learn much from those who train the Writing Center tutors to confer with students. Tutors are trained to respond to text without being directive. Instructors new to collaboration would do well to take heed of tutor training and techniques. Writing Center directors may conduct workshops, provide materials, or show videotapes of successful tutoring sessions which can help instructors new to this method of teaching to devise their own approaches. Faculty distrustful of the new system of assessment may also seek out the Director. Some faculty may fear that within a long-range system of writing and revision, writing collaboration may become collusion. These faculty may well seek out the reassurances of the Writing Center Director that tutors can and will be cautioned to remember neither to appropriate the student's text nor to be too directive. Here again is an opportunity for Writing Center Directors to educate faculty on the services that the Center can provide both students and faculty. Tutors will be needed to provide additional feedback, to ameliorate confusing or discouraging feedback from the clients' peers or from a perhaps over-directive instructor. They can help students who are uncomfortable with peer-evaluation and collaboration adjust to this technique in the classroom because they have experience helping students adjust to it in the center. Writing Center staff has the advantage of previous training and insight in dealing with problems that individual instructors or departments may be encountering for the first time.

Assessment of writing by portfolio is a concept of increasing interest and burgeoning practice because it offers direct assessment of writing over a period of time. Because it offers so much potential, schools across the country are investigating various applications of portfolio evaluation. The effects of portfolio evaluation on Writing Centers will be to increase the number of its current clients from writing courses and the number of clients from other disciplines as portfolio evaluation causes writing to become more important across the disciplines. Portfolio evaluation, because it is by and large a collaborative endeavor, also increases communication and collaboration among faculty, thereby potentially increasing another client base that is often largely unknown in many Writing Centers. The institution of portfolio evaluation requires careful consideration of potential problems on each campus, but it also provides a wide range of opportunities that

Writing Center Directors need to explore. Perhaps the next time that particular Writing Center Director with the pained expression confronts the issue of portfolio evaluation, it will be with a smile on his face.

Works Cited

Anson, Chris, Lillian Bridwell-Bowles, and R. L. Brown, Jr. "Portfolio Assessment Across the Curriculum--Early Conflicts." Three papers presented at the *National Testing Network in Writing*. Minneapolis, April 1988.

Belanoff, Pat, and Peter Elbow. "Using Portfolios to Increase Collaboration and Community in a Writing Program." *WPA: Writing Program Administration* (Spring 1986): 27-40.

Bridwell-Bowles, Lillian. "The Politics of Negotiations: a Case Study of Assessment at a Large University." *National Testing Network in Writing*, Atlantic City, April 1987.

Burnham, Christopher C. "Portfolio Evaluation: Room to Breathe and Grow." *Training the New Teacher of College Composition.* Ed. Charles W. Bridges. Urbana: NCTE, 1986. 125-138.

Camp, R. and Pat Belanoff. "Portfolios as Proficiency Tests." *Notes from the National Testing Network in Writing* 7 (1987): 8.

Ede, Lisa. "Writing as a Social Process: A Theoretical Foundation for Writing Centers?" *The Writing Center Journal.* 9:2 (Spring/Summer 1989): 3-13.

Elbow, Peter. "Portfolio Assessment as an Alternative to Proficiency Testing." *Notes from the National Testing Network in Writing* 6 (1986): 3, 12.

Elbow, Peter and Pat Belanoff. "Portfolios as a Substitute for Proficiency Examinations." *College Composition and Communication* 37:3 (October 1986): 336-339.

-------. "State University of New York, Stony Brook: Portfolio Based Evaluation Program." *New Methods in College Writing Programs: Theories in Practice.* Eds. Paul Connolly and Teresa Vilardi. *Options for Teaching* 9. Joseph Gibaldi, series editor. New York: MLA, 1986. 95-105.

Evans, Peter J.A. "Writing, The English Program, and The Writing Folder." *English Quarterly* (Summer 1985): 44-52.

Ford, James E. and Gregory Larkin. "The Portfolio System: An End to Backsliding Writing Standards." *College English* 39:8 (April 1978): 950-955.

Malbec, Toby W. "Using Interviewing Techniques," *Writing Lab Newsletter* 8 (June 1984): 5-6.

Martin, Wanda. "Dancing on the Interface: Leadership and the Politics of Collaboration." *WPA: Writing Program Administration* 11:3 (Spring 1988): 29-40.

Meyer, Emily and Louise Z. Smith. *The Practical Tutor*. New York: Oxford UP, 1987.

Murray, Donald. "The Maker's Eye: Revising Your Own Manuscript." *Learning by Teaching: Selected Articles on Writing and Teaching*. Portsmouth, NH: Heinemann, 1982. 68-71.

Tutoring Technical Students in the Writing Center

Donald Samson
Eastern Michigan University

As technical professionals in business and government stress the importance of communication skills in the technical professions, and as writing across the curriculum programs develop, more and more faculty in the sciences and technology ask their students to write. In an article that all writing center directors and staff should know, Alfred Powell has described the writing assignments he uses in a course in organic chemistry, assignments with different purposes, formats, and audiences. As Powell and other technical faculty consider what students should write in their courses to prepare them for writing in their work, so too do teachers of professional writing courses. Elizabeth Tebeaux has offered valuable suggestions for writing course design based on surveys and studies of professionals' communication needs.

Such efforts to help technical students develop their writing abilities will increase the numbers of upperclass technical students seeking help in writing centers. Also, the growing number of technical students for whom English is a second language will increase the demand for writing center tutoring. *Newsweek* has reported that "foreign nationals now receive a quarter of the natural-science Ph.D.s and more than half of the engineering Ph.D.s awarded in this country" (53). Consequently, as writing center staff consider how writing centers will change and expand in the next decade, they must consider how to meet the growing need to serve technical students in the writing center.

This essay focuses on writing center tutoring of technical students (majors in the sciences, engineering, computer science, nursing, etc.) by communication students (majors in English, technical writing, journalism, or other areas in the liberal arts). It considers the preparation of writing center staff to tutor technical students and the preparation of technical students for tutoring. Also, it suggests how peer tutoring of technical students can benefit the communication student tutors beyond providing them with teaching experience.

When technical students make use of the writing center to get help with their writing and often with their English in general, it is usually provided by communication students or faculty. (Although some writing centers have technical students able to tutor other technical students in writing, most centers have communication students tutor all the clients.) Technical students and communication students both benefit from peer tutoring in a writing center. Technical students get valuable help with their communication skills, and communication students gain valuable teaching experience. To make peer tutoring as valuable as possible, however, the writing center director should recognize the needs and abilities of both types of students and prepare both groups for the tutoring that will develop their abilities to communicate and prepare for writing in their later work.

As Thom Hawkins noted in an earlier collection of essays on writing centers, writing center staff "face new instructional challenges, but also are in a superb position to make discoveries about language development and composition," when they work with a "new clientele" such as technical writers or Asian immigrants (xiv). Clearly, working with such groups provides valuable educational experience for the tutors in the teaching of writing, but there are some questions about how to make the tutoring as effective as possible. For example, Stephen North suggested that we should test the assumption that peer tutoring benefits a tutor as much as it does a client (33). And university officials outside writing centers and English departments raise questions about peer tutoring. To understand better the problem of using communication students to tutor technical students in the writing center, we might consider two basic questions about tutoring technical students in a writing center. Can writing center staff and writing faculty defend peer tutoring against the attacks of educational leaders who question its efficacy? How well prepared are writing center tutors for peer tutoring of technical students, and how can they be prepared better?

Writing center staff assume that peer tutoring works and we should use it to promote learning by tutors as well as by clients. As Kenneth Bruffee put it, "peer tutoring made learning a two-way street, since students' work tended to improve when they got help from peer tutors and tutors learned from the students they helped and from the activity of tutoring itself" (1984,4).

However, we must recognize objections to peer tutoring. In 1989, William Chace, the President of Wesleyan University, questioned the effectiveness of collaborative learning in a speech to civic and education leaders in San Francisco. Chace said: "The ways in which we cherish democracy and equality have allowed us to permit, and sometimes encourage, the fictitious notion that a classroom of 24 students and one teacher actually holds 25 experts. After two decades of teaching experience, I want to assert that this is not so" (124).

Clearly, Chace extends the argument against collaborative learning (and peer tutoring). We do not expect all (or any) of the students in a class to be experts, and we do not expect writing center tutors to be expert in the various fields represented by writing center clients. Chace is careful to avoid the extreme that some have argued: that collaborative learning is often the blind leading the blind. But Chace's criticism of collaborative learning may have a point: How can tutors help technical students with their writing when the tutors know very little about what the students are writing about in their technical courses, or they are unfamiliar with the types of documents commonly written in the students' fields? How effective can peer tutoring and collaborative learning be when some students do not understand basic terms and concepts from other students' fields? In this situation, can tutors do much more than help with mechanics?

Doubts about the effectiveness of writing center work with technical students often translate into a lack of support for the writing center from department heads and deans in the sciences and technology. But to fund a writing center adequately, directors are finding that they must solicit support from across the disciplines, not just the English Department. To defend peer tutoring in the center, to convince faculty in the sciences and technology that writing center staff will be able to help technical students with writing in their fields and not just with writing in English courses, with writing and not just correction of mechanical errors, the director may need to argue that the peer tutors in the writing center are prepared to tutor technical students.

Some writing center staff automatically assume that peer tutoring is effective. Will we be able to continue to make this assumption without defending it, especially when tutors know very little about what their clients are writing about?

Assessing Tutor's Preparation To Work With Technical Students

Writing center staff often work with technical students enrolled in freshman English or a freshman- or sophomore-level humanities course. Occasionally they work with upperclass or graduate technical students -- and this will more often be the case as prospective employers increasingly stress communication skills. When technical students are working on papers for English and humanities courses, writing center staff are "at home" in the subject matter and can offer suggestions about content as well as organization and style. But when technical students bring to the center assignments in science or technology -- lab reports, for example -- writing center staff are often unfamiliar with the material and consequently cannot help their peers with the content of their writing or with organizational strategies that are content-driven. Writing center staff should remember that technical students are striving to enter a knowledge community different from ours. Can the writing center tutors who are communication students or faculty help technical students enter that community when the tutors are not members of it and perhaps do not even know the basic principles underlying that community?

To illustrate this problem, a quiz for writing center staff. Identify the major accomplishments of the people listed below:

Geoffrey Chaucer	Werner Heisenberg
Fyodor Dostoyevski	Dmitri Mendeleev
Ralph Ellison	Albert Michelson
George Eliot	George Ohm
Nathaniel Hawthorne	Erwin Schrodinger
William Shakespeare	Alfred Werner

Most writing center staff will have little trouble with the names in the list at the left, but they won't do well with those on the right. Gary Olson has observed that "English majors are not necessarily the best tutors; a student with patience, a receptive attitude, and a facility in explaining complex ideas often will prove to be a better tutor than someone who simply displays a good knowledge of the material" (1984b,92). And Linda Bannister-Willis has rightly argued that "literacy is not, or should not be, discipline-conscious. One of the best ways to demonstrate that to the doubting student is to have a center tutor reveal that he or she is a geography major" (138).

How much can writing center tutors help technical students enter the knowledge community they wish to enter when many tutors don't recognize the names of famous scientists, names that technical students learned in freshman physics and chemistry? The problem becomes even greater when tutors try to help students write reports that involve the scientific principles developed by people whose names the tutors don't even recognize. An analogous problem is that of the technical editor who does not understand the subject matter in the document to be edited: all he or she can do is proofread.

In *The Writing Lab Newsletter*, Cheryl Krapohl focused on the common ground of peer tutor and client: "As a peer tutor I have the power that a professor lacks to involve a fellow student in the class work, for the tutee and I are on the same level--we think alike." The idea of peer tutors and tutees thinking alike may be useful when tutors work with freshman composition students and some other clients. But it doesn't always work with technical students who visit the writing center, because peer tutors and technical students may think alike as students, but they often do not know alike.

Preparing Students For Writing Center Tutoring

The recruitment of tutors for the writing center has been addressed by a number of writers, including Joy Rouse, who identifies teacher education majors as good candidates, given their training and interest in teaching. Traditionally, most tutors have been upperclass communication students, although Victor Puma has reported success with first-year students as tutors. One group that has not been utilized as much as it should be is technical writing majors, who will go on to work with technical staff in writing situations in business and government. Upperclass technical writing students should possess the communication skills and interest in science and technology that could enable them (with training) to tutor technical students effectively.

Whatever the tutors' majors, they must be more knowledgeable than the 55% of the respondents to a 1988 National Science Foundation survey who did not know that the Earth orbits the Sun in one year (*Newsweek*, 56). They will need training to tutor effectively. And those who will be tutoring technical students might be given additional training to prepare them to tutor technical students.

One common solution is to have communication students study technical writing. This can be effective, because it introduces students to types of documents technical professionals produce. Technical writing is usually taught on the junior level and above, so that students have at least some upperclass course work in their majors, and some technical background, before they take a course designed to help them communicate information from their fields. But it is not always a good answer, because technical writing courses vary widely in their ability to help students learn how to communicate technical information. But technical writing is often taught at the sophomore level in a four-year school, and this can be very difficult, because the students usually do not have as much technical information to communicate as do juniors and seniors. Then the course becomes an extension of freshman composition, with descriptions of mechanical pencils instead of dorm rooms or Goodman Brown.

If writing center tutors take an upperclass course in technical writing, they will be better prepared to tutor upperclass and graduate technical students enrolled in technical writing courses, because they will have been introduced to the principles of effective technical writing that Fearing and Sparrow have discussed. Most of the students remanded to the center as part of their work for these courses will need help with principles of style and mechanics, but many will also need help organizing and developing material. Clearly, it would be appropriate to have writing center staff only at the advanced undergraduate and graduate levels, perhaps with course work in technical writing. Then the tutoring can be more effective peer tutoring. Upperclass technical students have better command of concepts and principles in their field, and they have a better sense of the writing that work in their fields will require. The upperclass tutors have had more training in writing, and their educational backgrounds are broader (or at least should be). The technical students can teach technical concepts to non-technical peer tutors, through the writing assignments they complete for writing center conferences. And the technical students can learn from those peer tutors how to write better. So knowledge is shared, and the students come to know, not just think, alike.

Many writers have reported that students learn how to teach writing better from tutoring their peers in a writing center. Learning through teaching has been established as a valuable pedagogical technique. But peer tutors can learn much more than how to teach writing better. They should, because many will not go on to be teachers of writing. Although most discussions of writing center tutors assume that the tutors will go on to be teachers, many go on to be writers in business or government. This will be more and more the case as students discover that they can earn far more as technical or business writers than they could as teachers.

To enable writing center tutors as well as technical students to profit from collaborative peer tutoring in the writing center, the director must prepare both groups for peer tutoring.

Preparing Tutors for Tutoring Technical Students

To train students to tutor technical students, the writing center director must be committed to helping people present different kinds of information in different formats. And he or she must encourage that commitment in the writing center tutors. Also, the director should encourage communication students to learn as much as they can about the writing done in their fields. Various articles have addressed the types of writing professionals do; a valuable one by Kitty Locker would be a good place for tutors to begin their research.

One good way to prepare writing center tutors to work with technical students and faculty is to hear faculty in the sciences and technology discuss the weaknesses they see in their students' writing and identify those qualities of writing that are most highly valued in their field. It can be very useful for tutors to learn that in professional work in technical fields, conventional report formats are very common and writers are expected to adhere to them, not reshaping the conventions as some writers of literature have done to achieve greatness. As Dorothy Winsor said, "For an engineer to be accepted as an engineer, he or she must write and speak in the already-created forms and tongues of engineering" (67).

Fearing and Sparrow have suggested talking with technical writing instructors for guidance on tutoring technical students (215-216). More recently, Lady Falls Brown has suggested that having a technical writing instructor speak to the tutors about technical writing can give the tutors "an idea where they might begin when called upon to tutor a technical writing student" (8). These writers do not identify faculty in the students' technical fields as resources, but these faculty (such as Alfred Powell) should be recognized as important sources of information about technical students' writing difficulties and their writing responsibilities in their professional work.

With the guidance of technical faculty, tutors can learn more about what technical students write in their fields. They can identify weaknesses to prepare for before they meet their clients (without expecting the weaknesses and creating a self-fulfilling prophecy). They can help technical students identify the writing skills they will need in their work. And most important, when faculty from the sciences and other fields become more aware of the goals, operation, value, and needs of the writing center, and when the center serves technical students well, the center will enjoy support from across the university.

The guidelines Fearing and Sparrow suggest for training writing center tutors are valuable, but learning about technical writing or even taking a course in it may not be enough preparation to tutor technical students effectively. Often, technical students have difficulty explaining technical concepts or presenting technical information because they don't understand the concepts or information. When this is the case, it will be very difficult for tutoring to be effective unless the tutor understands the concepts or information well enough to recognize that the student's problem lies in understanding the material rather than in communicating it. Only peer tutors with some background in science and technology will be able to help here. Those who have studied technical writing but do not have a technical background might be helpless.

Communication students who tutor technical students should be encouraged to become familiar with basic technical concepts, as preparation for teaching writing or for writing in business or government. A writing center director does not need a technical background to do this. He or she can identify resources that would help writing center tutors gain this familiarity, through handouts as simple as the list of major scientists in the Appendix. Also, the director could arrange for faculty or graduate students in technical fields to speak on concepts from those fields. But the best way to help tutors get familiar with scientists and technical concepts might be to encourage technical students to write about scientific and technical concepts in their field, with the writing center tutors, not professors, as their audience. This serves two useful purposes: the technical students get valuable practice writing for an audience different from technical faculty, and the communication students are introduced to those technical concepts.

A final suggestion for preparing writing center tutors to work with technical students concerns tutors' attitudes. Tutors need to be guided to recognize and address the students' weaknesses in writing but also to appreciate technical students' expertise. As Kenneth Bruffee has said, an important goal of "peer criticism is to increase tutors' respect for other students' minds, and to increase their ability to work collaboratively" (1980b,78). This ability is important because most writing in business and government is collaborative and depends on expertise in different areas. Writing center directors should encourage tutors to respect technical students' abilities and interests, as they must to function effectively as teachers or as writers in business or government. Also, tutors' attitudes will be sensed by technical students and sooner or later communicated to their faculty, who will increasingly be called on to support the center's work.

Clearly, positive reinforcement by tutors is important in developing clients' writing ability. As Gary Olson put it: "The single most important technique to teach tutors is the ability to offer the student positive reinforcement. It is impossible to overemphasize how important this is" (1984c,161). An excellent way to provide that reinforcement is to give technical students a chance to succeed in their writing by asking them to write about something they know about and are interested in. Having them write about technology in order to inform the tutor helps them grasp the concepts of purpose and audience. When tutors guide clients through global writing problems such as audience analysis and organization and postpone work on sentence-level problems until the global problems are solved, the technical students can concentrate on informing the audience. And if they are successful, the tutors can say honestly that they learned from the writing.

Having technical students write about technical subjects is an excellent way to break down the typical power structure in the writing center (in which tutors "know" and clients do not). The writers know, and the tutors become clients resembling the readers the technical students will address in their writing later as professionals in the technical field. Then technical students practice communication to tutor the tutors, and they don't see the work as drudgery.

Preparing Technical Students for Tutoring

Technical students need different guidance to profit from (and contribute to) tutoring in a writing center. In the students' first visit to the writing center, the director and the tutors should encourage the students to plan to discuss their writing center work and their writing with faculty in their departments as well as with writing center staff.

Also, the writing center director could discuss with technical students in their first visit to the center the writing they do in their technical courses and in liberal arts courses, and the differences between the writing they do in school and the writing they will do in their work. For the tutoring to be effective, the students must believe in the importance of effective writing. One way to convince them that writing skills are important is to have them interview professionals in their field about the importance of writing in their work. This assignment works well in technical writing courses, and technical faculty support it as a valuable assignment in technical students' work in the center.

The writing center director should also encourage technical students to bring materials from their technical courses to the center and work with those materials. With this subject matter, the students can feel comfortable in the center and develop a good attitude toward working on their writing. The director should emphasize the importance of writing for non-technical peers as well as for professors of science or engineering or English. Technical students need to be challenged to present basic concepts in their field clearly to the tutors as practice for later situations in which they will present technical information to a lay audience.

In an initial or early conference, directors or tutors should help technical students understand that most writing in business is collaborative, that they will be working with others to prepare most documents they work on. Technical students should be led to see that the writing center situation is one that mirrors how they will handle much of the writing in their work. Tutors can find valuable information about collaborative writing in recent collections of essays such as that edited by Richard Louth and Ann Scott. Also, tutors should recognize the difference in aims of writing in academia and in business. As Kenneth Bruffee put it, "in most academic setting we write mainly to be judged. In real life we write mainly to be understood" (1980b,78). When writing in school is done for evaluation purposes, Joy Ritchie suggests, "Students then leave school conceiving of writing as an act of retrieving a fixed body of information and putting it into a correct form to meet the requirements of the teacher and the institution" (159). Writing center staff should help technical students understand these differences between writing in school and writing at work.

Finally, technical students need to be encouraged to believe in their ability to write, especially if they aren't very good at it. Technical students often are very uneasy in their work in a writing course or in a writing center. They are often considered poor writers because they are poor editors or poor proofreaders, or because they are not adept at analysis of literature or of themselves. Many have been conditioned by English teachers to view themselves as poor writers. The best way to encourage them as writers is to have them write about what they are interested in and what they know about: science or technology. Just as we should not patronize them in writing courses by asking them to write about mechanical pencils or Tinkertoy assemblies, so we should not limit them to analysis of literature or to essays of self-discovery in their writing in a writing center. As writing center tutors develop better understanding of the technical students' fields and report formats and develop assignments that are more appropriate for technical students, technical students will have greater success in their writing, be more positive about their work in the center, and report more favorably about their writing center experience to faculty in their departments.

Benefits For Writing Center Tutors

In addition to valuable teaching experience and other benefits to future teachers summarized by Kenneth Bruffee (1980a,146), writing center tutors gain added benefits from tutoring technical students. As the profession of written communication develops (technical communication is said by the Department of Labor to be the fastest growing field in the 1990's), more and more communication student tutors will enter communication work in business and government rather than teaching. Students who wish to prepare for work in technical or business communications can derive four main benefits from tutoring technical students in a writing center.

First, tutors can gain a truer sense of the kind of people who work in technical fields. Many technical students enjoy mathematics and experimentation in a laboratory setting far more than communication students do. Most have enjoyed chemistry lab far more than English class. They may read as enthusiastically as any literature major, but they tend to read non-fiction or science fiction rather than traditional literature. They don't write like Faulkner (they may never have read him). Odds are they write more like Hemingway (they may have liked something by him). Forget Chaucer, Spenser, Austen, Lawrence, Woolf, Barth, Bellow, etc. So they may not have a great deal in common with their non-technical peers as far as their backgrounds and interests in reading and writing are concerned. But the scientific material they study and delight in can fascinate a writing center tutor who drops his or her guard of ignorance and is willing to learn about it as a peer tutor. (A student who won't drop that guard or develop that interest will not make a good tutor or teacher or professional writer.) Also, tutors who work with technical faculty or graduate students get even broader exposure to technical work and the people who do it.

Second, writing center tutors working with technical students can become familiar with technical terms and concepts. Too few tutors are familiar with basic concepts such as force, mass, acceleration, inertia, gravitation, electricity, magnetism, fission, fusion, oxidation, reduction, metabolism, integral and differential calculus, algorithm development, stress, strain, torque, and moment. Familiarity with these basic concepts would allow tutors to address matters of content in technical students' writing and would prepare tutors for writing work in business or government. Also, these concepts are excellent topics for technical students to write about in their work in the center, and the students' papers can be used to educate other tutors.

Clearly, tutors cannot be expected to understand all of these technical concepts, or even some of them, as well as technical students do. But some familiarity with these concepts can be very useful. Technical students are often remanded to writing centers because they cannot explain such concepts clearly. The work these clients do in the writing center can become writing to learn if their audience, the peer tutors, can ask the right questions to help them understand what they are writing about. Rarely in their work later will technical students present technical material to readers that know nothing about the science or technology involved. In the writing center, they should practice communicating information to readers who have some understanding of the basics. Readers who have some familiarity with the topic rather than none are a much harder audience to write for. Tutors with some technical background can help technical students prepare for that more demanding challenge.

As teachers or writers, writing center tutors will find familiarity with these technical concepts useful in working with technical students or technical staff. Clearly, the tutors cannot master these concepts for or through peer tutoring, but they can gain familiarity with them as they prepare to tutor technical students and by tutoring students who are writing about these concepts.

A third benefit for writing center tutors can be valuable experience helping technical students overcome three main writing difficulties many technical professionals have: competence in English, awareness of audience, and a positive attitude toward writing.

More and more technical students and professionals write and speak English as a second language, as the statistics presented earlier on PhD's indicates. One benefit for peer tutors of technical students in the writing center is the opportunity for tutors to work with ESL students and gain valuable experience for teaching or professional work in writing.

Second, technical professionals have difficulty remembering that non-technical people often know very little about the technology they know so much about and are so interested in. It is important for the writing center tutors to help technical students recognize this. Having the tutors serve as the audience of technical discussions, rather than technical faculty, can help technical students recognize the need to determine the limits of their audience's familiarity with the subject.

A third difficulty technical professionals have with writing is a tendency to see writing as an ancillary burden that detracts from their technical work. When technical students and professionals write, they want to be done with it quickly, to communicate the information and just stop. If writing center tutors understand this attitude, they can explore it with technical students as they revise technical discussions for the tutors. Tutors can help the technical students recognize the importance of developing their subjects adequately when they write documents in their work.

A final benefit for writing center tutors is familiarity with different documents used to present technical information. Technical students will have to produce certain kinds of documents -- proposals, progress reports, feasibility studies, and so on -- and writing center tutors can help technical students learn about those documents.The most basic document technical professionals write, however, the report on laboratory research, is one that more and more writing center tutors are unfamiliar with. Most English majors and other communication students don't have experience presenting observations of behavior and numerical data to support conclusions. They should learn how to, however, so they can work more successfully with writers and with documents that present such information. (Any student considering communications work in business or government should have technical course work that involved laboratory work.) In addition to research reports, it would be valuable for writing center tutors to have some familiarity with technical proposals, to help students and faculty with grant applications in the sciences, which are significantly different from grant applications in the humanities. This is one way a writing center can assist college or university faculty directly, generating greater campus-wide support for the center.

Conclusion

Ten years ago, Leonard Podis described a training course for peer tutors that had at its base the conviction "that the ideal tutor should strive to be knowledgeable and helpful," knowledgeable "about writing and rhetoric" (70). Podis further indicated that he meant "knowledge about language, discourse, and composition." Podis wrote in 1980. In the 1990's we must address better the other knowledge an effective peer tutor in a writing center should have, especially a tutor of technical students. We need to help tutors understand that writing teachers should be familiar with the subject matter their students are writing about, to be able to do more than comment superficially on the process the students are using.

Also, we should make the writing center a clearinghouse of information on effective communication across the disciplines, providing information on effective writing from technical journals as well as from writing journals. Articles by technical professionals such as Norman Cheville can be very useful with technical students and faculty, who tend to value them all the more when the discussions are written or published by specialists in their fields.

As writing center directors and staff investigate new directions for writing centers, we should recognize the need to continue to expand the purpose and activities of writing centers. Writing centers are expanding their clientele to serve the entire college or university, and even a school's neighboring community. As tutors in the centers work more and more with technical students and staff, they need to know more about science and technology, so they can tutor technical clients effectively. If the tutors go on to teach, they will be able to teach writing more effectively to all students. And if they choose not to teach but instead work as writers in business or government, they themselves will be better prepared to write about science and technology.

Appendix

Scientists that Writing Center tutors might investigate to prepare to tutor technical students:

Anders Angstrom
Svante Arrhenius
Amedeo Avogadro
Hans Bethe
Niels Bohr
Ludwig Boltzman
Robert Boyle
J. N. Bronsted
Henry Cavendish
Jacques Charles
Charles Coulomb
Francis Crick
Marie Curie
John Dalton
Louis de Broglie
Christian Doppler
Albert Einstein
Gabriel Fahrenheit
Michael Farraday
Enrico Fermi
Alexander Fleming
Thomas Graham
Otto Hahn
Werner Heisenberg
William Henry
Heinrich Hertz
Irene Joliot-Curie
James Joule
William Thompson, Lord Kelvin
Johannes Kepler
E. O. Lawrence
Antoine Lavoisier

Heinrich Lenz
Joseph Lister
T. M. Lowery
James Clerk Maxwell
Barbara McClintock
Lise Meitner
Dmitri Mendeleev
Gregor Mendel
Friedrich Miescher
Albert Michelson
Robert Millikan
Henry Moseley
Isaac Newton
George Ohm
Blaise Pascal
Louis Pasteur
Linus Pauling
Max Planck
Ernest Rutherford
Frederick Sanger
Erwin Schrodinger
Arnold Sommerfeld
Nikola Tesla
George P. Thomson
Sir J. J. Thomson
James Watson
James Watt
Alfred Werner
Thomas Young
Sonya Kovalevskaya
Henri Le Chatelier

Works Cited

Bannister-Willis, Linda, "Developing a Peer Tutor Program." *Writing Centers: Theory and Administration*. Ed. Gary A. Olson. Urbana: National Council of Teachers of English, 1984. 132-143.

Brown, Lady Falls. "Stable Concept / Unstable Reality: Recreating the Writing Center." *The Writing Lab Newsletter* 14.8 (April 1990): 6-8.

Bruffee, Kenneth. "Peer Tutoring and the 'Conversation of Mankind.'" *Writing Centers*, ed. Olson. 3-15.

----------. "Staffing and Operating Peer-Tutoring Writing Centers." *Basic Writing: Essays for Teachers, Researchers, and Administrators*. Ed. Lawrence Kasden. Urbana: National Council of Teachers of English, 1980. 141-149.

----------. "Two Related Issues in Peer Tutoring: Program Structure and Tutor Training." *College Composition and Communication* 31 (1980): 76-80.

Chace, William. "Do Universities and Their Students Owe Anything to the Future?" Speech to The Commonwealth Club of California, March 17, 1989. *The Commonwealth* 83.13 (March 27, 1989): 124-129.

Cheville, Norman. "Publishing the Scholarly Manuscript." *Veterinary Pathology* 23 (1986): 99-102. See also H. Peter Lehmann, Wanda Townsend, and Philip Pizzolato, "Guidelines for the Presentation of Research in the Written Form." *American Journal of Clinical Pathology* 89 (1988): 130-136.

Fearing, Bertie, and W. Keats Sparrow. "Tutoring Business and Technical Writing Students in the Writing Center." *Writing Centers*, ed. Olson. 215-226.

Hawkins, Thom. "Introduction." *Writing Centers*, ed. Olson. xi-xiv.

Krapohl, Cheryl. "Late Night at the Writing Center: Service Station Or Oasis." *The Writing Lab Newsletter* 14.2 (October 1989): 9.

Locker, Kitty. "What Do Writers in Industry Write?" *The Technical Writing Teacher* 9 (Spring 1982): 122-127.

Louth, Richard, and Ann Scott, eds. *Collaborative Technical Writing: Theory and Practice*. (Association of Teachers of Technical Writing, 1989).

Newsweek. "Not Just for Nerds." 115.15 (9 April 1990): 52-56.

North, Stephen. "Writing Center Research: Testing Our Assumptions." *Writing Centers*, ed. Olson. 24-35.

Olson, Gary A., ed. *Writing Centers: Theory and Administration.* (Urbana: National Council of Teachers of English, 1984).

----------. "Establishing and Maintaining a Writing Center in a Two-Year College." *Writing Centers*, ed. Olson. 87-100.

----------. "The Problem of Attitudes in Writing Center Relationships." *Writing Centers*, ed. Olson. 155-169.

Podis, Leonard. "Training Peer Tutors for the Writing Lab." *College Composition and Communication* 31.1 (February 1980): 70-75.

Powell, Alfred. "A Chemist's View of Writing, Reading, and Thinking Across the Curriculum." *College Composition and Communication* 36 (1985): 414-418.

Puma, Vincent. "The Write Staff: Identifying and Training Tutor-Candidates." *The Writing Lab Newsletter* 14.2 (October 1989): 1-4.

Ritchie, Joy. "Beginning Writers: Diverse Voices and Individual Identity." *College Composition and Communication* 40 (1989): 152-174.

Rouse, Joy. "Tutor Recruitment and Training at Miami University." *The Writing Lab Newsletter* 14.8 (April 1990): 1-3.

Tebeaux, Elizabeth. "Redesigning Professional Writing courses to Meet the Communication Needs of Writers in Business and Industry." *College Composition and Communication* 36 (1985): 419-428.

Winsor, Dorothy A. "Engineering Writing/Writing Engineering." *College Composition and Communication* 41 (1990): 58-70.

More Science in the Writing Center: Training Tutors to Lead Group Tutorials on Biology Lab Reports

Karyn Hollis
Villanova University

A search through the last seven annual bibliographies of writing center scholarship published by *The Writing Center Journal* turned up only one article on tutoring students from the sciences (Feirn). Rare in writing center lore are success stories involving, for example, "A Stratigraphic Study of the Panamanian Isthmus," or "The Chemical Reaction Rate of Chromium EDTA Complexes," or "The Interception of 233Pu Deposition by Fruits." We are far more likely to encounter articles and colleagues describing productive work with students in the humanities or social sciences. Currently, the "hard" sciences don't appear to be central to most writing center activity. This often unrecognized situation presents obvious theoretical, pedagogical and political problems for writing center work. If, as we believe in theory, everyone benefits from instruction in the writing process, our science students are probably deprived. They are unlikely to find the one-on-one tutoring in writing they need anywhere besides the writing center. Relatedly, without writing center experiences, science students probably will not have the opportunity for collaboration and evaluative feedback that research shows improves writing (Diederich 22). They will not learn the value of reader response as a cue to revision. Furthermore, most writing centers are the cornerstones of writing across the curriculum programs on their campuses. If we are not working with science students, can we truly claim to be the campus-wide undertaking we should be? And how long before administrators cite this neglect as a reason to cut funding? In short, writing centers are running serious risks by not strengthening ties to science departments.

Such was the case with the writing center at Dickinson College until very recently. Statistics tabulated at the end of the semester showed that only a dozen or so of our 1,000 appointments were from students in the sciences. Ironically, science faculty were anxious for us to help their students become better writers and had encouraged their students to take papers to the writing center for one-on-one feedback. When students did bring their papers to the writing center, however, both student and tutor complained that the sessions were unproductive. Why? The perception was that the tutor couldn't understand the subject matter sufficiently to comment usefully on science papers or lab reports. While it has been argued that tutor "ignorance" can even be an advantage in the Writing Center (Hubbuch), perhaps this is not the case with science writing where the vocabulary is far more specialized, style and format more prescriptive and subject matter more esoteric (at least for most of us).

We tried to hire more peer tutors from the sciences, but science majors told us that they could not spare the time to work in the writing center. Next we set up peer editing groups in science classes themselves. But while certain benefits accrued from the science students' knowledge of their subject matter, they had no particular expertise in composing, organizing, or polishing their prose. Nor did this approach get science students into the Writing Center, thus reinforcing the impression that what we really did was a writing-in-the-humanities or social sciences.

We finally concluded that the best solution was to have groups of science students meet in the Writing Center with our tutors. The Biology Department was enthusiastic about this method and organized their students in groups for evaluating lab reports. This arrangement combined the biology students' knowledge of subject matter with the tutors' expertise in writing. After some groups had met, however, we began to hear the same old complaint about the tutors: "It is very hard for writing center tutors to help us if they don't understand what we're writing about or how we should write it."

In an effort to attain the respect and confidence of the science students, we decided to rethink our approach. We developed a new way to familiarize ourselves with lab reports and devised a more successful group process for our tutorials. Since many tutors had never even seen a lab report before their experience in the Writing Center and were quite shocked by scientific "jargon," portions of our tutor training sessions were devoted to scientific writing in general and biology lab reports in particular. We called on members of the Biology Department to talk to us. One explained that scientific writing was supposedly clear, direct and simple, yet these characteristics had to be achieved without using the first person pronoun. Scientists rely heavily on passive constructions. "A scientist wouldn't write, 'I poured the acid into the beaker;' she explained, but 'The acid was poured into the beaker.' " We also studied in detail the contents and organization of the lab report. I devised a handout listing the basic requirements of each section. Tutors were surprised to learn that just as the expository essay has a conventional format, so does the lab report. This handout is reproduced below.

Contents of Laboratory Reports[1]

A. Title

1). Summarize in less than 10 words the contents of the report

B. Abstract

1). Include a statement of hypothesis or purpose of the experiment

2). Mention the principle(s) or theory involved

3). Briefly describe the method of experimentation

4). Report the significance of the results.

C. Introduction

1). Give the reader sufficient background (properly documented) to understand the historical development of the concepts and principles under study

2). Define terms in context of the experiment

3). Describe the experimental design and give reasons for choosing this method

4). Present a detailed discussion of the purpose of the experiment, concluding with the hypothesis under consideration

D. Materials and Methods

1). Carefully describe the procedures and equipment used so that replication of the experiment is possible

(A simple statement that you followed the directions in the laboratory manual --properly cited--is often sufficient.)

E. Results

1). Report the data you obtained in the laboratory, organized into tables, graphs, charts, etc., without discussing its implications

2). Present this information in sequence and label it clearly with descriptive titles and numbers

3). Follow tables and charts with brief textual explanations

F. Discussion

1). Relate your findings to existing knowledge on the topic

---

[1]This handout was compiled from information in a leaflet distributed by the Biology Department, Dickinson College; information in Robert Day's book on science writing, pp. 28-55; information from "Appendix D- Writing Lab Reports" of Dolphin's *The Biology Laboratory Manual* pp.380-382; and my own additions suggested by the pedagogical nature of lab report writing.

2). Explain the logic that allows you to accept or reject your original hypothesis.

3). Discuss the theoretical significance and implications as well as any practical applications of your findings

4). Acknowledge and attempt to explain any inconsistencies

5). Make suggestions for the improvement of techniques or experimental design

G. Literature Cited

1). Use Dolphin's version of name and year citation format: e.g., Bird, W.Z. 1980. *Ecological aspects of fox reproduction.* Berlin: Guttenberg Press. 316 pp.

2). Dolphin advises against using footnotes, recommending instead that the author's name and the date of publication be placed in parenthesis in the text. e.g, (Bird 1980).

Although providing this format alone is helpful to peer tutors, becoming familiar with actual lab reports is even better. There is no substitute for studying samples of student prose from the sciences. The Biology Department provided us with sample lab reports for this purpose, and I review them with tutors in the following way. Two versions of every section are juxtaposed to show tutors the strengths and weaknesses of each. Examples of these reports are duplicated below, followed by commentary and criticism. Since we try to coordinate curriculum with the Biology Department, sometimes our tutors will do this same report in their Writing Center peer groups, but even when they encounter different ones, tutors say that seeing the "real thing" beforehand is immensely helpful.

Sample Lab Reports: Mendel's Laws of Heredity as Illustrated by the <u>Drosophila melanogaster</u>

Abstract I: The purpose of this experiment with Drosophila melanogaster was to study and verify important principles of Mendelian genetics. Specific crosses were set up to observe the concepts of dominance-recessiveness, segregation and independence, and autosomal and sex chromosome inheritance, of first and second filial generations. After performing the crosses, the results verified the laws of heredity.

Commentary:

Although countless stylistic and organizational comments could no be doubt be made about each of the writing samples included here, I will point out only the most obvious flaws and successes. As for "Abstract I," tutors will easily see that most of the information called for in the lab report sheet is here. The purpose of the experiment is made quite clear; the particular laws of Mendelian genetics under consideration are listed as well as the physical characteristics (phenotypes) associated with them. However, this writer omitted the important methodological means of the Punnett Square and Chi-square test which are used to determine if the flies produced in the experiment correspond to the theoretical predictions based on Mendelian and other genetic principles. Stylistically, the last sentence, which begins "After performing the crosses ... ," contains a dangling modifier. It is also important to point out the unidiomatic use of "dominance to" instead of "dominance over." Furthermore, the first word of a compound scientific name is capitalized and the entire appellation is underlined (or italicized)

Abstract II: This experiment tested the autosomal and sex chromosome models of inheritance for the traits, eye color and wing size. Here, male and female, wild and mutant <u>Drosophila melanogaster</u> were anesthetized and placed in vials to mate and produce an F1 generation. This F1 generation was then anesthetized and put in fresh vials to mate and produce an F2 generation. In an attempt to predict the phenotypes of the filial generations, Punnett Squares were utilized.

Commentary:

In comparison with the first abstract, this one is clearly deficient. The main problem is that it is overly specific. The purpose of the experiment is not explicitly stated, while the characteristics to be observed ("eye color," and "wing size") are mentioned without an explanatory context. Similarly, the writer detailed a part of the experimental method ("anesthetized and placed in vials)," but did not explain how these particulars fit into an experimental logic. Concerning methodology, Punnett Squares were incorrectly linked to phenotypes, and the role of the Chi-square test was omitted. Worse yet, the results of the experiment were not given.

Introduction I: Mendel's laws are very important in the study of genetics. By using Mendel's principles, it is possible to predict the proportions of offspring phenotypes (physical characteristics) and genotypes (genetic combinations) that result from certain crosses of <u>Drosophila melanogaster</u>. Mendel's principle of dominance and recessiveness states that when an organism is heterozygous, containing two different alleles, only one of the alleles is expressed. This allele is dominant, and it masks the recessive allele. (Johnson, 1983) According to Mendel's law of segregation, an organism has two alleles for every characteristic and these alleles separate during anaphase I of meiosis so that each gamete receives one allele of each homologous pair. (Dolphin, 1983 and Johnson, 1983) Another important principle, the law of independent assortment, says that genes on homologous chromosomes separate independently of each other during meiosis. (Johnson, 1983)

In addition to Mendel's laws, the distinction between autosomal and sex chromosome inheritance is an important concept. Since both males and females have the same autosomes, traits carried on these chromosomes are inherited in the same proportions for both sexes. However, other traits are passed to descendants through the sex-linked genes of sex chromosomes. Because females have two X chromosomes and males have an X and a Y chromosome, the probability of inheriting certain characteristics differs between the two sexes. In <u>Drosophila</u>, for example, the genes for eye color are sex-linked and found on the X chromosome. The genes for wing size, on the other hand, are located on autosomal chromosomes. (Dolphin, 1983)

As discussed by Dolphin in 1983, one of the best experimental organisms used to study genetics is the <u>Drosophila melanogaster.</u> It is a complex organism with relatively few (eight) diploid chromosomes which gives quick results in comparison with other organisms. A hypothesis that can be made about the outcome of the crosses is that the <u>Drosophila</u> will reproduce and distribute genetic characteristics in proportions that correspond to the predictions based on Mendel's laws of genetics.

The Chi-square goodness of fit test is used to determine if the observed results fit the expected results. When there is perfect agreement between the observed and expected results, the value of Chi-square is zero. When the difference between observed and expected results is great, the value *of Chi-square is large. To determine whether it is too large, indicating poor experimental agreement, the calculated Chi-square value must be compared to a theoretical Chi-square value for similar experimental designs. To use the table in the back of the laboratory manual, the degrees of freedom (n) must also be calculated.*

Commentary:

The complexity of the material (at least for the non-science major) becomes readily apparent in the "Introduction" section. But since many of the concepts are defined, tutors may be able to understand them in context. This writer has done a good job of discussing the principles involved and documenting the source of his/her information. An hypothesis is stated clearly; however, there are several problems of content and organization.

Not enough background information is given to place the principles under study in an historical context. A little more information about Mendel and his experiments would be appropriate. Organizationally, the two sentences in paragraph three should be separated. The first one which discusses the advantages of the fruit fly for this experiment would be better placed earlier in the first paragraph. In that way, the reader understands why the fruit fly was chosen for genetic research. The second sentence of the third paragraph seems better as the last sentence of the section, logically following the contextual and background information. The fourth paragraph, which explains the experimental method, is more seriously flawed. Rather than an explanation of how the actual Chi square statistic works, we need an illustration of how the test will help reveal whether or not Mendel's principles are illustrated in the crosses of the Drosophila.

Introduction II: Gregor Mendel, an Austrian monk and scientist, discovered the basic laws of genetics when he worked out a conceptual model of how certain characteristics are inherited in pea plants. No one appreciated Mendel's work until the early 1900's when his theories were verified repeatedly. Mendel's methods provide a sound model for research, in that he asked simple questions, collected data, derived his explanations from analyzing the data, and published his results.

Biologists looked for the best experimental organism to use in studying more complex inheritance patterns. Thomas H. Morgan and others found the common fruit fly to be a perfect experimental animal for several reasons. The fruit flies reproduce in ten to fourteen days, so that results could be quickly obtained. Development goes from fertilized egg to adult, so that morphological, physiological, and developmental inheritance could be studied. And also, the diploid number of chromosomes in the fruit fly is only eight, which allows the researcher to determine on which chromosome a gene for a particular trait is located.

The significant principle being tested here is the appearance of certain traits on sex chromosomes-sex linked genes. Wing size is not a sex linked gene. The results of a cross, for example, between NN and Nn are independent of whether the mother or father has the Nn. However, eye color is sex-linked and the sex of the parents is important due to a recessive gene located on the x chromosome. Since this gene for eye color is located only on the x-chromosome, the male is haploid for that trait. So the genotype for this trait is the same as a homozygous female. The appearance of genes on sex chromosomes affects the occurrence of phenotypes in males and females.

Commentary:

This writer has included more historical information regarding Mendel's work than the previous one, but neglected to define and mention the specific laws of heredity involved in the experiment. The second paragraph is devoted to the rationale behind using the fruit fly for research but gives a little too much detail. In the third paragraph the writer chooses to concentrate on the concepts of autosomal and sex-linked inheritance but neglects the equally important concepts of dominance-recessiveness, as well as Mendel's Laws of Segregation and Independent Assortment. This writer needs to explain how these principles and laws will be illustrated through fruit fly crosses predicted with Punnett Squares and verified with the Chi-square test. Finally, the sources of his/her information need to be properly cited.

Materials and Methods I: Experiments were set up and performed according to the instructions on pages 219-224 in The Biology Laboratory Manual (Dolphin, 1983).

Materials and Methods II: The materials used in this investigation can be found in the exercise on Mendelian genetics. (Dolphin, 1983) The most important supplies were the Drosophila

*cultures. They consisted of red-eyed, normal-winged homozygous flies
and white-eyed, vestigial-winged homozygous flies. The procedures
were followed exactly as written in the lab manual.*

Commentary:
Although brief, the first version of this "Methods" section contains
the necessary information. The title of the biology lab manual should,
of course, be underlined. The second version adds some non-essential
details. The period in the first sentence of this version should be placed
after the parenthetical citation, not before.

Results:

Table 1

F1 Cross: Red-Eyed Normal-Winged Females With White-Eyed, Vestigial
Winged Males

Female Alleles:		$X+N$	$X+N$
	Xmn	$X+Xm\,Nn$	$X+Xm\,Nn$
Male Alleles	Yn	$X+Y\,Nn$	$X+\,Y\,Nn$

$X+=$ *red-eye allele* $N =$ *normal-wing*
$Xm =$ *white-eye allele* $n =$ *vestigial wing*
$Y=$ *sex chromosome without eye-color locus*

*This table shows the genotypes that could be expected from this cross
of F1 generation fruit flies. The phenotypes would include 2 red-eyed,
normal-winged females and 2 red-eyed, normal-winged males.*

Table 2

F2 Cross: Red-Eyed, Normal-Winged and Red Eyed, Vestigial Winged
Females with Red-Eyed, Normal-Winged and White-Eyed, Normal-Winged
Males

Female Alleles		$X+N$	$X+n$	$Xm\,N$	$Xm\,n$
	$X+N$	$X+X+NN$	$X+X+Nn$	$X+Xm\,NN$	$X+Xm\,Nn$
Male Alleles	$X+n$	$X+X+Nn$	$X+X+nn$	$X+Xm\,nn$	$X+Xm\,nn$
	YN	$X+YNN$	$X+YNn$	$Xm\,YNN$	$Xm\,YNn$
	Yn	$X+YNn$	$X+Ynn$	$XmYNn$	$Xm\,Ynn$

This Table shows the genotypes that could be expected from this cross of F2 generation fruit flies. The phenotypes would include 6 red-eyed, normal-winged females; 2 red-eyed, vestigial winged females and 3 red-eyed, normal-winged males; 3 white-eyed, vestigial winged males; 1 white-eyed, vestigial winged male.

Commentary:

Due to the largely numerical nature of the typical "Results" section of a lab report, only one student version is given here, and it is much abbreviated. This writer has done a good job of labeling his/her tables and following them up with explanatory text. We omit this section in our writing center peer group tutorials unless a student has a specific question about his/her data.

Discussion I: An analysis of the data of the F1 and F2 generations shows that, in general, inheritance of eye color and wing type is in agreement with the principles of genetics. The principle of dominance and recessiveness is verified by this experiment. In Table 1 we see that in the cross X+ N with Xm n, all of the offspring had normal wings. This shows that normal wings are dominant over vestigial wings.

To verify the Law of Segregation and the Law of Independent Assortment, a Punnett Square was devised to compare genotypes with the observed phenotypes. For example, in Table 1 we see that the genotype X+ N X+N of the female produces four different combinations (Law of Independent Assortment). Furthermore, each of these combinations contains one gene for each characteristic, X and N. (Law of Segregation) Since the observed results are the same as the expected results, it can be concluded that the Law of Segregation and the Law of Independent Assortment are illustrated here.

The predictions made for the F1 generation, revealed that about fifty percent of the offspring should be males with identical characteristics and fifty percent should be identical females. Looking at Table 1, it is clear that this is true. In other crosses, some unexpected results were observed. These may have come from experimental errors, death of some of the flies, or immature F1 offspring that did not yet emerge from the pupal stage at the time of offspring counting.

The F2 results also corresponded to the predictions made. Table 2 shows the genotypes for one set of crosses performed. The expected ratio was 6:2 or 3:1 for females and 3 :3:1:1 for males. Observed results show this to be the case.

Chi-square tests were used to determine the acceptable variability between the observed and the expected results of crosses II and III of the F2 generation. For three degrees of freedom, 95% of the values should be below 7.8. The Chi-square value for cross II was 3.65 and the Chi-square value for cross III was 4.5. Both of these are acceptable variations. The sexes for crosses II and III can be tested separately. The value for the females of cross II was 6.6, which was acceptable. The value for the males was 12, which was an unacceptable variation. Cross II should have produced a ratio of 3:1:3:1. This discrepancy may have resulted from many of the flies dying. Cross III (Table 2) produced males and females in correct proportions. The Chi-square value for the males was 5, and was acceptable. The value for the females was .797 and it needed to be less than 3.8 to be an acceptable value.

Another important concept studied in the Drosophila was the inheritance of genes found on sex chromosomes. This principle is illustrated by the fact that the males of the F1 generation always had the same eye color as the homozygous female parent. This shows that the eye color gene is found on the X chromosome and not on the Y chromosome. However, by studying the F2 generation (crosses II and III), it can be seen that in some cases the male offspring inherit a different eye color from the female parent. This can be explained by the fact that the females of these crosses are heterozygous for eye color and they can contribute the recessive gene to a male offspring.

Genes for wing characteristics, on the other hand, are found on autosomal chromosomes. By observing both the F1 and F2 generations, it is apparent that the inheritance of wing type has no relation to the sex of the organism. Males and females have an equal opportunity to receive either wing type.

By studying Drosophila melanogaster and comparing the inheritance of traits to known information about genetics, I can accept my hypothesis that Mendel's laws correctly describe how heredity works. One way to improve the experiment and get more accurate results is to put more

flies in each vial so that a greater number of offspring will be produced.
This would also decrease the errors that occur when some of the flies
die.

Commentary:

Most of the requirements for the "Discussion" section are met very
well here. The laws and principles under study are reviewed and the
procedures for verifying them are detailed. Findings are related to
existing knowledge and inconsistencies are explained. In the last
paragraph, the student should be cautioned against using the first person
pronoun as this is not customary in scientific writing.

Discussion II: By performing the Chi-square goodness of fit test for
the crosses, the acceptability of the results can be determined. The
results for cross II of the F2 generation cannot be accepted because the
experimental Chi-square value of 14.96 is greater than the theoretical
Chi-square value for 3 degrees of freedom, which is 7.8. The class data
also cannot be accepted for the F2 generation of cross 11 because its
experimental Chi-square value of 23.94 is greater than the theoretical
Chi-square value for 3 degrees of freedom, 7.8.

The results for the F2 generation of females for cross III had a
experimental Chi-square value of 0.96. This value is less than the
theoretical Chi-square value for 1 degree of freedom, which is 3.8.
Therefore, the variation is within an acceptable limit and results
conform to expectation. The class results for the female offspring of
cross III, however, did not conform to expectation. The experimental
Chi-square value of 22.33 is greater than the theoretical Chi-square
value for 2 degrees of freedom, which is 6.0. The male offspring of
cross III had a Chi-square value of 8.65 and the class data for the male
offspring of cross III had a Chi-square value of 31.72. Both of these
values are greater than the theoretical Chi-square value for 3 degrees of
freedom, 7.8, and, therefore, cannot be accepted as fitting the expected
outcome.

The expected phenotypic ratios for cross III differed for males and
females because the gene for eye color is a sex-linked gene which occurs
on the X chromosome. The allele for red eyes is dominant over the
allele for white eyes. If a male fruit fly receives an X chromosome from
a mother that has an allele for white eyes, he will have white eyes

because the Y chromosome does not carry an allele for eye color. A female fruit fly, because she has two X chromosomes, may be heterozygous for the alleles. Thus, because the gene for eye color is a sex-linked gene on the X chromosome, the expected phenotypic ratios for cross III differ for males and females.

There are a few possible reasons for the fact that the female offspring in the F2 generation in cross III fit the expected outcome, while the male offspring did not. The female offspring pupate before the male offspring. Therefore, the fruit flies may have been counted before all of the males were able to pupate and the observed results would not match the expected results. The flies recorded as having vestigial wings might have been flies which just emerged from their pupal cases, whose normal wings had not yet fully expanded. This mistake seemed to occur where the class data shows offspring where the expected results predict none, such as red-eyed, vestigial-winged flies in the F2.

Commentary:
While this student obviously did the required computations involving the crosses, this "Discussion" section is seriously flawed. It is very difficult to relate any of the mathematical information to the principles of genetics. There is hardly any mention of Mendel's laws; the hypothesis of the experiment isn't given even though the logic of the Chi-square is explained.

Literature Cited I:

Dolphin, Warren D. 1983. The Biology Laboratory Manual. Dubuque: William. C. Brown Company Publishers. 385 pp. Johnson, Leland G. 1983. Biology. Dubuque: William C. Brown Company Publishers. 1105 pp.

Commentary:
The documentation style is flawed. The title of the books should be underlined and only the first word of the title is capitalized.

Literature Cited II:

Dolphin, Warren 1983. Biology laboratory manual . William C. Brown Company: Dubuque. p. 65.

Johnson, Leland 1983. Biology. William C. Brown Company: Dubuque. p.65.

Commentary:
The page numbers are incorrect. They should refer to the total page numbers in the book.

In any tutor training sessions devoted to scientific writing, the recurring stylistic problems typical of this genre should be emphasized. Since science writers avoid the first person pronoun, an overly passive and nominalized style often emerges and wordy, circuitous prose is the result. Other common stylistic problems are misplaced and dangling modifiers, faulty agreement of subject and verb or pronoun and antecedent, and vague referents. Unintimidated by esoteric subject matter, peer tutors should be able to spot these problems easily.

Our group process requires that when the biology students come to the writing center, they bring enough copies of their lab reports to share with all members of their group. The writing center tutors, sometimes working in pairs, lead discussion and begin the session with a review of what the "Abstract" section of a lab report should contain. Rather than going through each lab report from beginning to end and risking long, boring monologues, every student reads his/her"Abstract" section in turn. When all the "Abstracts" have been read and commented on by peers and peer tutors, they proceed likewise to the "Introduction" section, then to "Materials and Methods," "Results," "Discussion" and "References" sections. Using this "comparative" approach, it is generally apparent which student papers have fulfilled the requirements of the section and which haven't. An additional benefit is that each time tutors hear a section they pick up useful information about it. One final point about this process, it is absolutely essential that the biology students understand the notion of collaborative work. It should be carefully explained to them, and they need to be encouraged to help each other. Point out to them that scientists often work in teams.

Using peer group tutorials, we have succeeded in bringing larger numbers of science students into our writing center, and we are beginning to lose our reputation as humanities or social science focused. To do this we had to venture into areas of very unfamiliar subject matter and, perhaps, concern ourselves with content more than we would normally do. But while our tutors have a better understanding of the goals of the experiments, the terminology used, the likely problem areas, etc., they are still far from the level of expertise most biology students have attained. Thus the weight of authority still rests with the student writers. In any case, it could be that writing centers are also more involved in matters of content in humanities and social science than we realize. Certainly the basic form of expository papers with which we are very familiar acts as an heuristic device for generating and evaluating content. At any rate our focus on the form and content of biology lab reports in our tutor training sessions is one that is working for us, and we recommend it to others who are looking for ways to approach the sciences.

Works Cited

Chapman, David W. "Checklist of Recent Writing Center Scholarship: April 1988-March 1989." *Writing Center Journal* 10.1 (1990) 54-58.

Day, Robert A. *How to Write and Publish a Scientific Paper*. Phoenix: Oryx Press, 1988.

Diederich, Paul B. *Measuring Growth in English*. Urbana, IL: National Council of Teachers of English, 1974.

Dolphin, Warren D. *The Biology Laboratory Manual*. Dubuque, Iowa: William C. Brown and Company Publishers, 1983.

----------. "Appendix D: Writing Lab Reports and Scientific Papers." By Warren D. Dolphin. *The Biology Laboratory Manual*. Dubuque, IA: William C. Brown , 1983. 380-382.

---------. "Mendelian Genetics." By Warren D. Dolphin. *The Biology Laboratory Manual*. Dubuque, Iowa: William C. Brown and Company Publishers, 1983. 216-226.

Feirn, Mary. "Writing in Health Science: A Short Course for Graduate Nursing Students." *Writing Lab Newsletter* Jan. 1989: 5-8.

Hubbuch, Susan M. "A Tutor Needs to Know the Subject Matter to Help a Student with a Paper: Agree____ Disagree____ Not Sure____." *Writing Center Journal* 8.2 (1988): 22-30.

Jacoby, Jay. "Checklist of Recent Writing Center Scholarship: April 1983-March 1985." *Writing Center Journal* 5.2 and 6.1 (1986): 46-51.

---------. "Checklist of Recent Writing Center Scholarship: April 1985-March 1986." *Writing Center Journal* 7.1 (1987): 44-51.

---------. "Checklist of Recent Writing Center Scholarship: April 1986-March 1987." *Writing Center Journal* 8.1 (1988): 43-48.

---------. "Checklist of Recent Writing Center Scholarship: April 1987-March 1988." *Writing Center Journal* 9.1 (1989) 61-66.

Johnson, Leland G. *Biology*. Dubuque, Iowa: William C. Brown, 1983.

"Laboratory Reports." Mimeograph. Dickinson College Biology Department. Carlisle, PA: No date.

Creating a Learning Center to Assist Developmental Studies Students Across the Curriculum

Curtis E. Ricker
Georgia Southern University

In the not-too-distant past, schools and their instructors were protected by the fairly widespread belief that students who had not learned had simply not paid attention or tried to master the presented material. Rita and Kenneth Dunn note that in the first half of this century, teachers singled out crowded homes, hunger, family chores, illness, national origin, and religious backgrounds as those factors which caused the lack of academic progress, but those were the days before educators had learned to use intelligence quotient scores, socioeconomic status, or insufficient environmental stimulation as reasons for failures of their students. Later in the fifties and sixties, increased student populations, extensive mobility, and belligerent student attitudes became widely accepted reasons for inadequate achievement (1). Overall, the rapid growth of post-World War II America and the accompanying social upheaval provided additional factors to consider.

During the seventies, however, public opinion gradually underwent a complete reversal, and as a result, in present times the blame for the low achievement of students is often placed directly on the schools, the instructors, and the instructional programs or pedagogical methods that are being used. The public is increasingly focusing its attention on the many functional illiterates who receive diplomas at the various levels of education and who are then pushed out into the job market, only to be condemned to a life of unemployment, marginal employment, or welfare. Public concern has moved from voter unhappiness to taxpayer suits claiming educational malpractice, and as a result, many legislators have voiced anti-education attitudes and submitted bills that would reduce ˋ funding for education while strengthening the accountability laws that would link fiscal support to better performance. Rita Dunn, Kenneth Dunn, and Gary E. Price claim that a series of court actions, each burrowing successively deeper into schools' vulnerability, has focused attention on an individual's right to expect results from his or her education and on a demand for greater accountability from the educational personnel who were supposed to have provided it (420).

Because college instructors are attempting to educate more and more students with varying levels of intelligence and diversified cultural

263

backgrounds, pedagogical methods of the future might need to be different from approaches used in the learning institutions of past years. These disparate students have had varied emotional and psychological experiences, and unlike previous generations, they have also had wide exposure to highly stimulating technology. For some of these students, attempts to place them into a traditional classroom environment and to group them in a manner that is administratively convenient are increasingly unsuccessful without individualizing the instruction that they receive.

Daniel U. Levine maintains that the educational system must recognize that no one standard approach is suited to the needs of all groups of students (143). As a consequence, instructors must be prepared to handle different types of students differently and often must rely heavily on individualized instruction. Such individualization of instruction is not impossible, and it is exactly what many courts and legislatures are demanding. At the federal level, Public Law 94-142 requires the diagnosis, development or related teaching prescriptions, and individualization of instruction for all handicapped persons.

Special laws also apply to the talented and gifted. Musgrave notes that many educators espouse the virtues of individualized instruction, yet few teachers actually practice individualized instructional strategies in their classrooms (ix). With current teaching loads at most institutions, many instructors simply do not have the time to allow for individualized instruction. Because of its effectiveness with special students groups, however, institutions need to develop methods for its use.

One special group of college students who often need individualized attention are the educationally disadvantaged students who populate the growing developmental studies departments in colleges and universities. A useful definition of educationally disadvantaged students was developed by the Florida Community College Inter-institutional Research Council for its 1970 study of compensatory education practices in twenty-four Florida community colleges. This study concerned students "considered to be educationally disadvantaged because of either one or a combination of the following conditions: low ability, low achievement, academic under-preparation, psychosocial maladjustment, cultural or linguistic isolation, poverty, neglect, or delinquency" (Schafer, Boddy, and Bridges 2). Many students from ethnic minorities, because of cultural and environmental backgrounds that have limited access to the majority culture, are also often so labeled (Rees 8).

The Carnegie Commission's 1970 report, "A Chance to Learn: An Action Agenda for Equal Opportunity in Higher Education," indicated that the proportion of blacks in the American college population was less than half of the proportion of blacks in the country's population as a whole and that approximately half of the blacks in college attended predominantly black institutions (15). Harcleroad cites reports from the United States Census Bureau which indicate that working to increase the survival of disadvantaged students will become increasingly important in American education. During the last five years of the 1960's, the number of black students enrolled in college more than doubled. However, in 1970 a clear disparity still existed between the number of whites and blacks who finished college in the twenty-five to twenty-nine year old age group. In this group, only ten per cent of black students and other minorities had completed college as compared with 17. 3 per cent of the white group (140).

Fortunately, however, increasing numbers of black and other minority students are entering higher education. Recent reports in *The Chronicle of Higher Education* note encouraging gains in minority attendance at colleges and universities but caution that the college-going rate for black and Hispanic high-school graduates still continues to trail that rate for white high-school graduates (Evangelauf A1). Indeed, most colleges and universities have made conscious efforts to recruit educationally disadvantaged students from minority groups. While doing so, these institutions must realize the special problems that exist for students moving from culturally deprived environments into the seemingly hostile and foreign culture of the college or university. Gordon Morgan indicates that there are two basically different approaches being taken by colleges and universities in assisting students to meet these problems: the remedial approach and the cultural difference approach. In the first, the colleges place the students into classes designed to remediate academic deficiencies; in the second, the instructors intimately acquainted with the problems of the culturally different group and with the use of methods based on language technology and experiences close to the students teach the students (4). Many programs place heavy emphasis on language training and improvement of communication skills. However, valuable compensatory programs include activities such as tutorial services, special counseling on a group or individual basis, special financial aid programs (including work-study programs, loans, grants, and scholarships), and special housing and classroom facilities.

Developmental studies programs are not, of course, only for minority students. Most colleges and universities have strengthened their remediation efforts in order to increase retention of all students, including minorities. The Carnegie Commission's 1971 report "Less Time, More Options: Education Beyond the High School," reports that while more people are attending college, only about half of entering college students will survive to receive a bachelor's degree (44).

A number of specific services are critical in order to increase the incidence of survival in all forms of higher education. While successful retention of underprepared students depends on many things, most educators quickly assert that a critical ingredient is, as Fred Harcleroad so aptly states, "the relationship between the faculty and the students" (144). Concerned faculty members do make the difference in retention of disadvantaged students. The students need to work closely with their instructors and develop a relationship that encourages learning. And while that relationship begins in the classroom setting, the numbers involved discourage effective remediation.

Because all students differ, their problems differ, and so too must the approaches to remediation for those problems differ. Ideally, an instructor would work out specific strategies for dealing with individual students in response to the information and resources available in each given case; consequently, the first step in the remediation process must be diagnosis. Diagnosis is pointless unless instructors use the information that they gain to shape remedial teaching, and remedial efforts not directed by diagnosis are invariably grossly inefficient. In practice, however, the gap between diagnostic and remedial efforts may be quite real. Unfocused, random teaching is as arbitrary and inefficient as indiscriminate testing and over-diagnosis are.

Instructors can eliminate, or at least narrow, the gap between diagnostic and remedial efforts if they keep in mind the questions for which they intend to find answers throughout the sequence of remedial instruction. The first question instructors need to answer is whether an adapted (more slowly paced instruction), a corrective (repetitive group instruction), or a remedial (individualized instruction) program is appropriate. The answer is important not because it dictates the nature of subsequent instruction but because, in effect, it sets the expectations and establishes the context for the instruction that follows. Having decided, for example, that a particular student is a disabled learner rather than a slow learner, the next question for the instructor is to decide if corrective help is likely to be adequate or if remedial help is also necessary.

The answer depends on the use of careful diagnosis to determine the degree and nature of the disability. The very severely disabled learners may need intensive remedial help outside the regular classroom. Additionally, instructors may also consider the students' reactions to group situations; while one student might benefit from the give-and-take often found in a group setting, another might become hopelessly lost. The make-up of the instructors' classes is also relevant. If a number of students share similar strengths and weaknesses, corrective teaching may be feasible, whereas students with unique problems might best learn from individualized instruction. The instructors need to answer most of these questions, at least tentatively, at the survey level of diagnosis.

At this point, a learning center that is staffed for tutorial work in all areas of the curriculum becomes invaluable. Individualized instruction of the nature that many developmental studies students need for remediation is simply not feasible in the traditional classroom setting at most colleges and universities. If the instructor can refer the student to a trained tutor who can work individually or in small groups with that student, the needed remediation is more likely to occur. Close communication between the instructor and tutorial personnel can guide the individualization of instructional material to match the needs of the student.

Recognizing that the need for supplemental individualized instruction exists in all curriculum areas, some colleges and universities have moved to broaden the role of writing centers to combine writing instruction with studies from all areas of the curriculum in tutorial centers. At Georgia Southern University, for example, tutorial services are provided for all students- -not just those in the Developmental Studies program in a Learning Resource Center, located in the university library. Any instructor can refer students to the Center for help in any subject matter--including writing. In addition, since the Learning Resources Center is one stop on the mandatory orientation tour, almost all students can locate that one area on campus where they can go to get or be referred to help in any subject. This center, which supplements the Writing Center in the English Department, contains both the Academic Computing Center and the Tutorial Center.

Heavily used by students from all subject areas, the Academic Computer Center is equipped with IBM and Apple/Macintosh computers in a networked environment. Many of these stations are linked to the mainframe computers of the university System Computing Network, providing access to Plato, the Cyber, and much computer-assisted instruction. Computer software is also available in multiple subject areas, and student assistants are available to help users. In addition, students are allowed to use this equipment for coursework from any class or personal work.

The Tutorial Center division of the Learning Resources Center offers an alternative to the customary Writing Center approach. Available to any student on campus, the Tutorial Center assists those experiencing difficulty with academic assignments or wishing to improve their academic skills. The peer tutors in the Tutorial Center are supervised by faculty from the Department of Developmental Studies in the areas of English, mathematics, reading, and study skills-- instructional areas covered in the University's Developmental Studies program. One-on-one tutorials are supplemented by small group work, computer-assisted instruction, audio and videocassettes, and selected texts. Faculty from all the academic departments regularly present workshops that relate to specific instructional areas, and tutors from each academic department maintain regular schedules. And because the Tutorial Center has such close ties to the Department of Developmental Studies, those "at-risk" students who are initially placed in developmental studies courses become acquainted with the assistance available from the Center during that crucial transition period of their freshman year.

In order for such a tutorial system to work, close communication between the teacher and the tutoring center must exist. The most basic information obtained through the instructor's diagnosis that must be communicated to the tutor is an estimate of the level at which remedial instruction should begin. Related questions that the instructors might ask are many: What is the exact status of the students' skill mastery in the specific area of difficulty? Do the students have any special problems with motivation? In what areas, if any, are they experiencing success? What additional information can other specialists supply? Answers to questions such as these will direct both the tutors' strategies for remediation and their quest for additional information. Usually, however, the instructor will not be able to gather all of the essential information before the actual remediation begins. In most cases, the teaching process itself will uncover the necessity for additional information which will, in turn, lead to even further diagnosis and modifications in teaching. The tentative diagnosis, however, provides a rationale for the proposed treatment, which then serves as a guide to the first steps in the remediation process.

Again, the learning center tutors must work out specifics of remediation in view of the information and resources that are available in each case. Nevertheless, knowledge about learning principles is extremely useful in the planning of remediation efforts. Perhaps the most important is that the tutors must secure the learners' cooperation. Active participants are more efficient learners than passive spectators, and ultimately, the success or failure of remedial efforts will depend on the involvement of the learners. The individualized instruction that a learning center can offer is a particularly effective remediation strategy, for it helps in establishing a rapport between the tutors and the students, a rapport that encourages learning. Students have a much harder time getting through individual tutoring sessions without participating than they have getting through class sessions. Keeping the students actively participating in the learning is simply much easier in this type of teaching situation. In addition, correct diagnosis is more likely when the student is actively participating in a more individualized teaching situation than when he or she is a passive member of a group.

In addition, effective instruction must also begin on the learners' level. The tutors must constantly keep in mind what the students' present skill development and capacity levels are. Such an awareness is much easier when looking at one student in a one-to-one or small group situation than when facing a whole classroom of people. Furthermore, while the students in a given class may share many of the same needs for remediation, at some point they have individual problems that need to be solved individually. To solve these problems, the tutors of course also need access to and familiarity with a wide variety of instructional materials at various levels which will permit the implementation of individualized instruction. Once again, such teaching occurs more easily in a learning center situation than in a classroom.

To aid remediation efforts, reinforcement of any successes that the students may experience must be available. In many instances, a successful experience provides its own reinforcement. In fact, an underlying assumption of remedial education is that small steps insure correct responses and that these correct responses are rewarding to the learners. A related assumption is that the students will have immediate knowledge of results; they will know whether or not their responses are correct. This latter knowledge is particularly important if the learning experience is to be reasonably self-sustaining.

One of the main attractions of the tutoring situation is the opportunity to provide the students immediate feedback on their learning attempts. Ultimately, of course, the students must come to recognize their own problems and to derive satisfaction from their successes, but as developmental studies students, they will need considerable coaching along the way.

The learning center personnel must also make sure that learning tasks and materials are meaningful. Various research studies demonstrate that students master meaningful tasks and materials more readily than materials that have either limited meaning or tasks that the students do not clearly understand (Mickelson 14). The problem in remediation, however, is not merely to be sure that the presented tasks and materials have inherent meaning, for few instructors actually present useless materials. Instead, the question is whether the materials are meaningful for the particular students and whether the students understand the assigned tasks fully. In order to learn efficiently, students must understand what their instructors are presenting. Interaction with a tutor allows close monitoring of the students' understanding of the materials presented; plus, in a more individualized situation, the tutors can judge more effectively whether or not the given tasks match correctly the students' particular needs. With traditional classroom situations, the teachers usually gear the assignments for the majority of the class members' needs without carefully monitoring how closely the assignments are meeting each individual student's needs. Tutors in a learning center could monitor the individual more carefully, supplementing where necessary with addition work.

For effective remediation, students must also engage in activities that will facilitate remembering. Researchers usually approach the study of memory by studying forgetting, and most psychologists agree that the primary cause of forgetting is interference (Kausler 225). Old learnings tend to stand in the way of new learnings with new learnings tending to blur old learnings because similarities in what a person knows and what that person is freshly learning tend to merge; this merging of old and new learning causes interference with both efficient learning and remembering. Tutors of developmental studies students can combat interference by stressing the unique features of each piece of newly learned material and by making sure that the students understand those features; the clearer the differentiation, the less likely interference will cause forgetting. However, while merging together causes interference and forgetting, a similar process enables students to grasp useful relationships and to generalize; consequently, tutors should not refrain from pointing out the similarities and relationships between the old and the new learning when appropriate.

But transfer to new tasks and situations is better when students are able to discover important relationships and generalizations for themselves. Consequently, the learning sequence should be structured so that students are lead to the place where relationships and generalizations are clear and where self-discovery is the next step. The teachers' role, then, is not to impose relationships but to provide the setting that permits them to emerge. The necessary next step is to provide opportunities for the students to apply the relationships they have learned. Because the students often need individual help and attention as they attempt to generalize about what they are learning, learning centers can be an excellent place for drawing from the students the relationships and similarities that they see among the ideas they are studying. Such personal attention simply cannot be done to the same extent in the traditional classroom setting.

With some tasks, the best method for facilitating remembering is to provide for overlearning. In the basic skills area, repetitive practice or drill may help to teach a number of tasks through overlearning. Once more, the learning center is an ideal situation for such an activity. Computer-assisted instruction may also be useful for these repetitive drills. By performing such procedures over and over again, students can remember the process for when they must perform on their own. When working with the students in an individualized setting, the tutors can judge effectively how much repetition is needed and the point at which mastery occurs.

Evidence clearly indicates that spaced or distributed practice will produce better results than massed practice (Underwood 245). Studies also suggest that spaced practice does improve long-term retention (Keppel 110). Other research indicates that spaced practice may be preferable because it permits the dissipation of reactive inhibition (Otto 14). Reactive inhibition is a negative drive that results from sustained performance, and its effect is decreased learning efficiency. For these and other reasons, developmental studies students need to schedule frequent work sessions that are shorter than the traditional class and that may occur more frequently. The individuality of the learning center allows for this flexibility.

Still another benefit of the individualized attention that students can receive in a learning center is the accessibility to the students so that the tutors can monitor motivation. Motivation that is too intense is likely to be accompanied by distracting emotions and limited cue utilization, both of which interfere with efficient learning. Some researchers have suggested that learning is facilitated until motivation reaches an intermediate level and that any further increase in motivation results in decreased learning efficiency (Weiner 885). Intense motivation appears to be particularly debilitating when the learning task is complex. Movement along a continuum that goes from healthy achievement motivation to anxiety to fear will differ greatly from student to student, so generalizing about optimum motivation for individuals is difficult. Tutors who are sensitive to symptoms of anxiety and fear, however, can adapt their motivational techniques as needed. Some students may need a great deal of constant encouragement while others may resent it. The learning center provides the ideal setting for dealing with such personal, individualized problems and for helping students maintain a sense of balance, for the tutor can monitor each student individually and change when needed, a feat that an instructor would find most difficult -- if not impossible -- to accomplish in the classroom.

Some years ago Ernest Hilgard expressed his belief that a person's tolerance for failure is based largely upon a backlog of success (486). Students who have a past history of success experiences in learning have that history to sustain their efforts when they encounter difficulty. Developmental studies students, on the other hand, expect to fail in academic areas and have little reason to try again when they fail at a given task since they lack a backlog of success. An extremely important function of the learning center tutors, then, is to see that all of the students add to their stores of success experiences, for a reserve of success experiences will help to sustain the students in their other efforts. Because of the increased personal contact time with each student, the learning center provides a perfect opportunity to provide positive feedback on the good performances of the students, thereby increasing their reserves of success experiences. The students can be praised for each successful application of learned material as they actually work.

In short, individualized instruction that a learning center allows in all areas of the curriculum may be an extremely valuable pedagogical strategy, particularly for meeting the needs of high-risk developmental studies students. With its roots in the teaching methods of classical times, such a strategy recognizes the need to teach the whole person. Through the various activities in which the students at the learning center participate, they are able to focus on their individual problems, obtain the necessary help they need to remediate those problems, and learn through immediate feedback how effectively they have mastered the necessary material. Also, in addition to the academic help that they receive, the students who participate have the opportunity to develop a close working relationship with their tutors, a relationship that helps foster learning through the development of self-esteem and confidence. For these reasons, it is a particularly effective teaching method for remediation and for retention of disadvantaged students, a group of students who benefit greatly when given personal, individual help.

Works Cited

Carnegie Commission on Higher Education. *A Digest of Reports of the Carnegie Commission on Higher Education.* New York: McGraw, 1974.

Dunn, Rita, and Kenneth Dunn. *Teaching Students through Their Individual Learning Styles.* Reston: Reston, 1978.

Dunn, Rita, Kenneth Dunn, and Gary E. Price. "Diagnosing Learning Styles: A Prescription for Avoiding Malpractice Suits." *Phi Delta Kappan* 58.5 (Jan. 1977): 418-20.

Evangelauf, Jean. "1988 Enrollments of All Racial Groups Hit Record Levels. " *The Chronicle of Higher Education.* 11 April 1990, A :1+.

Harcleroad, Fred F. "Disadvantaged Students and Survival in College. " In *New Teaching, New Learning,* edited by G. Kerry Smith, 138-148. San Francisco: Jossey-Bass, 1971.

Hilgard, Ernest Ropiequet. *Theories of Learning.* 2nd ed. New York: Appleton, 1956.

Kausler, Donald H. *Readings in Verbal Learning.* New York: Wiley, 1966.

Keppel, Geoffrey. "Facilitation in Short- and Long-Term Retention of Paired Associates Following Distributed Practice in Learning." *Journal of Verbal Learning and Verbal Behavior* 3 (1964), 91-111.

Levine, Daniel U. "Differentiating Instruction for Disadvantaged Students." *The Educational Forum* 30. 2 (Jan.1966): 143-46.

Mickleson, Norma I. "Meaningfulness: A Critical Variable in Children's Verbal Learning." *The Reading Teacher* 23 1969): 11-14.

Morgan, Gordon D. *The Ghetto Student: A Descriptive Essay on College Youth from the Inner City.* Iowa City: The American College Testing Program, 1970.

Musgrave G. Ray. *Individualized Instruction: Teaching Strategies Focusing on the Learner.* Boston: Allyn, 1975.

Otto, Wayne. "Reactive Inhibition as a Contributor to School Failure." *Journal of Special Education* 1 (1966): 9-15.

Rees, Helen E. *Deprivation and Compensatory Education: A Consideration.* Boston: Houghton, 1968.

Schafer, Michael I., Eugene Boddy, and Winston T. Bridges, Jr. *Implementing the Open Door: Compensatory Education in Florida's Community Colleges; Phase I: Questionnaire Analyses.* Florida Community Junior College Interinstitutional Research Council, 1970.

Underwood, Benton J. "Ten Years of Massed Practice on Distributed Practice." *Psychological Review* 68 (1961): 229-47.

Weiner, Bernard. "Motivation." In R. L. Ebel and V. Noll (Eds.). *Encyclopedia of Educational Research.* 878-88, 4th ed. New York: Macmillan, 1969.

Writing Centers In Context:
Responding To Current Educational Theory

Christina Murphy
Texas Christian University

Having come into prominence in the last forty years as an important aspect of supplemental instruction, writing centers are essentially constructs of the postmodern world. As such, they reflect the educational philosophies and socio-political currents shaping American society and contending for paramountcy in the second half of the twentieth century.

In *Education Under Siege*, Stanley Aronowitz and Henry A. Giroux describe this conflux of competing ideologies as "the conservative, liberal and radical debate over schooling" (iii). The conservative perspective envisions a schooling system in which "the mastery of techniques is equivalent to progress" (2). The model that underlies the conservative perspective is that of education as a type of regimented and highly authoritarian training for future roles within society.

The liberal vision is of schooling "as a broad preparation for life, as an effective means to reproduce the kind of society and individual consistent with western humanist traditions" (5). The paradigm that guides this view is that of liberation, the vast capacity education possesses for freeing -- through intrapersonal enrichment -- the varied capacities individuals are endowed with as pre-actualized potentials.

The radical view conceptualizes the process of education as a microcosm of the power relations and oppositional politics that exist in any society and any historical era. Educators, thus, "are, perhaps unwittingly, clerks not only of the state, but also of the class that dominates it," and they exemplify the Marxist view that "the ruling ideas of any society are the ideas of the ruling class" (6). Like the liberal view, the radical paradigm envisions education as liberatory but adds a broader dimension to this concept by emphasizing that schools should "promote ongoing forms of critique and a struggle against objective forces of oppression" (Giroux xviii).

The contemporary concept of the writing center has emerged from the matrix of these conflicting ideologies and the responses to educational issues favored by each. Initially, in the 1940's and 50's, writing centers were established to address the instructional problems of weaker students by strengthening their writing and critical thinking skills and thus better preparing them for the academic experience (North

276

436). Since the early writing centers were extensions of English departments, they emerged from the humanities as their root discipline and embodied the liberal concept of developing students' potentials and facilitating their intellectual growth.

Interestingly, though, the writing centers formulated upon this basis also served to foster the conservative agenda of having task-oriented students working to achieve the "markers," or measurable objectives, by which both intellectual progress and mastery of the techniques of literacy could be measured. The result of this inadvertent merging of objectives was a difficult, if not uneasy, alliance that has affected the design and axiological underpinnings of writing centers ever since.

From the conservative perspective, writing centers are effective when they advance a student's mastery of skills -- specifically, grammar, mechanics, vocabulary, and sentence complexity and variety. The energy of the conservative view pushes writing centers in the direction of becoming remediation centers to rectify deficiencies in the language arts training students are expected to have received in high schools. Writing centers should serve, too, the ancillary purpose of diagnostic assessment of students to detect weaknesses and to offer supplemental, corrective instruction, often of a drill/review nature. Philosophically, there is an "overwhelming emphasis on immediate, empirically measurable objectives" and "a tendency to consider such short-term prespecified outcomes (behavioral objectives, skill acquisition, grade equivalency achievement) as conceptually adequate to guide research and development" (de Castell, Luke, MacLennan 4).

From the liberal perspective -- in which literacy education is the catalyst for the empowerment of intellectual abilities -- the conservative model of the writing center (and of literacy education) is anathematic. It represents reductionism by asserting that a complex intellectual task like writing can be understood in terms of a mechanistic model of parts being put together to make a whole. The concomitant focus upon learning these separate parts as "skills" narrows the time and attention given to higher-level cognitive processes -- specifically those involved in the formulation and evaluation of ideas -- and de-emphasizes their value. Equally reductive is the role of the tutor, who functions as a quasi-technician in diagnosing skill levels and designing appropriate models for remediation that will produce the highest number of measurable results for the largest number of students in the shortest time frame.

Within the liberal model, recognition is given to the nature of the bond established between tutor and student that facilitates learning through individual attention and instructional approaches. Students learn how to develop their analytical and critical thinking skills through dialogic exchanges with the tutor. The paradigm for this method is apprenticeship learning in which the craft of writing is learned by an apprentice writer from a more experienced and knowledgeable writer, the tutor, who is also able to articulate aspects of his or her craft. The tutor is, in essence, an additional instructor who supplements and enhances the learning processes initiated by the classroom teacher, and the tutor's teaching skills and capacity to guide students in their learning processes are highly valued. Obviously, this factor is considerably more difficult to measure than the factors that can be quantified under the conservative model.

As writing center practice sought to address the changes in education that occurred in the 1960's and 70's, the tension that had existed in attempting to balance the philosophical and methodological oppositions inherent in the conservative and liberal models was intensified by three factors: the shift in pedagogical emphasis in writing instruction from product to process; increased enrollments in writing classes and the emergence of radical challenges to the value of the educational process as traditionally structured.

With the shift in pedagogical emphasis in writing instruction from the written product -- which focused upon the formal aspects of writing (such as grammar and mechanics) -- to the writing process -- which emphasized the cognitive acts involved in composition--it became clear that writing and the teaching of writing were much more complex acts than originally imagined (Moffett 195). This focus upon the writing process of each individual writer contributed to a backlash against the conservative philosophy with its strong emphasis upon normative standards of instruction and assessment and a concomitant "rediscovery" of the liberal emphasis upon the uniqueness of each student as a learner.

To many writing theorists and instructors, writing centers seemed to be an important medium for addressing both the formal and cognitive aspects of writing instruction by providing students access to training in the fundamentals of written expression as well as tutoring in the heuristics involved in conceptualizing the writing process as a whole. In addition, the emphasis writing centers placed upon tutorial conferences reinforced the uniqueness of the student as a learner whose intelligence, talents, and writing processes could not effectively be addressed by the unitary practices of the conservative model.

Increases in college and university enrollments during the 1960's and 70's and proportional increases in the number of students assigned to writing classes greatly accelerated the use of writing centers as a form of supplemental instruction. Writing instructors who had from two to four classes of twenty-five students or more often found they simply could not focus the amount of time and attention necessary to help each student develop ideas dialectically and to mature in his or her writing skills. If, for example, a teacher were to meet individually for a half hour with 100 students in a single week, that teacher would be conferencing for 50 hours -- a gargantuan, if not impossible task, given that teacher's additional academic duties. Thus, the writing center, with its emphasis upon providing tutoring to students and complementary instructional assistance to the writing teacher, seemed a practical, effective, and pedagogically sound medium for providing an institutional response to important needs in writing instruction.

How this institutional response was to be shaped, however, brought writing centers into conflict once more with the opposing philosophies of the conservative and the liberal models. The liberal response is perhaps best exemplified by Stephen M. North in "The Idea of a Writing Center":

> Maybe in a perfect world, all writers would have their own ready auditor -- a teacher, a classmate, a roommate, an editor -- who would not only listen but draw them out, ask them questions they would not think to ask themselves. A writing center is an institutional response to this need . . . .Writing centers are simply one manifestation--polished and highly visible -- of a dialogue about writing that is central to higher education. (439)

The conservative response to this same situation of increased enrollments and larger class sizes in writing courses, coupled with the expansion of the educational process in the 1960's and 70's to admit a wider range of differently prepared students, was to focus upon the writing center as an institutionally sanctioned medium for recodifying educational processes of instruction and assessment. The call was for writing centers to exemplify a return to instruction in the basics and to work toward a hegemonic sense of the educational enterprise.

Ironically, the strength of this demand was intensified in the 60's and 70's by the emergence of the computer as a technological tool for writing instruction. The inclusion of computers and software for literacy instruction in the educational process represented a significant philosophical statement, for, as Harry Braverman indicates in *Labor and Monopoly Capital*, technology embodies social relations, and the computer is value-laden. Aronowitz and Giroux phrase this position even more compellingly:

> We would argue that the introduction of computer mediated learning, often presented entirely in its technological mode, is only part of a larger shift in the ideology of schools, proposed by conservatives and rapidly becoming hegemonic in all discussions of the [literacy] "crisis." This larger shift proposes that school ambience no longer conform to the surrogate family metaphor, but more or less self-consciously adopt a market orientation in the learning process itself. (190-91)

Walter J. Ong voices the liberal objection to this view by arguing that "deep familiarity with complex technologies encourages taking machines as models for everything; ultimately it encourages thinking of consciousness itself as simply a technology and even of the human being as a kind of machine" (190).

While the conservative philosophy encouraged writing centers to embrace a hegemony of educational standards and objectives, the radical perspective argued for the ideal of counterhegemony. In the radical view, writing centers should serve as advocates for literacy by respecting and encouraging multiple literacies rather than by enforcing only one definition of literacy -- or literacy with a capital L.

As the conservative pressures intensified for the type of competency testing that emphasized one definitive standard for assessing cognitive skills and writing abilities in our culture, feminist and Marxist critics found an ally in writing centers that emphasized a multiplicity of approaches to writing instruction and assessment. Writing centers, with their focus upon individual tutorials and one-on-one assessments of students' writing skills as well as their avowed and actual function of serving a myriad of student populations with different language skills and belief systems, could serve as an alternative to competency tests that emphasized normative rather than individual concerns. Proponents of feminist and Marxist rhetorical theory argued that focusing upon ways that writing centers could emphasize multiple views of writing instruction and assessment and could incorporate these perspectives into university-wide writing programs provided one of the richest and most challenging opportunities for change within the university.

While the conservative, liberal and radical views of how education is to be conducted represent socio-political formulations and develop from historical influences, these opposing positions also represent differing philosophies of the function of knowledge within a culture. Certainly, within the conservative model there is an effort to incorporate into writing instruction the objectivity traditionally associated with the sciences and to reconceptualize the process of literacy education as a social science rather than as a branch of the humanities.

In contrast, the liberal and radical perspectives reject the false scientism of the conservative model and propose, instead, an interpretive or hermeneutic approach that embraces ambiguity and denies the relevance of positivist goals to literacy education. Louis A. Sass in "Humanism, Hermeneutics, and the Concept of the Human Subject," for example, argues that

.. both humanists and hermeneuticists are heirs to the intellectual tradition of Romanticism, itself largely a reaction against the Enlightenment tradition of objectivism. . . . Indeed, both these groups can be called *humanistic* in a broad sense -- if by this we mean committed to developing an approach respectful of the special characteristics of human experience and action, and free of the positivism, mechanism, and reductionism of 19th-century physical sciences and the social sciences modeled on them. (222)

Philosopher Jurgen Habermas conceptualizes the conflict between these two positions of scientism and humanism as a struggle between differing "cognitive interests," which, in turn, generate their own rhetorics and epistemologies. Scientific rhetoric is "empirical-analytic" discourse underlain by a technical interest in interpreting and controlling natural phenomena. Humanistic interests involve a "historical-hermeneutic" discourse in which there is an emphasis upon understanding meanings rather than upon interpreting data objectively (*Knowledge* 197). Jerome D. Frank argues that "the fundamental problem may be that traditional scientific methods have been devised to discover relationships between facts, that is, objectively definable, measurable, repeatable phenomena. Facts can be confirmed or disconfirmed by the objective criteria of the scientific method; meanings cannot" (298).

Frank's focus on meanings and Habermas' assertion that the rhetoric of each discipline or "cognitive interest" represents a meaning-making activity that structures an epistemology raise interesting questions over what role writing centers are to play in present and future debates about literacy education. All theorists, for example, whether conservative, liberal, or radical, tend clearly to perceive literacy "as a source of autonomous behavior, and illiteracy is presumed to contribute to powerlessness; literacy is mind-expanding and a source of freedom; illiteracy is a cause of enslavement" (Stevens 7). The debate, thus, is not over the value of literacy, but over the means by which literacy is to be valorized and implemented as a societal objective. Paulo Freire, for example, in *Pedagogy of the Oppressed*, argues that definitions of what shall constitute literacy and who shall possess this knowledge are intimately connected with the power relationships that structure historical eras, and W. Ross Winterowd states in *The Culture and Politics of Literacy* that "defining literacy is not idle semantic debate or academic hair-splitting but is almost always a consequential political act" (4).

At present, writing centers seem caught up in the debate between the conservative emphasis upon empiricism and the "technicization" of writing instruction and assessment and the liberal and radical goal of "conscientization" described by Freire in *The Politics of Education: Culture, Power, and Liberation*:

> The starting point for such an analysis must be a critical comprehension of man as a being who exists in and with the world. Since the basic condition for conscientization is that its agent must be a subject (i.e., a conscious being), conscientization, like education, is specifically and exclusively a human process. It is as conscious beings that men are not only in the world but with the world, together with other men. Only men, as "open" beings, are able to achieve the complex operation of simultaneously transforming the world by their action and grasping and expressing the world's reality in their creative language. (68)

One response to the dilemma created by the two different epistemological views of literacy that John Wilson calls the "society-oriented or utilitarian purposes" and the "purposes benefitting the individual human being as such, not as a role filler in a particular society at a particular time" (30) resides in Habermas' description of a third sphere of intellectual activity, or "cognitive interest," which he defines as the "empirical-critical." Using Marxism and Freudian psychoanalysis as examples, Habermas contends that empirical-critical intellectual activity is characterized by an emancipatory interest combined with a capacity to reflect critically upon the fundamental premises of one's own epistemology and ideology. As Habermas states, "The critiques which Marx developed as a theory of society and Freud as metapsychology are distinguished precisely by incorporating in their consciousness an interest which directs knowledge, an interest in emancipation going beyond the technical and the practical interest of knowledge" (*Theory*).

Since it is apparent that contemporary writing centers are involved with both dimensions of knowledge as Habermas defines them, the emancipatory and the technical/practical, they offer potentials for what Freirean critics describe as the capacity for transcendence. As Henry Giroux explains in his introduction to Freire's *The Politics of Education*, "As a referent for change, education represents a form of action that emerges from a joining of the languages of critique and possibility" (xiii). Salvatore R. Maddi, in an interesting essay titled "On the Problem of Accepting Facticity and Pursuing Possibility," discusses the potentials for possibility in this fashion:

> It is clear that, according to existentialism, the best thrust of human functioning is toward possibility. Minimizing facticity leaves one's options open for personal growth through new experiences. This way lies freedom, renewal, richness, sensitivity, deepening understanding, sophistication in the best sense. But facticity cannot be avoided completely. It is inherent in our experience, not only in our own limitations, but also in what we have become, even if in that becoming we have pursued possibility vigorously. Hence, our sense of what is possible is intertwined with what we perceive as given, and the dynamic balance between the two gives our lives its particular flavor. (183)

Both Giroux and Maddi focus on a "sense of what is possible" within the given constraints of facticity. Ironically, for writing centers, the "dynamic balance" between possibility and facticity is more difficult to attain than for other components of the educational system, largely because writing centers are administrative constructs of the present century and are not a discipline in the traditional sense of the arts, humanities, natural sciences, and social sciences. As a result, writing centers come into being to address specific needs on specific campuses, and the pragmatic truth or "facticity" is that writing centers reflect and serve the "social context" of which they are a part. Winterowd states that "literacy is always grounded in a social context" (11), and so, too, is the significance of any writing center.

On most college and university campuses, writing centers are instructional hybrids composed of a balance between administrative aims and the traditional practices of writing instruction that reflect writing centers' early alliance with English departments directly and indirectly with the humanities. From different perspectives, this hybridism represents, at once, the limitations of writing centers in educational settings and their transformative possibilities. Essentially, the dispute centers upon whether writing centers will serve instructional aims of self-efficacy and self-enrichment or administrative aims of the quantitative assessment of identifiable literacy skills.

This dispute, however, is not so easily dichotomized, for what also needs to be considered is the enormous power writing centers possess, by virtue of their very hybridism, to bridge administrative and instructional aims through what Toby Fulwiler describes as a "comprehensive long-term program to develop more fully all the interrelated learning and communication skills of the whole campus community" (124). Thom Hawkins states that "the growth of writing centers is but one part of a search for new vitality in the humanities" (xi), indicating that a major aspect of a writing center's ability to generate a new vitality in the humanities is the writing center's capacity to bridge disciplines in a common search for the most effective long-term methods to instruct students and encourage their intellectual growth. In this regard, a writing center can serve as a true "center" for an outreach amongst disciplines, and even for a community and regional outreach that offers the type of transformative and liberatory educational experiences described by Freire in which philosophy and practice join for social transformation. Hawkins also focuses upon the important outreach role writing centers play in assisting faculty with writing

instruction and in drawing faculty from a range of disciplines into the
structuring of writing curricula:

> If writing centers are to continue making substantial
> contributions to classroom practices and curricula, if they
> are to reach a productive and long-lasting maturity, they must do
> more than patch together fragments of successful practices. To
> begin with, writing centers can ally themselves with faculty who
> are redefining what it means to teach writing. Writing centers are
> not alone in meeting the challenge of teaching the new
> constituency of nontraditional students and the new methodologies
> of collaborative learning. Faculty from various departments look to
> the writing center for knowledge and expertise in these areas, but
> also for a place to share experiences, to compare notes .... In
> years to come there will be an increasing demand on writing centers
> to participate in campuswide efforts to improve the teaching of
> writing. (xiii)

The potential writing centers have to transform the rhetorical
communities of college and university campuses by extending and
redefining the dialogue on literacy education represents their most
significant power and makes them agencies for change within
academics. In composition studies' efforts to define a metatheory and
metamethod to address such questions as "what topics and problems
should a field address? What relations hold among theories? What
grounds would justify choosing one over another?" as Louise Wetherbee
Phelps suggests in *Composition as a Human Science* (183), clearly
writing centers can play an important role--precisely because they are
hybrids of the two most pervasive and influential conflicts of
interpretation operating in American society today, "between positivist
or objectivist modes of inquiry and interpretive ones, more relativistic
and subjective" (Phelps 184).

Developing out of and exemplifying both traditions of theory and
method, writing centers manifest the potential inherent in the bridging
of different discourse communities. Defining toward what ends this
potential will be used represents one of the more significant and
challenging issues affecting literacy education today. Since each of the
philosophies of education, the conservative, liberal, and radical, makes
legitimate claims on what the character and identity of a writing center
should be within the educational system, determining whether writing

centers will be humanistic or technopragmatic; hegemonic or counterhegemonic; liberatory or objectivist; multi-disciplinary in outreach or centripetal in focus; remedial or multi-based are all important challenges that will need to be addressed as writing center practice moves forward into the next century.

Works Cited

Aronowitz, Stanley and Henry A. Giroux. *Education Under Siege.* South Hadley: Bergin & Garvey, 1985.

Braverman, Harry. *Labor and Monopoly Capital.* New York: Monthly Review Press, 1974.

de Castell, Suzanne, Allan Luke, and David MacLennan. "On Defining Literacy." *Literacy, Society, and Schooling: A Reader.* Ed. Suzanne de Castell, Allan Luke, and David MacLennan. Cambridge: Cambridge U P, 1986. 3-14.

Frank, Jerome D. "Psychotherapy, Rhetoric, and Hermeneutics: Implications for Practice and Research. *Psychotherapy* 24 (1987): 293-302.

Freire, Paulo. *Pedagogy of the Oppressed.* New York: Seabury, 1973.

--------. *The Politics of Education: Culture, Power, and Liberation.* South Hadley: Bergin & Garvey, 1985.

Fulwiler, Toby. "How Well Does Writing Across the Curriculum Work?" *College English* 46.2 (1984): 115-25.

Giroux, Henry A. Introduction. *The Politics of Education: Culture, Power, and Liberation.* By Paulo Freire. South Hadley: Bergin & Garvey, 1985. xi-xxv.

Habermas, Jurgen. *Knowledge and Human Interests.* Boston: Beacon, 1970.

--------------. *Theory and Practice.* Boston: Beacon, 1973.

Hawkins, Thom. Introduction. *Writing Centers: Theory and Administration.* Ed. Gary A. Olson. Urbana: NCTE, 1984. xi-xiv .

Maddi, Salvatore R. "On the Problem of Accepting Facticity and Pursuing Possibility." *Hermeneutics and Psychological Theory: Interpretive Perspectives on Personality, Psychotherapy and Psychopathology.* Ed. Stanley B. Messer, Louis A. Sass, and Robert L. Woolfolk. New Brunswick: Rutgers U P, 1988. 182-209.

Moffett, James. *Teaching the Universe of Discourse.* Boston: Houghton Mifflin, 1968.

North, Stephen M. "The Idea of a Writing Center." *College English.* 46.5 (1984): 433-46.

Ong, Walter J. "Reading, Technology, and Human Consciousness."
Literacy as a Human Problem. Ed. James C. Raymond.
University: U of Alabama P, 1982. 170-201.

Phelps, Louise Wetherbee. *Composition as a Human Science:
Contributions to the Self-Understanding of a Discipline*. New
York: Oxford U P, 1988.

Sass, Louis A. "Humanism, Hermeneutics, and the Concept of the
Human Subject." Messer, Sass, Woolfolk 222-271.

Stevens, Edward W., Jr. *Literacy, Law, and Social Order*. DeKalb:
Northern Illinois U P, 1988.

Wilson, John. "The Properties, Purposes, and Promotions of
Literacy." *Literacy, Society, and Schooling: A Reader*.
Ed. Suzanne de Castell, Allan Luke, and David MacLennan.
Cambridge: Cambridge U P, 1986. 27-36.

Winterowd, Ross W. *The Culture and Politics of Literacy*. New
York: Oxford U P, 1989.

CONTRIBUTORS

Katherine H. Adams is Director of Writing Across the Curriculum and associate professor of English at Loyola University in New Orleans. Her professional activities include being director of Loyola's Law School Writing Center, editor of the *ATAC Newsletter*, and an officer of the Association of Teachers of Advanced Composition, and organizer and first director of the Smokey Mountain Writing Project, an affiliate of the Bay Area Writing Project. She has published articles and reviews in *College Composition and Communication, Rhetoric Society Quarterly, Rhetoric Review, Teaching English in the Two-Year College, Freshman English News, The Writing Instructor, Journal of Teaching Writing, Arizona English Bulletin, Teaching Writing,* and other journals, and she co-edited a special issue on cultural literacy for *The Clearing House*. Her advanced writing textbook, *The Accomplished Writer*, was published by Prentice-Hall in 1988. She has also co-edited an essay collection, *Teaching Advanced Composition: Why and How*, for Boynton/Cook (1990). She is currently working on *A History of Professional Writing Instruction in American Colleges* for SMU Press.

James Addison is Director of the Writing Center and associate professor of English at Western Carolina University. He has published and presented numerous papers on writing and rhetoric, most recently including "Style and Technical Writing" in *Technical and Business Communications* (NCTE, 1989) and work at CCCC and NCTE. He is currently interested in how scientific and technical writing form communicative texts and how the composition of these texts are affected by the role of the tutor in the writing center.

Don Bushman is Assistant Director of the Writing Center at the University of Tennessee and a former writing center tutor at Illinois State University. He is a Ph.D candidate in English, with research interests in rhetoric and composition studies. He has presented papers at various national writing center-related conferences, and is working on an annotated bibliography of writing center research over the last twenty years. In the Writing Center at UT, he works with tutor-training and computer-assisted tutoring software.

Robert D. Child has served as a Board Member for the National Writing Centers Association and the East/Central Writing Centers

Association, has published articles on writing centers in *The Writing Center Journal, The Writing Lab Newsletter*, and *Teaching English in the Two-Year College*. Additionally, he has presented papers on writing center theory and practice at CCCC and other national conferences. He currently directs the English Fundamentals Program for Education majors at Purdue University, where he is pursuing a Ph.D.

Irene Lurkis Clarke has a B.A. in Music from Hunter College, New York, an M.A. from Columbia University in English, and a Ph.D from the University of Southern California in English with a concentration in nineteenth-century British Literature. She is currently the director of the Writing Center at the University of Southern California where she is also in charge of two computer labs. Her book *Writing in the Center: Teaching in a Writing Center Setting* (Kendall/Hunt, 1985) won an award from the National Writing Centers Association as did her article "Collaboration and Ethics in Writing Center Pedagogy," published in *The Writing Center Journal* in 1988. She has published in *Teaching English in the Two-Year College, The Journal of Basic Writing, The Writing Lab Newsletter, The Writing Center Journal, Research in Word Processing Newsletter*, and *College Composition and Communication*. She is currently working on a book concerned with research papers in the composition course to be published by Harper/Collins.

Ruth Dobson is a reading instructor at the University of Missouri-St. Louis who conducts the ESL graduate writing support groups.

Sallyanne H. Fitzgerald currently directs the Center for Academic Development which houses the University of Missouri at St. Louis Writing Center. She has tutored both in a California community college writing lab and in the UM-St. Louis Writing Center where she developed the tutor training program. The current chair of the Midwest Writing Centers Association, Dr. Fitzgerald has presented papers on writing centers and published in the *Writing Lab Newsletter, Research and Teaching in Developmental English, Exercise Exchange*, and *Freshman English News*.

Karyn L. Hollis received her Ph.D. in Rhetoric, Linguistics, and Literature from the University of Southern California. She began her career at Dickinson College, a small liberal arts institution, where she developed a Writing Center and Writing across the Curriculum Program. She has since joined the English Department at Villanova University to work in the writing program there. She founded the Progressive Composition Caucus, edited its newsletter for seven years and has also chaired the CCCC Committee on the Status of Women in the Profession. Her articles have appeared in *The Writing Instructor* and *Writing Lab Newsletter*.

Bradley T. Hughes is Director of the Writing Lab and Director of Introductory Courses in the English Department at the University of Wisconsin at Madison, where he has taught for the past six years. At Wisconsin, Hughes has also been involved with developing and leading faculty seminars on writing across the curriculum. As part of of IBM's advanced education project, Hughes has written *Comp-U-Talk*, a networked computer program for use in writing across the curriculum courses. He has presented papers on writing centers, composition instruction, writing across the curriculum, and computers and composition at numerous professional conferences, including ADE, CCCC, and the Midwest Writing Centers Association, and has been a keynote speaker at the Midwest College Learning Center Summer Institute. He has published articles in *Illinois English Bulletin*, *Collective Wisdom: A Sourcebook of Lessons for Writing Teachers* (Random House, 1988), and *Computers and Composition*.

Jay Jacoby is an associate professor of English at the University of North Carolina at Charlotte where for the past five years he has directed the composition program. He formerly directed The Writing Resources Center and was the 1986-87 President of The National Writing Centers Association. Jacoby holds graduate degrees in English from Villanova and the University of Pittsburgh. He was an 1981 Fellow of the Brooklyn College Institute for the Teaching of Peer Tutors. His research is widely published, including articles in *CCC*, *The English Journal*, *The Writing Lab Newsletter*, *The Writing Center Journal*, and *CEA Critic*.

Nadene A. Keene is an assistant professor at Indiana University at Kokomo where she works in the Learning Enhancement Center and teaches a wide range of writing courses -- basic writing, freshman composition, advanced expository writing, and advanced technical writing. She also teaches an introductory linguistics course and a literature course which focuses on ethnic and minority literature. While completing her doctoral degree at Illinois State University, she focused her research on gender studies. Since then, her research interests have expanded to include writing centers, assessment, and pedagogy. She has published articles in *Indiana English, Illinois English Bulletin*, and *The Proceedings of Writing Centers Association: East Central*. Her most recent article "The Dollmaker: Betrayal in Art and Academia" will be published in the forthcoming feminist anthology *Wisdom in the Bones: Autobiographical Literary Criticism*.

Richard Leahy has taught at Boise State University since 1971 and has directed the Writing Center since its inception in 1979. He holds degrees from the University of San Francisco, the University of Iowa, and the University of California, Davis. He has organized several regional writing center conferences in the Rocky Mountains and the Inland Northwest, and has frequently presented at regional conferences and at the NCTE and CCCC. From Fall 1987 through Spring 1990 he served on the Executive Board of the National Writing Centers Association and the Editorial Board of *The Writing Center Journal*. He has published several articles on teaching writing, writing centers, and writing across the curriculum in *The Writing Lab Newsletter, The Writing Center Journal, College Teaching, Idaho English Journal, Oregon English*, and *Washington English Journal*.

Peggy Mulvihill is the current Writing Center supervisor at UM-St. Louis. She began the graduate writing support groups at UM-St. Louis. She is a published poet, Coordinator of Communications for the Center for Academic Development, and has presented her research at CCCC, NCTE, NADE, and at the Sixth Conference on Computers and Writing.

Christina Murphy is the Director of the Writing Center and Associate Director of the Center of Academic Services at Texas Christian University. She is Editor of *Freshman English News* and Chair of the Texas Association of Writing Centers. Her articles on rhetorical theory have appeared in a range of journals including *North Dakota Quarterly, Writing Center Journal*, and *Chronicles of Culture*. Her book on Ann Beattie was published by G.K. Hall in the Twayne series, and her textbook on critical thinking skills was published by

Prentice Hall. Her B.A. is from Temple University and her M.A. and
Ph.D. are from the University of Connecticut.

Janice Witherspoon Neuleib, Ph.D., University of Illinois, 1974,
began the University Writing Center at Illinois State University in
1976. She directed it until 1986 when she became director of the newly
formed University Center for Learning Assistance, a position she
continues to hold. She teaches courses in tutoring reading and writing
and graduate courses in pedagogical theory. She has served as project
coordinator for Illinois State University's three-year NEH sponsored
collaborative teaching institute on literature and writing. She has
published in *College English, CCC, The Journal of Teaching Writing,
The Writing Center Journal,* and *The Writing Lab Newsletter,* as well
as contributing to books on writing centers.

Stan Patten is an assistant professor of English at the University of
North Carolina at Charlotte where he directs The Writing Resources
Center and is associate director of the UNCC Writing Project. He holds
graduate degrees in English and philosophy from Purdue University.
His work has appeared in *The Writing Lab Newsletter, Carolina
English Teacher,* and *Feminist Future.*

Curtis E. Ricker, head of the Department of Developmental Studies
at Georgia Southern University, is an assistant professor holding a joint
appointment in English and Developmental Studies. With an
undergraduate background in English, chemistry, and biology, and
graduate degrees in English literature and English composition, he is
interested in the effects of writing across the curriculum programs,
particularly upon developmental studies students. He continues his
research in remediation and writing across the curriculum, drawing on
his varied teaching experience. Besides presenting numerous papers at
national and state meetings, he has published in *Notes on Teaching
English,* and co-authored *Reading/Writing Relationships,* a textbook for
combined reading/English developmental studies classes.

Donald Samson has a B.A. in English from Cornell University and
an M.A. and Ph.D. in English literature from the University of North
Carolina at Chapel Hill. He has taught literature and writing at
Meredith College and the University of Tennessee, and now teaches
technical writing and Shakespeare as an associate professor at Eastern

Michigan University in Ypsilanti. For two years, Dr. Samson was a senior Writer/Editor for Martin Marietta Corporation. Dr. Samson's published work has appeared in *Technical Communication, IEEE Transactions on Professional Communication, The Journal of Technical Writing and Communication, The Technical Writing Teacher*, and *Proceedings of the International Technical Communication Conference*. He is writing a textbook in technical editing to be published by Oxford University Press.

Maurice Scharton, Ph.D., Kansas State University, 1976, has directed the writing assessment program at Illinois State University since 1980. He participated in the design of the University Center for Learning Assistance where he works with tutor training and test development. He teaches rhetorical theory and writing. He has published in *College English, Research in the Teaching of English, The Journal of Developmental Education,* among others. He consults regularly on test development and implementation and has directed a state grant on assessment in the schools.

Jeanne Simpson, after earning her doctorate at Illinois State University, established the writing center at Eastern Illinois University in 1981. She is now Director of Writing Across the Curriculum at Eastern as well as coordinator of a freshman orientation seminar. A former president and founding board member of the National Writing Centers Association, she has published in *Writing Lab Newsletter, The Writing Center Journal, Journal of Teaching Writing*, and *Computer-Assisted Composition Journal*. She is also author of *The Elements of Invention*. Jeanne has made presentations at many regional and national conferences, including CCCC, NCTE, Midwest Writing Centers Association, the Penn State Conference on Rhetoric and Composition, East Central Writing Centers Association, and others.

Ray Wallace is Director of the Writing Center at the University of Tennessee where he is an assistant professor. He has published writing center research in *The Writing Center Journal, Focuses*, and *The Writing Lab Newsletter*, and has published other writing-related research in *TESOL Quarterly, The Computer-Assisted Composition Journal, The NCTE Classroom Practices Series, Exercise Exchange*, and other journals. He is an elected member of the Executive Board of the

National Writing Centers Association, on the editorial board of *The Writing Center Journal*, an MLA International Bibliographer in Linguistics, and an AP Composition Reader for the Educational Testing Service. He has presented writing center-related research at CCCC, International TESOL, the World Congress of the International Reading Association (in Australia), the National Peer Tutoring Conference, and the Southeastern Writing Centers Association Conference. He is currently completing a writing across the curriculum text for Wadsworth.

Henry Wilson is Assistant Director of Composition at the University of Tennessee, and a former writing center tutor and member of the Writing Center Advisory Board at Western Carolina University. Currently, he tutors and teaches a wide variety of courses at UT-Knoxville, and is pursuing the Ph.D in English with an emphasis on rhetoric and composition studies. His current research deals with the writing center's role in writing across the curriculum, a subject on which he completed an M.A. thesis.

William C. Wolff studied Latin and Greek, English, and Philosophy at Fordham University from which he took his A.B. and A.M. He earned his doctorate in rhetorical theory at Rutgers University studying under Janet Emig and Robert P. Parker. Presently, he edits *Focuses*, a journal linking rhetorical theory to composition programs and practice in the classroom and in the writing center. He also directs the University Writing Center at Appalachian State University in Boone, North Carolina where he is an associate professor of English.